The Cost of Being a Girl

Yasemin Besen-Cassino

The Cost of Being a Girl

Working Teens and the Origins of the Gender Wage Gap

TEMPLE UNIVERSITY PRESS
Philadelphia • Rome • Tokyo

TEMPLE UNIVERSITY PRESS
Philadelphia, Pennsylvania 19122
www.temple.edu/tempress

Library of Congress Cataloging-in-Publication Data

Names: Besen-Cassino, Yasemin, author.
Title: The cost of being a girl : working teens and the origins of the
    gender wage gap / Yasemin Besen-Cassino.
Description: Philadelphia : Temple University Press, [2018] | Includes
    bibliographical references and index. | Description based on print
    version record and CIP data provided by publisher; resource not
    viewed.
Identifiers: LCCN 2017018199 (print) | LCCN 2017020816 (ebook) |
    ISBN 9781439913505 (e-book) | ISBN 9781439913482 (cloth (alk.
    paper) : alk. paper) | ISBN 9781439913499 (paper : alk. paper)
Subjects: LCSH: Wages—Women—United States. | Teenage girls—
    Employment—United States.
Classification: LCC HD6061.2.U6 (ebook) | LCC HD6061.2.U6 B47
    2018 (print) | DDC 331.4/21530973—dc23
LC record available at https://lccn.loc.gov/2017018199

To Dan

Contents

Acknowledgments

This project would not have been possible without the help of many friends, colleagues, and study participants. Michael Kimmel has been an amazing mentor. I thank him for his encouragement and guidance. James Rule has been a strong supporter of this project from its inception, and I thank him for his theoretical perspective and for asking difficult questions. Tim Moran and Naomi Rosenthal have also read the book and given me feedback. I thank them for their valuable comments. I am grateful to Mary Gatta, Richard Ocejo, Lauren Rogers-Sirin, Toni Pole, Meredyth Krych-Appelbaum, and Jay Livingston for their encouragement and suggestions. I also thank the wonderful editorial team at Temple University Press, especially editors Ryan Mulligan and Micah Kleit. In addition, I thank the three anonymous reviewers for their insightful comments.

I thank my colleagues in the Sociology Department at Montclair State University, who have encouraged me and discussed the project with me at various stages. I especially acknowledge Laura Kramer, whose encouragement and discussions on gender helped me throughout the project. I thank my dean, Rob Friedman, and provost, Willard Gingrich, for their support of this project.

A very early descriptive version of Chapter 1 was published as Yasemin Besen-Cassino, "The Cost of Being a Girl: Gender Earning Differentials in the Early Labor Markets," *NWSA Journal* 20, no. 1 (2008): 146–160. I thank the Johns Hopkins University Press for their permission to use the title and ideas from the article. The research for Chapter 1 was supported with a grant from the W. E. Upjohn Foundation. I thank the foundation for its invaluable support.

I thank my mom and dad, Zeynep and Edip Besen, who always fostered my intellectual curiosity and believed in gender equality.

Julian Besen-Cassino has been my biggest (and littlest) supporter: he cheered me on throughout the project and tried to teach me that puffins are not small penguins.

The biggest thanks go to Dan Cassino. He encouraged me to write this book, he read the entire manuscript and gave me comments, and he helped me come up with pseudonyms for the many participants in my study (which is harder than you might think). He not only makes the best coffee in the tristate area, but he makes the best conversation.

The Cost of Being a Girl

Introduction

> *I do not demand equal pay for any women save those*
> *who do equal work in value. Scorn to be coddled by*
> *your employers; make them understand that you are in*
> *their service as workers, not as women.*
> —Susan B. Anthony, "The Revolution"

Kiara[1] is sitting in her car, parked in the parking lot of a major sporting-goods chain, changing from her polished and professional reception-ist's outfit of a frilly blouse, black pants, suit jacket, and black heels to a more athletic-looking top and sneakers. Kiara, twenty, is an African American college student majoring in sociology at a large state university, where she runs track and field. She is hoping to go to graduate school and eventually become a social worker. She started working in her early teens and has always had a job in the service sector, working for large chains and franchises, often struggling to find part-time jobs in service or retail. For the past year, she has been juggling two jobs: as a receptionist at a physical therapy center for children and as a sales associate in the apparel section of a major sporting-goods retailer. When you ask her how much she works, she says she works part time, but in the past year, she has been averaging twelve to fifteen hours per week as a receptionist and twenty-five to thirty hours per week at the sporting-goods store, putting her above forty hours most weeks.

Because she does not get enough hours at either job to pay her bills, she keeps both, even though she is not happy with the working conditions at either of them. She has shoe boxes thrown at her because she cannot accept expired coupons, and she listens to parents shouting at her because of insur-ance companies' high deductibles. Her schedule has been so hectic in the

---

[1] All names of participants and businesses are pseudonyms, and identifying characteristics have been changed.

past month that on Saturdays, she leaves her shift at the physical therapy center at 4:30 P.M. instead of 5:00 P.M. (if the last parent pays early) just to make it to her second job at the sporting-goods store. Every Saturday in the past month, she has changed out of her office-appropriate professional attire into her sporty outfit in her car. To maintain the appearances required by the two employers, she constantly invests in two wardrobes. Despite the increasing demands and her rising investments in the jobs, her hourly pay has remained unchanged, and her employers have failed to give her enough hours at either job.

Emily, similarly, has been working as a babysitter since she was twelve years old. Today, she is a twenty-one-year-old double majoring in social sciences and education, with plans to become a teacher. She first started babysitting for her neighbors' newborn baby nine years ago, when the parents were out to get dinner on Friday nights. She continued babysitting, and now she takes care of up to four siblings after school, driving them to and from school, scheduling playdates and after-school events, coordinating extracurricular activities and hobbies, and doing light cleaning, laundry, and cooking and running errands. The previous week, with numerous school cancellations and adverse weather conditions, was so hectic that she missed her own classes. Despite her heavy workload and ever-increasing job demands, she has not had a pay raise for a long time. Her job description kept changing, including more tasks, more children, and more unpaid preparation time, yet her paycheck is essentially the same as when she began babysitting. Still, she does not feel that she can ask for more money.

When scholars talk about the gender wage gap, they focus on years of peak earning potential, the effect of marriage and motherhood (Correll, Benard, and Paik 2007; Ridgeway and Correll 2004), unequal divisions of household chores (Bianchi, Robinson, and Milkie 2006; Bittman et al. 2003), balancing work and family responsibilities (Bose and Bridges-Whaley 2011), gendered expectations of workplace habits (Britton 2000), structural and cultural barriers against advancement (Alessio and Andrzejewski 2000; Garcia-Lopez 2008; McGuire 2002), and the willingness and ability of women to negotiate higher salaries or better work conditions (Babcock and Laschever 2003; Bowles, Babcock, and Lai 2007). But stories like those of Kiara and Emily tell us that gendered inequality in the workplace starts much earlier than such concerns suggest, and a true understanding of the gender pay gap requires an understanding of the gendered inequalities faced by the youngest workers in our society. The pay gap does not start when women are thirty or forty. It has roots in the work of children as young as twelve, and if our society wants to eliminate the pay gap, it needs to understand how it begins.

Kiara and Emily are two examples of many young women who work part time while still going to school. Working part time as a student is a quintessentially American phenomenon (Greenberger and Steinberg 1986) with roots in early American farms. Throughout American history, adolescents have always worked, and today, almost every student works sometime before the end of high school (Besen-Cassino 2014; Herman 2000; Marsh and Kleitman 2005; Manning 1990; Mortimer 2005; Zimmer-Gembeck et al. 2006). According to the U.S. Bureau of Labor Statistics, since the 1950s, the part-time employment of sixteen- to nineteen-year-olds has been a constant component of our economy, with substantially higher rates of participation in the labor force in the summer than during the school year. During the 1980s, teen participation in the labor force increased substantially, reaching peak participation rates. After the recession of the late 2000s, labor-force participation rates for sixteen- to nineteen-year-olds declined, with teenagers finding themselves in competition with older workers who are recently unemployed or immigrants (Bureau of Labor Statistics 2011; see also Sternheimer 2016). Because of the economic recession of the late 2000s (Pew Research Center 2015) and increasing economic inequality in the labor market (Bureau of Labor Statistics 2014), the increase in the number of teenagers in general, and the more demanding hiring standards of retail and service sector jobs (Besen-Cassino 2014; see also Casselman 2016), a smaller percentage of teenagers holds jobs compared with the previous decade.

Despite a decrease in employment rates after the recent economic recession, teenagers continue to be solidly integrated into our workforce. In *When Teenagers Work*, Ellen Greenberger and Laurence Steinberg observe that "the large teenage, part-time labor force that staffs the counters of fast-food establishments, waits on customers in retail stores, assembles parts in industrial settings, and cleans motel rooms and office buildings has become such a familiar part of our social landscape that we may fail to note its unique character or to ponder its social significance" (1986, 3). In both the service sector and freelance jobs like babysitting, many young women are strongly entrenched in our workforce. Therefore, work experience, along with all potential problems of labor markets, such as the gender pay gap, begin much earlier than the onset of the completion of formal education and the onset of full-time employment.

The gender wage gap is one of the most persistent problems of labor markets and women's lives. Today, an average full-time working woman makes eighty-two cents for every dollar a man makes, according to the Bureau of Labor Statistics (2013; see also Kimmel 2015; Hegewisch and Edwards 2012; Hegewisch and Williams 2013; Wade and Ferree 2015). The gender wage gap has improved substantially over the years: in 1820, women earned thirty-five cents for a man's dollar, which increased to fifty-six cents in 1930, sixty cents in 1970, and seventy-two cents in 1990 (Wade and Ferree 2015). However, the closing of the gap is not due to massive increases in women's pay but rather to the substantial decline in men's wages due to loss of high-wage, skilled manufacturing jobs (Fligstein and Shin 2003; Fortin 2008; Goldin and Katz 2007; Hegewisch and Edwards 2012; Kimmel 2015). Despite the rapid gains of the 1970s and 1980s, the rate of progress in closing the gap has been stagnant (Blau and Kahn 2004; Fontin 2008; O'Neill 2003). The gender wage gap is such an important social problem that in 1996, President Bill Clinton declared a day in April to be National Pay Inequity Awareness Day; the date signifies that an average woman has to work until early April of the next year to reach a man's earnings from a given calendar year.

This inequality has long-term effects. Over a lifetime, the average woman will make $434,000 less in income than the average man. A college-educated woman will lose approximately $713,000 over the course of her career (Arons 2008). The wage gap also affects women's economic stability during retirement years, as it influences social security benefits (Calasanti 2001; Kimmel 2016; Wade and Ferree 2015). Despite improvement over time and slight variations based on sector and country—the gap is smaller among lower-paying jobs, higher among professional degrees, and higher among older workers—the gender wage gap remains a resistant problem in our current economy (Wade and Ferree 2015) and remains partially unexplained (Blau and Kahn 2006; Padavic and Reskin 2002; Valian 1999).

Why do women get paid less than men do? Researchers in and outside academia have offered a myriad of explanations. Typical explanations from the media include assertions that women have babies, women take time off from work for child care, women do more housework, women do not negotiate as much as men do, and women do not care about the money.

Typical academic explanations for the wage gap have three distinct orientations, which are discussed in more detail in Chapter 1. The first set of explanations, the human capital approach (Becker 1964), focuses on individual characteristics and highlights personal differences between men and women workers, such as differences in education, work experience, and credentials (England 1997; Gottfried 2013). This view argues that women are not paid as much as men do because they do not have the same credentials and work experience (Berk and Berk 1979; Blau and Kahn 2006; Bose and Bridges-Whaley 2011; Cohen and Huffman 2007; Hersch and Stratton 1997; Hochschild 1989; Mincer and Ofek 1982; Padavic and Reskin 2002; Ross 1987; Waldfogel 1998), rendering them less productive (Bose and Bridges-Whaley 2011, 201; Gottfried 2013). Scholars advocating this approach explain that these personal differences in human capital are mostly due to the maternal and domestic duties of women; they argue that having children, taking time off from work, child-care responsibilities, and unequal housework demands render women less productive, taking away time and investment in their human capital and resulting in unequal pay (Gottfried 2013). Even though prior research attributes much of the wage gap to individual differences in education, skills, and job experience, these factors do not explain all of the earnings gap (Altonji and Blank 1999; Blau and Kahn 2006; Fuller and Schoenberger 1991; Goldin 1990; Groshen 1991; Paglin and Rufolo 1990; Schilt and Wiswall 2008).

A second set of explanations, the occupational segregation approach, focuses on occupational characteristics and argues that men and women are paid differently because they work in different sectors, at different positions and occupations. This approach suggests that men are concentrated in more managerial positions, full-time positions, and positions with more authority and higher options for advancement (Blum, Fields, and Goodman 1994; Budig and England 2001; Cohen and Huffman 2007; England and Folbre 2005; Fuller 2008; Hearn and Parkin 2001; Huffman and Cohen 2004; Reskin and McBrier 2000; Reskin and Padavic 1994; R. Smith 2002) and that invisible barriers, or glass ceilings, prevent women from access to these higher-paying jobs (Cotter et al. 2001; Hultin 2003; Wright and Baxter 2000).

The third approach focuses on differences in values and beliefs about work and argues that men and women are paid differently because they value different aspects of work with differential emphasis on monetary gratifications. This approach suggests that men get paid more because they care more about money and material benefits, while women value more social, altruistic, and nonmonetary gratifications (Andreoni and Vesterlund 2001; Gottfried 2013). In addition, this approach finds that men tend to be more leadership oriented and competitive (Gneezy, Niederle, and Rustichini 2003; Kuhn and Weinberger 2005), which might result in higher pay.

These theories are vastly different in focus and approach. However, they all have one thing in common. No matter how they approach the problem of the gender wage gap, they all focus on *adult* employment, despite the fact that Americans begin working well before their education is completed. Looking at earlier work experiences includes a previously neglected portion of the workforce and provides a more comprehensive understanding of the wage gap. Today, work experience for many American teenagers begins as early as twelve years of age and remains an important social and economic component of teenagers' lives. Many teenagers do not work just a few scattered hours, either. According to the U.S. Department of Labor's "Report on the Youth Labor Force" (Herman 2000), 8 percent of fourteen-year-olds and 17 percent of fifteen-year-olds work over fifteen hours per week. There-fore, work is an important part of teenagers' lives in the United States, eco-nomically, socially, and in terms of providing identity (Besen-Cassino 2014). Teenage labor also constitutes a substantial portion of our service economy, with teenagers constituting 4 percent of the American service work force. Therefore, in studies of important social problems such as the gender wage gap, focusing on just the adult labor force reflects only a small and nonrep-resentative sample of our work force.

In addition, youth employment offers a natural social laboratory where many typical confounding factors are naturally controlled for, as many typi-cal explanations of the pay gap are not applicable for young workers. Twelve- and thirteen-year-olds are not married, and they generally do not have children. It could be argued that adult men and women may tend to have different job experiences and skills, but at these ages, boys and girls have the same education levels, job experiences, and skills. Any difference in the rates of pay between them, therefore, cannot be due to these sorts of background factors.

Finally, by looking at early employment experiences, we can trace the origins of the gender wage gap and pinpoint exactly when gender inequalities emerge and offer explanations. By understanding early inequalities, we can see how these early differences contribute to future inequalities.

Pay Gap: Prior Work

While the youth pay gap has not received much academic attention, the adult pay gap has been widely explored. Because work is an important part of people's lives and their identities, work has emerged as an important arena where gender inequality is played out (England and Folbre 2005; Gottfried 2013; Reskin and Padavic 1994). A wide range of scholars, including sociolo-gists, economists, and psychologists, have studied this persistent problem of labor markets and tried to answer why women get paid less than men do. To understand how these explanations may, and may not, apply to the youth labor market, it is important to explore each of them in more depth.

The first set of explanations of the pay gap, the human capital approach, focuses on individual factors and argues that women are simply more likely to have certain characteristics that lead people to be paid less. This approach argues that characteristics like education, job training, and years of experi-ence (Becker 1964) affect pay, and since women, on the whole, have fewer years of education, fewer advanced degrees, fewer certifications, and lower graduation rates, as well as fewer years of training and fewer years of job experience, women, in general, would be expected to be less valuable to the employer (Becker 1964; Bose and Bridges-Whaley 2011). This is reflected in pay: women's pay is lower because their human capital is lower, resulting in lower productivity (Bose and Bridges-Whaley 2011; Gottfried 2013).

Education is a determining factor in whether individuals work, which positions they have, which jobs they hold, and how much they earn. However, differences in education do not really explain sex-based differences in pay. While such differences in education have been offered as potential explanations historically, today such explanations would not be applicable (Blau and Kahn 2000, 2006; Bobbitt-Zeher 2007). Especially in recent years, women's participation in higher education has proliferated rapidly, with women's college attendance and graduation rates surpassing men's (Haveman and Beresford 2012). Despite much higher college attendance and completion rates by women, human-capital-approach scholars argue that women are concentrated in different fields than men are. For example, they point to lower participation of women in science, technology, engineering, and mathematics (STEM) fields (Prokos and Padavic 2005), business, and other higher paying positions (Bertrand, Goldin, and Katz 2010; Carrell, Page, and West 2010; Prokos and Padavic 2005; see also England and Li 2006; Reskin and Bielby 2005).

While there are no significant educational gender differences between men and women today, training is an area of significant gender differences. Partly due to cultural and social beliefs about gender roles, and partly due to employees' and educators' actions, women and men receive differential job training both in schools and at their jobs. For example, in high school, guidance counselors channel male and female students into different courses based on cultural biases of gender-appropriate jobs (Kane 1991). These occupational aspirations, choices, and suggestions are "shaped by individuals' assessment of their likely success in a given activity, and the individuals adjust their activities in light of the gendered expectations that others have of them" (Castagnetti and Rosti 2013, 632; see also Correll 2001, 2004; Ridgeway 2009; Ridgeway and Corell 2004; Winslow 2010).

Such biases are not limited to individual guidance counselors, but are reflected in our legal system. For example, federal law establishing vocational education specifies job training for male students and home economics for female students (Reskin and Padavic 1994). Apprenticeships, similarly, run by unions under the auspices of the U.S. Department of Education, often exclude women (Reskin and Padavic 1994). Even on the job, women receive less training (Carey and Eck 1984, 12). For example, employers train 44 percent of construction workers, whereas only 5 percent of secretaries receive training on the job (Carey and Eck 1984, 5, 18). Employers are willing to provide training for traditionally male jobs, whereas for traditionally female jobs (such as nursing or secretarial work), employers expect female workers to obtain the training on their own (Reskin and Padavic 1994). Today, the Department of Labor has created many apprenticeship opportunities, especially in newer fields like health care, and little information exists about gender inequalities in these new apprenticeship positions so far (Schilt and Wiswall 2008).

Similarly, male workers are more likely to be mentored than female workers. This is partly because men dominate managerial positions, but even when managers are female, they, too, tend to mentor male workers (Blau, Ferber, and Winkler 2006; Bose and Bridges-Whaley 2011). In addition to differences in their job training and mentoring, the human capital approach also argues that women do not have the same levels of job experience. On average, women today have less work experience than men do, but the gap in experience is fast closing (Reskin and Padavic 1994). The scholars of this view argue that the job experience gap is typically due to women's domestic and maternal obligations and often explained by interruptions in work due to childbirth and child-care obligations (Bose and Bridges-Whaley 2011; Gottfried 2013). For example, these scholars argue that because of child-care responsibilities, women work shorter hours, take time off from work, or even opt for jobs and sectors that have more flexible hours and shorter shifts to balance work and family obligations (Bose and Bridges-Whaley 2011; England and Folbre 2005; Gottfried 2013; Solberg and Laughlin 1995).

Pamela Stone, in her landmark book *Opting Out?* (2008), shows that high-income executive women feel they do not have child-care options and end up leaving their jobs mid-career because of a lack of family leave policies. In response to Lisa Belkin's *New York Times* article "The Opt-Out Revolution" (2003), which argues that highly educated women are leaving high-paying, high-prestige jobs when they have children because they prefer more traditional gender roles of child care, Stone shows that these women did not really have a choice. Many were offered more money and more responsibilities but not given any time off or any time away from work that would allow them to fulfill parental duties while retaining their jobs.

To the extent that such career interruptions decrease the overall levels of job experience women have, it is expected to contribute to the pay gap. Taking time off from work also presents challenges for many female workers: when female workers try to return to the workforce after taking time off for child care, many face difficulty in finding jobs that offer their previous pay and benefits, to say nothing of the loss of promotion opportunities (P. Stone 2008). This is closely connected to the lack of parental and family leave policies in the United States. The workplace makes the implicit assumption that "the prototypical human being is a self-sufficient rational economic man"

(Lynch 2010, 2). Reproductive work and care work are defined as all activities focusing on the provisioning and caring for children and the elderly, including "caring, feeding, clothing, teaching, and nurturing individuals" (Parrenas 2008, 12). While these activities are essential to the growth of our society, as well as important components of our productive economy, our economy still is based on the assumption that all workers are care-free (Lynch 2010), and therefore we offer limited parental leave, especially compared with other industrialized countries (Gottfried 2013).

Overall, the human capital approach has been criticized because by focusing on individual factors, it ultimately blames the victim. This view believes that the problem lies with individual differences and, therefore, individual workers. However, despite high levels of labor-force participation and significantly greater educational attainment by women, gender inequalities persist (Charles 2003; Charles and Bradley 2009; Gottfried 2013). Similarly, this view has also been criticized because experience differences and labor-force interruptions are not the main culprit. Stephen Rose and Heidi Hartmann (2004), in their study of men and women who have remained in the workforce continuously for fifteen years, show that women earned fifty-seven cents on the dollar, much lower than the often-cited seventy-seven cents. Therefore, even when women did not leave the labor force, they did not achieve equality in pay (Gottfried 2013). Furthermore, the cost of leaving the workforce is not the same for men and women: women experienced harsher losses for transitioning in and out of the workforce (Fuller 2008). Overall, even after controlling for individual characteristics, a substantial portion of the pay gap still remains unexplained (Blau and Kahn 2006; Fuller and Schoenberger 1991; Goldin 1990; Groshen 1991; Paglin and Rufolo 1990; Schilt and Wiswall 2008; Wood, Corcoran, and Courant 1993).

The second set of explanations, the occupational segregation approach, shifts the focus from individual attributes to occupational characteristics. This view argues that men and women are paid differently because they work in different jobs (Bose and Bridges-Whaley 2011; Reskin and Padavic 1994; Reskin and Roos 2002) with female-dominated jobs being lower-paying and lower-authority positions (England 2005, 2010; England and Folbre 2005). The effects of occupational segregation are not limited to the pay gap but can also reduce women's fringe benefits, pensions, and social security income (Calasanti 2001). For example, Toni Calasanti's (2001) quantitative work shows that because of accumulated inequality throughout the working years, what are considered the "golden years" of retirement are not as beneficial to women as they are to men.

Historically, since the Industrial Revolution and the rise of the cash economy, jobs have been sex segregated (England 2005, 2010; England and

Folbre 2005; Goldin 1990; Vallas, Finlay, and Wharton 2009). In the United States, occupational sex segregation, based on an index from 0 to 100, with higher values representing more segregation, fluctuated little between 1910 (69.0) and 1970 (67.6). However, the gender revolution of the 1970s led to a sudden drop in the index, which reached 59.8 by 1980 (Jacobs 1989). Throughout the 1980s and 1990s, the gap kept narrowing, but it has been stagnant since (Davis and Gould 2015). Despite some progress, men and women still work in different sectors in different industries and hold different jobs (Bielby and Baron 1986; Charles 2003; Charles and Bradley 2009; Hegewisch and Williams 2013; Reskin and Padavic 1994; Vallas, Finlay, and Wharton 2009). While the decline over time in the sex-segregation index is a welcome change, not all of it comes from women entering traditionally male jobs. The decline in the 1960s mostly stemmed from men's entry into traditionally female jobs (Reskin and Hartmann 1986). By the 1970s, women started moving into traditionally male jobs (Gottfried 2013). Especially with changing laws, affirmative action, and regulations that bar discrimination, women started entering many traditionally male sectors, such as broadcast reporting, bank management, and bartending (Reskin and Roos 2002). This was also bolstered by job growth in some sectors and the absence of qualified male workers in other sectors, allowing women workers to enter traditionally male fields.

Despite changes, the majority of men and women today still work in sex-segregated jobs (Charles 2003; Charles and Bradley 2009; England 2005, 2010; England and Folbre 2005; Gottfried 2013; Hegewisch and Williams 2013; Padavic and Reskin 2002). Because of sex segregation, women end up with lower pay and benefits because industries that employ mostly women tend to offer lower pay (Aldrich and Buchele 1989; Beck, Horan, and Tolbert 1980; Blau 1977; Coverdill 1988; England 2005, 2010; England and Folbre 2005; Ferber and Spaeth 1984; Hodson and England 1986). Typically referred to as the androcentric pay scale (Wade and Ferree 2015), jobs in which women are concentrated typically pay 5 percent to 21 percent less than jobs in which men are concentrated (Cohen and Huffman 2007). Once a job becomes dominated by female workers, it comes to be considered a woman's job, and the overall pay declines substantially (Gottfried 2013).

As Christine Williams (1992) shows in her study of male nurses, as men enter traditionally female industries such as nursing, not only do they get paid more and have higher opportunities of advancement, but the overall pay of the industry goes up. By the same token, as women enter traditionally masculine fields, not only do they face discrimination and sexual harassment (Kanter [1977] 1993; see also Yoder and Aniakudo 1997), but the overall wages decrease (Gottfried 2013; Reskin and Roos 2002). Psychologists Lynn

Liben, Rebecca Bigler, and Holleen Krogh (2001) also show that male occupations are associated with higher status than women's jobs. They presented ten- and eleven-year-olds with the fake occupations "clipster" (person who tests batteries) and "heigist" (a person who ensures water quality). When the children were told that these jobs were performed by men, the children gave these jobs a higher status ranking. Similar studies of college students confirm that the perceived prestige of the job increases if it is performed by a male worker. Jobs performed predominantly by women are not just lower in prestige, but they also are assumed to require fewer skills and be easier to perform (Hochschild 1983).

Sex segregation is not just on the industry level: even within the same industry there is sex segregation on the corporate level. Francine Blau (1977), for example, shows that in male-dominated occupations (such as accounting clerk, payroll clerk, or computer programmer), men outearn their counterparts because they work for higher-paying firms, while women are concentrated in lower-paying firms. Research also shows that women tend to be concentrated more in part-time jobs (England and Folbre 2005), while men are concentrated in full-time jobs (Blackburn et al. 2002; Gottfried 2013) with higher rates of moving in and out of the workforce (Fuller 2008). Therefore, even within the same job, women tend to be concentrated in more part-time jobs, not necessarily performing much fewer duties but getting paid substantially less, with fewer benefits and limited advancement opportunities.

Similarly, there is also sex segregation within job assignments. For example, women tend to be concentrated in nonmanagerial jobs, while men are overrepresented in managerial jobs (Kimmel 2015; Lorber 1994). This is also highly correlated with biases in perceptions of what makes a "good manager." Research shows that many qualities that are sought in a manager are traditionally masculine. However, recent research on women managers shows that when they exhibit such traditionally masculine characteristics, their evaluations decrease substantially. The same actions that are considered to be decisive leadership skills for men are evaluated negatively for women. Female managers are expected to be nice, caring, and nurturing, but when they do display these traditionally feminine qualities, they are often seen as less assertive (Kimmel 2015). A study of college professors shows that female professors get lower evaluations from students when they show leadership and authority (Boring, Ottobani, and Stark 2016). Anne Boring, Kellie Ottobani, and Philip Stark's research of student evaluations shows systematic and statistically significant bias against female instructors in student evaluations of teaching. Based on 23,001 student evaluations of 379 instructors by 4,423 students in six mandatory first-year courses in a five-year natural experiment at a French university, as well as on 43 student evaluations for four sections of an online course in a randomized, controlled, blind experiment at an American university, the research team shows systematic bias against female instructors. The bias against female faculty is reflected not only in their lower ratings but even in students' perceptions of seemingly objective and tangible actions, such as grading and returning assignments in a timely manner. This is especially important because these student evaluations of teaching are used in decisions of tenure and promotions.

On top of all this, women who are mothers face a motherhood wage penalty when applying for positions, as well as in their wages (Budig and England 2001). Overall, men outpace women in both male- and female-dominated jobs, creating a promotion gap as men advance at a faster pace (Padavic and Reskin 2002; Valian 1999). As a result, men tend to be clustered in higher-paying occupations and in managerial positions with greater pay, autonomy, and authority and more opportunities for advancement (Bose and Bridges-Whaley 2011; Budig 2002; England and Folbre 2005; Padavic and Reskin 2002; Reskin and Roos 2002; Schilt and Wiswall 2008).

A third view looks at differences in attitudes and values between men and women and explains the pay gap as a result of their differential work-related values and motivations (Fortin 2008). These differences occur because parents, peers, teachers, and the media socialize men and women into gendered values and behaviors from a very young age (Marini 1989; Subich et al. 1989; Kimmel 2000; Schilt and Wiswall 2008). Such early socialization might result in differential occupational choices for men and women: women might be encouraged to choose helping and nurturing professions to reinforce feminine traits, while men might be encouraged to choose higher-paying and higher-authority jobs to reinforce masculine traits (Kimmel 2000; Schilt and Wiswall 2008).

This view argues that men and women value different things in the workplace and their reasons for working differ substantially: men value making more money and having more authority, while women value social benefits (Reskin and Padavic 1994; Farrell 2005). The gender wage gap, in this view, has less to do with the actions of employers and more with how men and women are socialized. However, research by Ronnie Steinberg (1990) has conclusively rejected these claims and has demonstrated that men and women do not value different things at work. However, in the recent years, especially with the slowdown of the closing of the wage gap, there has been a renewal in interest in this strand of work (Blau and Kahn 2004; Fortin 2008). With renewed interest in differences in attitudes, new studies explore gender differences in values and motivations (Bowles, Gintis, and Osborne 2001; Fortin 2008).

Similarly, these scholars have argued that men and women do not show the same levels of job commitment: female workers are not as committed to their jobs as their male counterparts, and as a result they are not as productive (Reskin and Padavic 1994), limiting their value to the employer and, thus, their pay. Despite these claims, male and female workers show similar levels of productivity. However, male workers are more likely to receive tools to increase productivity in the workplace (Reskin and Padavic 1994). In the context of agricultural modernization, for instance, male agricultural workers have monopolized modern equipment and methods to increase their productivity, leaving more manual agricultural jobs to women (Boserup 1970).

In addition, many studies have found that male and female workers actually show similar levels of job commitment (Bielby and Bielby 1988; Gottfried 2013; Rose and Hartmann 2004). What affects commitment to jobs and productivity is not the sex of the worker but factors such as working conditions, job autonomy, and promotion opportunities. In fact, women show more commitment to jobs than men do at the same levels of job autonomy (Bielby and Bielby 1988). The assumption that job commitment is equally rewarded for both men and women is also problematic, as the social meaning of "job commitment" is not the same for both genders, and men and women are not rewarded in the same fashion. Rose and Hartmann's (2004) study of job commitment shows that even when women show the same level of strong labor attachment and work commitment, they are paid significantly less than men are.

Youth Labor in America

The Fair Labor Standards Act of 1938 sets the minimum age of work as sixteen. However, depending on the type and intensity of the work, fourteen- and fifteen-year-olds can work, especially in retail and service sector jobs. Nevertheless, freelance work often starts as early as twelve, with adolescents babysitting, shoveling snow, and doing yard work (Herman 2000).

Today, according to the Bureau of Labor Statistics (2016), the labor-force participation for all youth ages sixteen through twenty-four was 60.1 percent in July 2016. This is much lower than the youth employment rates of previous years; the youth labor-force participation rate peaked in 1989 at 77.5 percent. Despite the decline, which is seemingly tied to the aftereffects of 2008's economic downturn, youth labor-force participation rates are still very high, with many working and many still looking for work. Also, of course, youth employment during the summer months is also much higher than employment rates during the school year. Currently, youth labor-force participation rates are much higher for white youth (62.3 percent) than African American youth (56.4 percent), Asian youth (44.6 percent) and Hispanic youth (56.3 percent).

In addition, the labor-force participation for young men (61.8 percent) is also slightly higher than that of women (58.2 percent). The largest sector of employment for young workers is leisure and hospitality (25 percent), within which youth work is concentrated in restaurant services, with 18 percent working in retail. While retail and service sectors are the most dominant categories, smaller portions of youth are employed in agriculture (6 percent) and construction and manufacturing (12 percent).

Overall, despite the bouts of unemployment experienced by youth after the recent economic recession, young people's labor-force participation still remains high, and they constitute 4 percent of our overall workforce (Hirschman and Voloshin 2007). In addition, work is also a socially and developmentally important component of American youth's lives, providing young people with social space and a common vocabulary with which to relate to their peers, meet new people and socialize with friends, and help establish their identities (Besen-Cassino 2014). Even though youth employment has always been part of American culture, it has only emerged as a topic of sociological inquiry in the 1970s. In the 1970s, emerging studies started to document the prevalence of youth employment historically (Entwisle, Alexander, and Olson 2000).

In the second wave of research, during the 1980s, studies started focusing on the benefits of part-time work. This wave of research argued that part-time work helps young people find jobs in the future (D'Amico and Baker 1984; Stephenson 1980; Stern and Nakata 1989; see also Creed, Muller, and Patton 2003; Leventhal, Graber, and Brooks-Gunn 2001; Marsh and Kleitman 2005; Mortimer, Staff, and Oesterle 2003), reduces dropout rates (D'Amico and Baker 1984; McNeal 1997), improves school attendance (Marsh 1991; Mortimer and Finch 1986), and boosts academic performance (D'Amico and Baker 1984). According to these scholars, working while still in school has positive effects on both academic performance and future careers because it teaches important skills such as work ethic, discipline, and working with deadlines. They also find that working provides young people with a sense of accomplishment, making the transition to adulthood smoother. However, D'Amico and Baker (1984) show that these positive effects are mostly experienced by non-college-bound youth, with college-bound youth not experiencing the same benefits.

The optimism of scholars in the 1980s was followed by the third wave of research, which focused on the negative effects of employment for young people. These researchers found that part-time work lowers academic success, especially if teenagers work over twenty hours per week (Marsh 1991; Mortimer and Finch 1986; Steinberg and Dornbusch 1991; Steinberg, Fegley, and Dornbusch 1993). More recently, Herbert Marsh and Sabina Kleitman (2005) found that working had several negative outcomes, especially on achievement scores, grades, attendance, and educational aspirations.

Working also interferes with emotional development: working long hours, in particular, is linked to lower mental health indicators, including depression and lower self-esteem (Greenberger and Steinberg 1986; Marsh and Kleitman 2005); reduces interactions with family and friends (Finch et al. 1991; Greenberger and Steinberg 1986; Mihalic and Elliot 1997; Paternoster et al. 2003); and increases the likelihood of risky behavior, such as substance abuse (McMorris and Uggen 2000; Mihalic and Elliot 1997; Steinberg, Fegley, and Dornbush 1993) and crime (Hansen and Jarvis 2000).

Researchers in this era also started looking at work in a more nuanced fashion, taking into account the intensity of work and the number of hours young people spend working. When they take into account these factors, they find that working lowers academic success and decreases the likelihood of finishing high school. Noah Lewin-Epstein (1981), for example, shows that working more than nineteen and a half hours per week has detrimental effects on academic progress, as work takes time away from academic studies. Similarly, by taking into account both the number of hours worked and the intensity of work, Ellen Greenberger and Laurence Steinberg (1986) find that working interferes with emotional and psychological development during the teenage years because it takes time away from peers, family, and extracurricular activities.

Working can also have potentially negative effects on risky behaviors, such as crime and drug and alcohol use. However, the direction and magnitude of these effects are much debated in the literature. Barbara McMorris and Christopher Uggen (2000), for example, show that working increases alcohol use but that the effects are short-lived and do not translate into higher alcohol use in adult years. Sharon W. Mihalic and Delbert Elliot (1997), on the other hand, find that students who work in high school are more likely to consume alcohol and marijuana even over the long term, when they are twenty-seven and twenty-eight. David M. Hansen and Patricia Jarvis (2000) bring in another factor, showing that *where* students work matters in predicting risky behavior: they find that youth who work in family businesses are less likely to engage in risky behavior.

In more recent years, the research on youth employment has moved away from looking at the advantages and disadvantages of working and toward exploring inequalities in the workforce (Entwisle, Alexander, and Olson 2000). Rather than seeing employment as a static and equal experience for all youth, today's research focuses on the context and conditions of working (Entwisle, Alexander, and Olson 2000). In addition, bourgeoning studies problematize inequalities and different levels of access to jobs based on race and socioeconomic status. These contemporary inquiries move away from evaluating effects of work on passive subjects but, rather, see young people as active agents of their own lives (Besen-Cassino 2014; Liebel 2004).

In this book, as a response to this emerging research focusing on inequalities in the adolescent workforce, I explore the lived experience of gender inequality from the perspectives of the central actors: young people themselves. I aim to uncover when gender inequality emerges in early employment, identify the factors that contribute to gender inequality, identify the mechanisms through which these inequalities are reinforced in everyday lives, and show how these early inequalities are translated into gender inequity in the adult workforce.

Methods

To answer these questions, I adopt a multimethod approach using both quantitative and qualitative methods. The quantitative data help identify large-scale trends in our society and labor market. They also provide a context for the individual personal narratives and provide generalizability. For the quantitative analysis in this book, I draw on the National Longitudinal Survey of Youth (NLSY97). The NLSY97 is a large-scale, national, representative survey of American youth. The study consists of lengthy interviews, conducted periodically starting in 1997–1998, with American youth between the ages of twelve and seventeen. This ongoing cohort has been surveyed sixteen times to date, with the most recent round, Round 16, in 2013–2014. The NLSY97 not only provides a nationally representative sample of twelve- to seventeen-year-olds with a robust sample size of more than nine thousand participants but also offers the unique opportunity to track the same individuals from adolescence into adulthood. The NLSY97 is a very comprehensive study that collects information on many areas of young people's lives, including school, work, substance use, body image, and sexual activity. In addition, this dataset also provides extensive information concerning the family background and living arrangements of the children, including health, income and assets, participation in government programs, child-care arrangements, and parental expectations of youth. In particular, the dataset includes extensive information about work and the transition from school to work, including freelance and part-time jobs, and collects extensive information about youths' labor-market behavior and educational experiences over time. Employment information focuses on two types of jobs: "employee" jobs, where youths work for a particular employer, and "freelance" jobs, such as lawn mowing and babysitting. These distinctions enable me to study the effects of very early employment among youth through adulthood.

In addition, this is one of the rare datasets that collects such extensive information on the work habits of young people in the United States. While many datasets collect information on the formal economy, very little information exists on freelance jobs and early work experiences. Informal, freelance jobs such as babysitting, snow removal, and yard work start much earlier than the official age of work—sixteen—but very little information exists on these early work experiences. Among other benefits, this data allows the researchers to identify when and why the gender wage gap emerges and helps researchers isolate the effects.

Finally, it is important not to overlook the longitudinal nature of the NLSY97. The same participants have been contacted since 1997, and researchers have followed up with very detailed surveys on participants' work experience, as well as their social, economic, and political views and practices. Such a large-scale and longitudinal dataset allows us to see changes and trace the effects of early work experiences over time. Because it has been twenty years since the start of the NLSY97 in 1997, the dataset allows the researchers to study actual outcomes of early work experiences. Therefore, using this dataset, researchers can follow the same participants over the course of the past twenty years and identify how working as a teenager affected participants' future wages, future attitudes toward work, self-esteem, and identities. This is one of the only datasets that allow us to measure long-term effects, in addition to the short-term effects, of working as a teenager.

While the NLSY97 is the central quantitative dataset used in this book, I supplement this dataset with the World Values Survey (WVS). Especially in Chapter 1, I use the WVS to capture the values, motivations, and aspirations of youth and their effects on wages. The WVS also offers a reliable and comparable international dataset on youth ages sixteen to nineteen, including not only their work experience but why they work: their motivations, aspirations, and the things they value at work. Using this dataset, I model the work decisions of youth and compare and contrast male and female youth's work values and reasons for working.

I supplement these quantitative analyses with a detailed qualitative analysis. My qualitative data collection began in January 2016. Between January 2016 and September 2016, I conducted thirty-five in-depth, face-to-face qualitative interviews with young women, ages eighteen through twenty-four, who were employed as babysitters at the time of the interview. I also conducted twenty-five interviews with eighteen- to twenty-four-year-old women employed in the retail and service sectors. Out of the babysitters, 70 percent were white, 20 percent were African American, and 5 percent were Asian American; 10 percent self-identified as Hispanic. In addition, I interviewed twenty-five retail workers. These workers were 60 percent white, 30 percent African American, and 10 percent Hispanic.

I also interviewed three male babysitters. It was challenging to find male babysitters, as the field is dominated mostly by adolescent women, and I have included their experiences as detailed case studies. I use their lived experiences and firsthand accounts of babysitting to provide comparisons with those of the female babysitters.

The participants for the in-depth interviews—both babysitters and retail workers—were recruited through snowball sampling at one large state university and one private liberal arts college. Both locations are located in affluent, predominantly white suburbs of a major metropolitan city. These locations offer ample opportunities for retail and service-sector jobs as well as babysitting jobs. While the interviews are not meant to be representative of all jobs, they provide insight into the firsthand experience of work from the perspectives of young women and uncover the mechanisms though which inequality is transmitted and normalized. While these individual, in-depth interviews give detailed information on the lived experience of gender inequality in both retail and freelance jobs from the perspectives of the women, the quantitative data help generalize and provide context for these findings for better interpretation.

These interviews were ethnographic, qualitative, semistructured interviews, lasting approximately half an hour to two hours. I interviewed the participants at different places: school, work, offices, workplaces, and malls. I asked the participants about their present jobs, work conditions, gender relations at work, pay, promotions, aesthetic labor, emotion work, and job expectations, as well as about demographic information (full question guides are provided in the Appendix). I had follow-up interviews with some of the participants, as well, and have contacted many participants for clarification and verification. Because of institutional review board (IRB) restrictions, I did not interview any participants younger than eighteen. However, during the interviews, I asked questions about the participants' work histories and early work experiences.

These interviews were audio recorded and transcribed by hand, yielding approximately two hundred pages of transcribed notes. These notes were coded using the qualitative data analysis software NVivo, and I interpreted these interviews in light of the field notes and observations I kept throughout the interviews. I also took extensive notes based on my observations during their work shifts and on their body language as I interviewed some participants at their workplaces. I have adopted a grounded-theory approach (Glaser and Strauss 1965, 1967), letting the qualitative data and findings guide and inform theory. Both the babysitters and the retail and service-sector workers provided insight into the lived experience of workers in these jobs, as well as into the everyday experience of gender inequality. These personal accounts uncover the mechanisms through which gender inequality is experienced, normalized, and reinforced in everyday life.

Finally, I supplemented these in-depth qualitative interviews with personally administered original surveys. I administered approximately one hundred original surveys to eighteen- to twenty-four-year-old students about their past work experiences. These original surveys provide more background information on working youth as well as a detailed account of their past and present work experiences. Every participant in the face-to-face in-depth interviews was also given the survey. The surveys were especially instrumental in collecting detailed demographic information, such as household income, that participants are more reluctant to give in face-to-face interviews. Another advantage of the surveys, which were anonymous, was to give young workers an anonymous venue to talk more comfortably about some work issues, such as harassment and inequality in the workplace, as participants may be less likely to talk about sensitive and personal issues in face-to-face interviews. The surveys provided a safer space for the participants to talk about the problems in the workplace.

Overall, both the statistical analysis and the personal narratives focus on the work experiences of the young workers, while the individual stories help us understand the mechanisms through which gender inequality is experienced and reinforced. The quantitative analysis situates these individual narratives and accounts within a more representative setting, offering external validity.

I also supplemented the perspectives of the workers with additional perspectives from the employers. While this book's focus lies predominantly with the young workers, I designed an experiment to measure the biases of the potential employers for babysitters. Present and potential employers for babysitters may not admit to showing bias in hiring or giving raises; therefore, surveys and in-depth interviews do not capture the type and content of discrimination and bias among employers. Because of this social desirability bias—potential employers want to appear unbiased and objective—asking the participants directly in surveys or in-depth interviews does not accurately capture the extent of the bias. In many studies measuring bias in hiring, employment, promotions, or pay, scholars opt for an experimental design. András Tilcsik (2011), for example, uses an experimental study to measure the bias against LGBTQ employees. In a large-scale study, Tilcsik sent two versions of fictitious résumés to 1,179 job postings. While these fictitious résumés were otherwise identical, the control group received the résumé without any indication of the candidates' sexual orientation, and the experiment group received the identical résumé with an indication that the candidate was openly gay. Tilcsik shows that candidates who appear to be openly gay experience significant discrimination in employment. Furthermore, employers who emphasize stereotypically heterosexual male traits are more likely to discriminate against openly gay candidates.

Similarly, experimental research designs have been used to measure discrimination against candidates in the job market by many scholars. Stephen Crow, Lillian Fok, and Sandra Hartman (1998), for example, asked full-time employees in a southern city to pick six candidates from eight fictitious candidates for an accounting position. They concluded that participants were more likely to eliminate homosexual candidates than heterosexual candidates. Michael Horvath and Ann Marie Ryan (2003) asked a sample of undergraduates to rate résumés, experimentally manipulating the gender and sexual orientation of the applicants. They conclude that gay and lesbian candidates receive lower ratings than heterosexual men but higher than heterosexual women. Similarly, Crow, Fok, and Hartman (1998) presented different race, gender, and sexual orientation combinations for the participants as potential candidates for a job (e.g., white, heterosexual, female) to measure the magnitude and direction of discrimination.

The use of experimental methods in studying discrimination in the job market is not limited to discrimination against LGBTQ candidates, but such methods are used to measure prejudice against a wide range of candidates. Sonia Kang, Katherine DeCelles, András Tilcsik, and Sora Jun (2016) used them to measure the effects of race-based discrimination. Résumés containing cues to signal the racial and ethnic backgrounds of the candidates, such as names that could be perceived as African American and Asian American, result in significantly lower callback rates for candidates. Similarly, Lauren Rivera and András Tilcsik (2016) measured the effects of socioeconomic class bias in hiring using applications from fictitious candidates. The applications that signaled a higher-social-class background received more callbacks.

Shelley J. Correll, Stephen Benard, and In Paik (2007) used an experimental study to measure the extent of the motherhood penalty, by sending identical résumés that included subtle indicators that the candidate was a mother, and showed that these individuals faced significant discrimination. They found that mothers were perceived to be less competent and were recommended lower starting salaries.

Following in this tradition of using experimental designs to measure discrimination in the workforce, I designed an experimental study. In the experiment, 102 participants (recruited from Amazon's Mechanical Turk service) reviewed a vignette about a babysitter asking for a raise and then were asked how likely they would be to give the raise; they were also asked to rate their views of the babysitter. The respondents were 43 percent female, 79 percent white, and 11 percent African American. Almost half of the respondents (47 percent) were twenty-one to twenty-nine years old, 25 percent were thirty to thirty-nine, 13 percent were forty to forty-nine, 10 percent were fifty to fifty-nine, and 5 percent were sixty or older. Of the entire sample, 42 percent said that they currently had children under the age of eighteen living with them at home, 25 percent said that they regularly used a babysitter, and 31 percent said that they had used a babysitter regularly in the past. There were four versions of the vignette. Half of the respondents (49 percent) were asked to evaluate a male babysitter (Jake) and the other half a female babysitter (Molly; the names of the babysitters were the demographically "whitest" names in American in 2015, to avoid any racial confounds). The versions of the vignette also differed in the emotional investment the babysitter showed in the child. In one version, the babysitter says that he or she has "formed a strong emotional connection to the child" and brings homemade snacks (50 percent). In the other, the babysitter says that he or she would "like to continue in the position" and brings store-bought snacks to babysitting sessions.

In this study, the participants were asked to rate the babysitters, how likely they would be to give a raise, and to characterize the babysitters. The results, discussed in Chapter 2, show the extent to which women are penalized simply for asking for a raise, a finding that helps to explain why women may be so reticent to do so.

Overall, the book uses a multimethod approach, bringing together qualitative interviews, original surveys, and advanced statistical analysis, as well as experiments to capture gender inequality in the adolescent workforce.

The Plan of This Book

The book is organized into five chapters, with a substantive introduction and conclusion. In Chapter 1, "Origins of the Gender Wage Gap," I situate the problem of the pay gap at the intersection of the dominant theories. The human capital approach focuses on differences in individual characteristics between men and women to explain the pay differential. This view explains men's higher earnings as being the result of differential levels of education, experience, and skills, as well as, especially, the domestic and maternal duties of women. The occupational segregation approach focuses on differences in the jobs that men and women hold, arguing that the differential rates in pay are a result of the fact that men and women choose or are sorted into different jobs, resulting in differential pay. This approach argues that men's jobs tend to pay more and that women are concentrated in more flexible, part-time, and nonmanagerial jobs. In this view, much of the gap is driven by the percentage of women in an occupation: whether or not a job is a "woman's job" or a "man's job" determines the pay. I situate my research question about the teenage pay gap at the intersection of these dominant theories.

Youth of both sexes work while still in school in seemingly comparable jobs. These equal labor-force participation rates, perhaps, project the image of a gender utopia, in which the job segregation and the gender wage gap simply do not exist. However, when examined closely, the gender wage gap arises from this time of seeming equality. Using the NLSY97, this chapter shows that when teenagers are twelve to thirteen, there is gender equality in pay, but when they get to be fourteen to fifteen, we see the emergence of the gender wage gap, which widens with age. The youth labor market offers social laboratory-like conditions to study gender inequality in pay because it naturally controls for many typical explanations of gender inequality in pay. For instance, among adults, the gender wage gap is sometimes explained as being the result of differences in human capital. But by focusing on twelve- to sixteen-year-olds, we eliminate these confounding variables because boys in that age group rarely have more education, skills, and experience than girls do. Furthermore, the maternal and domestic duties that are often used as a reason for women's lower earnings simply are not applicable to the majority of teenage girls.

While the differences in the skills and responsibilities of girls and boys cannot be the cause of the early gender wage gap, Chapter 1 shows that the differences in earnings are largely due to the types of jobs that differentially employ young men and young women. Girls tend to concentrate in freelance jobs like babysitting, while boys tend to be concentrated in more formal jobs that typically pay more. Even within the same jobs, girls are socialized into more "feminine" jobs that require more social skills, while boys are encouraged to work with money in more physically demanding jobs. Overall, Chapter 1 identifies the jobs of white suburban youth as a site of gender inequality and traces the origins of an important social problem: the gender wage gap in early employment.

After comparing the effects of two dominant theories in the pay gap literature—the human capital approach and the occupational segregation approach—I focus on another dominant theory of the pay gap: values and motives. This theory suggested that men and women value different factors in the job. According to this model, women might value social benefits, while men value monetary benefits. In this chapter, I explore the reasons why teenagers work and what factors teenagers value in a job. Using the WVS, I show that boys and girls do not have different reasons for working. Both boys and girls in the same age group highlight the social benefits of the job and the status of the brand they work for, yet there are no gender differences in values or motives for working.

In Chapter 2, "Babysitters: Pricing the Priceless Child (Care)," I turn my attention to freelance jobs. In this chapter, I compare the gender differences in pay among freelance workers. Freelance jobs typically offer lower pay, no benefits, and limited hours. I find that as employee-type jobs become available, boys move into such formal settings, as girls remain in freelance jobs. Even within freelance jobs, we see gendering: girls are concentrated in babysitting, whereas boys are concentrated in snow removal and yard work, which pay more than babysitting jobs. While I have not found a substantial number of girls in snow removal and yard work jobs, boys in babysitting jobs have been increasing. Especially for babysitting small boys, many parents favor male babysitters, as they consider them more qualified to play with younger boys and teach them about sports. As a result, boys who offer babysitting services are seen as more entrepreneurial, and they receive higher pay. They are also not expected to take on other household tasks, such as doing house chores, cooking, or running errands, but rather are treated more professionally.

As babysitting is seen as quintessentially an adolescent young woman's job, young women have an easy time finding babysitting jobs, especially through informal networks. However, the same informal, weak ties that help young women find jobs also deter women from asking for more money. Many young women report not being able to successfully negotiate for higher wages.

Using the experimental study discussed earlier, I show that girls, when they ask for a raise, are more likely to be denied the raise and are characterized as manipulative. They are asked to show care to get the job; however, even caring young women are denied the raise because wage negotiation is seen as a noncaring act. Because of personal contact and informal ties, many young women who babysit end up not being able to leave babysitting to move to higher-paying jobs and, instead, end up performing more tasks for the same pay.

In Chapter 3, "Shop Girls: Gender Inequality in Retail and Service-Sector Jobs," I focus on the everyday lived experience of gender inequality from the perspectives of young women in retail and service-sector jobs. Based on in-depth qualitative interviews and first-person accounts, this chapter explores how girls in this age group experience gender inequality in their everyday lives. By focusing on everyday work experiences, this chapter illuminates the mechanisms through which gender inequality is sustained and reinforced. I show that affluent teenage girls are sought after by employers for high-end service-sector and retail jobs. However, my findings show that employers believe that girls work for social reasons, such as meeting new people and seeing their friends, and employee discounts. While I found no differences in values or motives between boys and girls in the age group of interest, employers tend to think of girls as working for just discounts, and they overemphasize their roles as consumers. Even though many boys the same age have expressed interest in discounts and association with a cool place to work, such as a gym, record store, bookstore, or a computer store, their choices are not viewed as consumption by employers. Furthermore, I find that girls are asked to spend more time at workplaces off the clock, working to help others.

In Chapter 4, "Race, Class, and Gender Inequality: An Intersectional Approach," I situate the gender discussion at the intersection of race and socioeconomic status. To do so, I explore the differences among young women in the United States and point to how racial and socioeconomic differences structure their work decisions, as well as influence how employers perceive these young women. Typically, the part-time jobs that young people tend to hold are service-sector and retail jobs with low pay, no benefits, and odd hours, including nights and weekends. However, despite the working conditions and limited monetary gratifications, these jobs have what Dennis Nickson, Chris Warhurst, and Eli Dutton refer to as "aesthetic labor" requirements (2004, 3). In other words, the workers need to look good and sound right (Nickson and Warhurst 2001). Especially in higher-end service-sector and retail jobs, girls have had more advantages than boys, with a greater ability to meet these aesthetic-labor requirements. In this chapter, I opt for an intersectional approach and show that not all young women share the same advantage: race and socioeconomic status are important factors. While affluent white women are sought after, lower-income women of color have a much harder time finding jobs, take longer to find jobs, are often shut out of the workforce, and often settle for lower-paying fast-food jobs, resulting in a wider wage gap. In Chapter 4, I also highlight, based on in-depth interviews, the differential expectations of aesthetic and emotion labor.

In Chapters 1–4, I focus on the work experiences of part-time adolescent workers—both in employee-type jobs and in freelance jobs—and discuss the short-term effects of gender inequality. These chapters identify the direction and magnitude of the pay gap through quantitative methods and isolate the causes. Chapter 5, "Long-Term Effects," shifts the focus from immediate gender inequality to long-term inequality. In this chapter, I explore how these early inequalities in the workplace translate into inequalities in the labor force. Using the NLSY97 data, I estimate the future wages of adult workers using their early work experience. These analyses show that inequalities, especially gender inequalities, translate into future jobs. This chapter shows that while working as an adolescent has a positive effect for men, the same benefits are not experienced for women. Women who work part-time as adolescents, in the long term, make less than their male counterparts. Furthermore, women who have worked, particularly in apparel sectors and in service sectors as servers, have body-image issues and report feeling overweight in the long term.

The Conclusion, "Work, Recession, and Future Direction," provides an overview of the findings of the book. I conclude my research on the adolescent labor force by summarizing the short-term and long-term effects of early work experiences in terms of gender inequality. In addition to understanding the short- and long-term effects of part-time work for gender inequality, I also discuss the implications of the late-2000s economic recession and offer projections about the future direction of the youth labor force and pay gap. In the past, Chris Tilly and Françoise Carré (2011) argued that retail and service-sector jobs were so abundant that teenagers got jobs if they passed the pulse test: every teenager who had a pulse could easily find a service-sector job with low pay and limited hours, no benefits, and limited promotion options. However, in recent years and since the economic recession, these jobs are no longer abundant. For the first time, young people are finding themselves in competition with many others and experiencing a limited number of employers that are hiring. When they do hire, service and retail sectors are exceedingly prioritizing aesthetic-labor requirements. I discuss the effects of the economic recession and the changing nature of service and retail, as well as freelance jobs, the rise of aesthetic labor, and important policy implications for gender equality.

Finally, in the Conclusion, I advocate for a gendered lens to explore these important social problems. With the economic recession of the late 2000s, many academic and nonacademic accounts point to the effects of not having part-time jobs or limited access to jobs on young people's lives. Many academic and journalistic accounts point to both the short-term effects of unemployment, decreased resources and social benefits, and important longer-term effects, the loss of job experience needed for future jobs and, subsequently, even lower future wages and retirement benefits. Yet I show that the effects of employment (and unemployment) are different for young women.

1

Origins of the Gender Wage Gap

The gender wage gap has been a persistent component of labor markets and women's lives. There has been lot of progress in closing the pay gap, with it narrowing substantially in the 1970s and 1980s, but the progress slowed substantially starting in the 1990s (Blau and Kahn 2006; Gottfried 2013). According to the U.S. Census Bureau, based on median annual earnings of year-round, full-time workers, the female-to-male pay ratio rose from 59.7 percent to 68.7 percent between 1979 and 1989 (Blau and Kahn 2005). Despite this rapid progress in the 1970s and 1980s, the ratio has been stagnant for the past few decades, and the progress seems to have plateaued since the 1990s (Blau and Kahn 2006; Reskin 1993; Reskin and Roos 2002). A small portion of the gender wage gap still remains unexplained. To explain this persistently unexplained portion, many scholars are searching for alternatives to study where and when inequalities emerge (Fortin 2008), especially looking at prelabor values and gender identities: masculinities and femininities and appropriate ways of doing gender (Kimmel 2000; Schilt and Wiswall 2008). In this chapter, I look at very early work experiences to understand how boys and girls learn to do gender (West and Zimmerman 1987) and potentially trace the origins of the gender wage gap. Since people enter the labor market at a young age, working in both freelance and employee-type jobs, early work experience can shed light on this persistent inequality. Is there a time of equality in the workforce? When does the first gender wage gap emerge? What factors contribute to the early gender inequality in pay?

To begin with, this chapter deals with two of the dominant theories of the gender pay gap: the human capital approach and the occupational segregation approach. The human capital approach focuses on men's and women's individual characteristics in explaining the pay gap (Altonji and Blank 1999; Becker 1964; Blau and Kahn 2006; Brown and Corcoran 1997; Fuller and Schoenberger 1991; Goldin 1990; Groshen 1991; Mincer 1962; Paglin and Rufolo 1990; Schilt and Wiswall 2008; Wood, Corcoran, and Courant 1993). According to this view, the pay differences between men and women can be explained by individual characteristics, such as differences in education and experience on the job (Bose and Bridges-Whaley 2011; Gottfried 2013). While this view has been popular in previous decades, some of the explanations are really no longer applicable. For example, this view argued that women were paid less than men because women are not as educated, do not have as many advanced degrees, or have lower graduation rates. However, while this might have been true in previous decades, today women outnumber men in college attendance and graduation. Over the past forty years, women's educational attainment has outpaced men's substantially (Haveman and Beresford 2012). Heather A. Haveman and Lauren S. Beresford (2012), based on their analysis of 2011 data from National Center for Education Statistics, show that in 1970–1971, women accounted for only 43 percent of all bachelor's degrees. By 2009, women earned 57 percent of all bachelor's degrees. Haveman and Beresford observe a similar trend in higher degrees, as well. Women earned 40 percent of all master's degrees in 1970–1971, whereas by 2008–2009, they accounted for 60 percent of master's degrees. In 1970–1971, women earned only 14 percent of all doctoral degrees, but by 2008–2009, they earned 52 percent of all doctorates.

Along with the rapid gains in educational attainment at all levels, the subjects, majors, and areas of specialization pursued by women have changed quickly as well (Haveman and Beresford 2012). Women have become more likely to seek out bachelor's and master's degrees in business, from 9 percent of business BAs and 4 percent of MBAs in 1970–1971 to 49 percent of business BAs and 45 percent of MBAs in 2008–2009 (Haveman and Beresford 2012). Even in science, technology, engineering, and mathematics (STEM) fields, there have been important changes, with STEM majors increasing from 18 percent female in 1970 to 38 percent in 2004 (Haveman and Beresford 2012; see also National Science Foundation 2007). There are some differences in specialization, with women being underrepresented in mathematically heavy subfields of finance and STEM fields (Bertrand, Goldin, and Katz 2010; Carrell, Page, and West 2009; Prokos and Padavic 2005). Despite significant educational gains, the pay gap persists (Charles 2003; Charles and Bradley 2009).

The human capital approach also argues that unequal pay is due to differences in experience (Gottfried 2013). As with the claims about differential levels of education, such claims are less compelling than they might once have been, as women have made substantial progress in increasing their job experience (Bose and Bridges-Whaley 2011). Forty years ago, only 41 percent of women (as opposed to 76 percent of men) were employed, but by 2009, 54 percent of women and 65 percent of men worked, closing the work experience gap (Haveman and Beresford 2012). One important factor contributing to the experience gap is the fact that women are also more likely to work part time (Goldin 1990; Jacobs 1989; Gatta and Roos 2005; Roos and Gatta 1999). Typically, part-time jobs offer little to no benefits and few opportunities for advancement, and they contribute little to women's careers. However, women often take these part-time jobs to balance child care and domestic duties.

Women may also have fewer years of job experience, which are due to labor market interruptions linked to parental leave, child care, and domestic duties (Bertrand, Goldin, and Katz 2010). Haveman and Beresford (2012) break the workforce into four age cohorts: twenty-five to thirty-four, thirty-five to forty-four, forty-five to fifty-four, and fifty-five to sixty-four. Among the youngest men, the median amount of job experience was 2.8 years, increasing to 5.2 years in the next age group, 8.2 years in the one after that, and 10.1 in the oldest age group. For women of all age groups, the median experience level was lower: 2.6 years, 4.7 years, 7 years, and 9.8 years, respectively—all lower than their male counterparts in the relative age groups (Haveman and Beresford 2012). There has been a rapid shift in the past few decades in attitudes toward working: today, attitudes toward working women and working mothers are overwhelmingly positive (Brewster and Padavic 2000), in a major shift from where they stood in the 1980s. However, even today, there remains a bias against mothers with small children working full-time (Treas and Widmer 2000). Especially with limited parental leave policies and in the absence of governmental programs that could help to balance work and family commitments, many women take time off from work or opt for reduced hours (Collinson and Collinson 2004; Jacobs and Gerson 2004). Jerry A. Jacobs and Kathleen Gerson (2004) find that women experience more work-family conflict than men do. Especially with recent changes in parenting and the increasing movement toward intensive mothering, more of the responsibility of parenting falls on the shoulders of women, where they are expected to be involved in all activities of the children. Women are more likely to be expected to tend to the everyday lives of their children rather than delegating to babysitters and nannies (Epstein 2004; P. Stone 2008). Expectations that mothers will chauffeur their children to structured activities, manage bake sales, volunteer at their children's schools, and coach sports teams make it increasingly difficult to find workplaces that will accommodate the demands of intensive parenting (Lareau 2003; Lareau and Weininger 2008). As a result, many highly educated working women leave the workforce or interrupt their careers to focus on intensive mothering (Belkin 2003; P. Stone 2008; Story 2005), either by choice or for lack of options.

In addition to childcare responsibilities, women also perform more housework than men do (Bianchi 2011; Bianchi et al. 2000; Bianchi et al. 2012; Sayer 2005). Today, among dual-earner couples, the division of chores is nowhere near equal: it is divided approximately two thirds to one third, with women performing two thirds of the house chores and men performing only one third (Coltrane and Adams 2001). In addition to the inequality in the division of chores, even individual tasks are gendered. For example, men are more likely to do more masculine tasks, such as mowing the lawn and barbecuing, while women are more likely to sew and iron. The tasks that men perform are typically not as time sensitive as women's tasks, either. For example, men are able to mow the lawn any day within the week based on their work schedule and availability, whereas everyday cooking, which is typically performed by women, has more immediate deadlines and more time pressures (Bittman et al. 2003; Coltrane 2010; Coltrane and Adams 2001). Similarly, typically masculine tasks, such lawn care, snow removal, and car repairs, can be subcontracted to others (sometimes even children can take over such tasks), while traditionally female tasks, such as everyday cooking, are much less likely to be performed by others. Overall, despite changes and progress, the bulk of the house chore responsibilities still fall on women, even when men and women work comparable hours. Because women are more likely to multitask and be responsible for house chores, they are more likely to be distracted, which may result in in lower workplace productivity.

Overall, this view argues that the pay gap can be explained through individual differences between men and women, resulting in lower productivity for women because they have fewer years of schooling, fewer credentials, and fewer years of experience (Corcoran and Duncan 1979; Duncan 1996; Goldin and Polachek 1987; Oaxaca 1973; Polachek 1981). Mary Corcoran and Greg J. Duncan (1979) for example, make use of the Panel Study of Income Dynamics to find that 44 percent of the observed gender wage gap is accounted for by differences in human capital. Solomon W. Polachek (1981), however, argues that even the measurement of human capital is a measure highly biased to privilege men and advocates for measurements to correct for such biases.

Alternatively, the occupational segregation approach argues that the wage gap is explained not through individual characteristics but through occupational factors. In other words, men and women do not get paid the same, not because they are different but because they work in different jobs (Gottfried 2013). In the past few decades, much progress has been made in occupational segregation, mostly with women entering traditionally male occupations (Reskin and Hartmann 1986; Reskin and Roos 2002), but relatively few men have entered women's jobs. Several studies have confirmed that sex segregation has very strong negative effects on wages (England, Hermsen, and Cotter 2000; Tomaskovic-Devey and Skaggs 2002).

Despite the difference in the two perspectives, these models have one thing in common: they focus on the *adult* work force, while work experiences often start much earlier. As noted previously, the majority of high school students work sometime during the school year, and they are even more likely to work during the summer (Staff, Schulenberg, and Bachman 2010). By the time they graduate from high school, most students have worked at some point either during the school year or the summer, so the gender wage gap potentially starts long before what has traditionally been measured. Wage differentials among teenagers, despite the prevalence of their work, have received scant academic attention. Two early studies point to boys and girls working in widely divergent sectors of the economy (Medrich et al. 1982; see also Goldstein and Oldham 1979), leading the authors to speculate that such different work arrangements may mirror differences of chore divisions at home. Lynne White and David Brinkerhoff (1981) find that boys and girls tend to work in different sectors, but their limited dataset includes young people between the ages of two and seventeen, a group dominated by people too young to have jobs of any kind. Simply because of the limitations of their data, they are unable to pinpoint what types of jobs young people work at and when the wage gap begins to emerge. In the early 1980s, Ellen Greenberger and Laurence Steinberg, in their article "Sex Differences in Early Labor Experience: Harbinger of Things to Come" (1983), explore gender inequality in the workplace for young workers. In their study, which remains the most comprehensive study of gender inequality in early labor markets, they point to gender differences in employment, sectors, and wages. They find that "the earliest experiences of boys and girls in the formal labor force mirrors sex differentials in the adult labor force. From virtually the moment youngsters go to work outside the home, they enter a labor force where the work of males and females is quite distinct" (Greenberger and Steinberg 1983, 481–482).

Based on their analysis, first, they find that adolescent girls work fewer hours in their first jobs than adolescent boys do and that adolescent girls have lower hourly wages. However, they offer only descriptive differences and do not delve into explanations of why such gender differences would exist, instead calling for more systematic studies of gender differences: "More systematic studies of children's early work are needed, however to clarify when boys' and girls' labor force participation begins, when boys' and girls' work moves in different directions, and when sex differences in hours of employment and hourly wages begin to emerge. The latter issue is virtually unexplored to date" (Greenberger and Steinberg 1983, 469). Unfortunately, despite the call for more studies to explain the gender wage gap in early years, data limitations have prevented many scholars from exploring these early inequalities in the past few decades.

This chapter aims to fill this gap in the literature and delve into gender differences in the teenage workforce. I situate my analysis at the intersection of these dominant theories, to help trace the origins of this persistent problem and also naturally control for many methodologically problematic confounds. Like a natural laboratory, focusing on these very young workers will help eliminate a wide range of confounds, including house chores, child care, and many other human capital explanations. Teenagers in this age group are not married and do not have children, and they do not have domestic or child-care duties.

The National Longitudinal Survey of Youth (NLSY97; described in detail in the Appendix) provides ample data on income and employment variables along with demographic information on youth. For comparison purposes and easier interpretation, the dataset is aggregated by age to enable analysis and explore changes over time. It is also separated into three cohorts: twelve- to thirteen-year-olds, fourteen- to fifteen-year-olds, and sixteen- to nineteen-year-olds. This dataset is particularly valuable not only in terms of the detailed, nationally representative data it provides on the employment characteristics of youth but also because of its inclusion of twelve- to fifteen-year-olds, most of whom are traditionally omitted from analysis of youth labor.

Typical accounts portray youth employment as "gender utopia" in terms of labor-force participation rates, a place where men and women seem to be, for once, on completely equal footing. If we focus solely on labor-force participation rates, in fact, we observe no significant differences (Figure 1.1). In none of the three age cohorts is there a substantial difference between boys and girls in terms of their labor-force participation rates. Among the twelve- to thirteen-year-olds, 36 percent of girls and 37 percent of boys work, among the fourteen- to fifteen-year-olds, 47 percent of girls and 51 percent of boys work, and among the sixteen- to nineteen-year-olds, 66 percent of girls and 65 percent of boys are employed. Such marginal differences mean that we can treat the labor participation rates, at least, as being approximately equal. Unlike when Greenberger and Steinberg (1983) found that boys were more likely to work than girls, for the past few decades, boys and girls have had

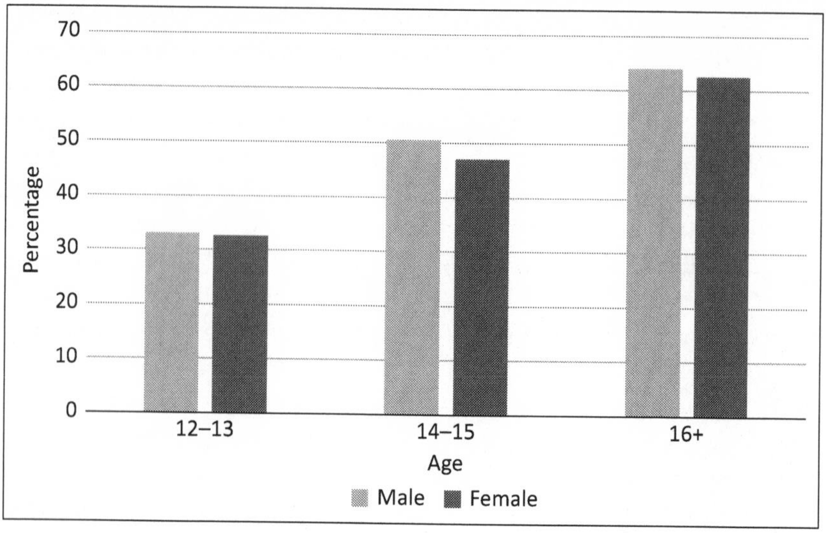

Figure 1.1 Labor-force participation by gender

comparable labor-force participation rates. This well-known finding, per-haps, leads to the perception of the youth labor market as a place of gender equality.

However, a lack of differences in the likelihood of youths working does not imply equality in all aspects of youth employment. While boys and girls of a certain age are equally likely to work, it is still possible that they receive differential pay for their work or are segregated into different types of jobs.

The Emergence of the First Wage Gap

In terms of earnings, we observe approximately equal annual median earn-ings for both genders during their early employment years, based on median annual earnings of dependent youth. Among the twelve- and thirteen-year-olds, boys, on average, make $120, while girls make only slightly more: $125. If for no other reason, this is important because it is the first instance of gender parity in earnings in the American labor force. As a further analysis shows, by the time the youth in the study are in the second age cohort, boys' earnings outstrip girls' substantially, with boys earning an average of $400 a year and girls earning only $266 annually. Thus, we first observe the gender wage gap among fourteen- and fifteen-year-olds, and it only grows with older cohorts. On average, sixteen- to nineteen-year-old boys make $950, grossing $200 more than their female counterparts.

Although the conventional and more reliable method of measurement, because of the low hourly pay at earlier ages and relatively lower work hours, is yearly wages, it is important to also look at the hourly pay rate. Parallel with the above findings, we observe that fourteen- to fifteen-year-old boys have higher hourly wages than girls of the same age. However, at these early ages, most working youth are engaged in freelance, nonhourly work. As freelance work is often paid on the basis of a completed task, rather than on an hourly basis, calculating hourly rates of pay lead to high standard deviations in the estimates of hourly earnings. Thus, annual earnings are a more reliable measure of earning power, but it is important to note that an analysis of hourly wages yields similar results to that of the annual wages.

What we can see from Figure 1.2 is that when youth are twelve or thirteen, we see no difference in pay, but when they get to fourteen or fifteen, we see the emergence of the gender wage gap, which widens with age. The mechanism behind this increasing gap is not immediately clear. Most of the traditional explanations of the gender wage gap fail when brought to bear on youth employment. Girls in these age cohorts would almost certainly not be less productive because of having children; similarly, there are not likely to be large differences in education, skills, credentials, or experience that would lead to differential pay. All of them have the same education (less than high school) and the same experience (basically, none).

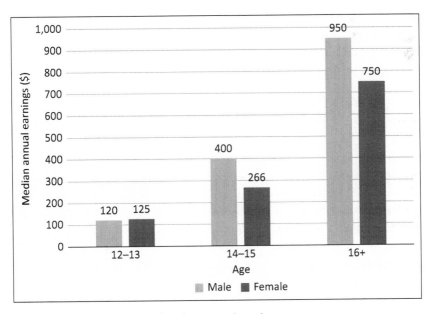

Figure 1.2 Median annual earnings by age and gender

Despite the fact that almost all individual explanations fail to account for the gender wage gap, the only applicable individual difference is the number of hours worked per week. It is important to note that boys might be working more hours than girls, resulting in the gender wage gap. Unlike our common perceptions, when we look at the aggregate data, girls and boys on average work almost equal hours, with girls working slightly more than boys. Based on the NLSY97 data, we can see that girls on average work 7.9 hours per week (standard deviation of 9.9), while boys work 7.2 hours per week (standard deviation of 9.9). Therefore, with similar standard deviations, we can see that girls work slightly more hours than boys do; therefore, there is no reason to suspect that differential hours of employment contribute to the gender wage gap.

Since the gender wage gap in youth jobs cannot be explained by individual differences such as differences in productivity, education, and experience, especially those due to domestic and maternal duties, we must look for alternative explanations. The second set of explanations in the literature focuses on structural factors such as the type of job. One potential explanation is that boys and girls, while having equal labor-force participation rates, may work in different types of jobs. In fact, the types of jobs that employ youth do seem to differ by gender. Among the fourteen- and fifteen-year-olds, girls are more likely to be employed in freelance jobs, such as babysitting, while boys tend to be employed in employee-type jobs, working at more regular hours at an organization for set rates of pay. Here, the U.S. Department of Labor defines freelance jobs as self-employment: typical examples of this type of work are babysitting and yard work. Employee-type jobs, however, are defined as working for an organization, such as a fast-food restaurant or a retail store.

Even though we observe the gendering of jobs within employee- and freelance-type jobs, which will be discussed in the following chapters at length, the gendering seems to be present at age twelve to thirteen, and the change over time seems to be slow. However, the largest effect is in the concentration of boys and girls in freelance- and employee-type jobs, respectively (Figure 1.3). It seems that teenagers adopt traditional gender roles quickly on entering the workforce, with the freelance- versus employee-type job distinction as the major difference.

The Making of the Gender Wage Gap

The overall analysis of the data shows a difference in the types of jobs taken by boys and girls, especially a marked concentration of girls in freelance jobs and boys in employee-type jobs, but we have yet to show that this is the cause

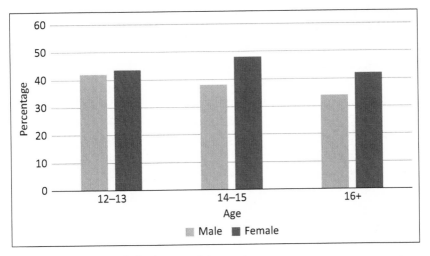

Figure 1.3 Participation in freelance work by gender

of the gender wage gap. First, there is no evidence to suggest differential pay for different types of jobs among the youth. The vast majority of youth employed in employee-type jobs receive the minimum wage, and there is no reason to believe that freelance jobs pay more to one gender than the other.

Second, the disproportionate employment of girls in freelance jobs cannot alone be the cause of the gender wage gap, as child labor laws restrict youth under 16 from employment. Therefore, the samples of twelve- to thirteen-year-olds and fourteen- to fifteen-year-olds are predominantly employed in freelance-type jobs (although exceptions do exist for agricultural workers, work in family businesses, and some other situations, they do not apply to most children). If the disproportionate employment of girls in freelance-type jobs explained the gender wage gap, we would not observe the significant pay differential for the fourteen- to fifteen-year-old cohort that we do, as relatively few of the teenagers work in employee-type jobs. Moreover, while the concentration of girls and boys in traditionally gendered jobs increases, this does not map onto the earliest signs of the gender wage gap. Even among the twelve- to thirteen-year-old cohort, where girls actually earn slightly more than their male counterparts, there is a concentration of girls and boys in traditionally gendered jobs. The extent to which job choice results in the discrepancy in pay needs to be tested.

The purpose of this analysis is to account for the effect of gender on income by controlling for all the possible confounding factors. Even though the number of hours does not differ for boys and girls, it is important to control for it as a confounding variable. In addition to the average number of hours worked per week, the regression analysis includes several variables representing structural explanations for the wage gap applicable to youth, such as the type of job (freelance versus employee-type), and demographic-control variables traditionally included in similar analyses, such as race (white or Asian versus nonwhite or Asian), age (as youth typically earn more as they become older), the socioeconomic status of the household (measured through household income, as a percentage of the local poverty level), and, of course, the gender of the respondent. The model uses all of these to explain the income of the respondent, logged in order to minimize the impact of outliers. Simply put, the existence of a difference in wages based on gender, rather than on hours worked or any other explanation, should be evident from a significant coefficient attached to the variable representing the gender of the respondent.

All of the predictor variables in the model have statistically significant effects on youth income. In interpretation of the table coefficients, it is important to note that all reflect changes in logged, rather than actual, income. The details of the model are presented in the methodological notes. The most important finding of this regression is in the coefficient attached to the gender of the respondent. Accounting for all the explanations applicable to the youth in our sample, including the number of hours worked and the nature of the job, girls can expect to earn about $93 less per year solely by virtue of their gender. While this may not seem like a great deal of income, it is very large relative to the mean earnings of a girl in the sample, which come out to only $606.76 per year. Thus, at these young ages, girls are making almost 13 percent less than boys, solely because of their gender.

Other factors in the model were used solely for control purposes to identify the pure effect of gender, but they also provide interesting comparisons by which we can better comprehend the magnitude of the effects of gender on income. It is interesting to see that the effects of race result in an average difference between white and nonwhite workers of $63, one-third less than the effect of gender.

The heteroskedastic maximum-likelihood regression also allows for the substantive interpretation of the causes of the variance in our model. (The details of the model are also presented in the Appendix.) As predicted, the variance in the model increases with age and income—the latter bolstering the assertion of depressed model fit due to reporting error in the dependent variable—but decreases with the interaction of the two, a striking result, especially given the relative strengths of the coefficients. This can be interpreted to mean that as youth become more like adults—as they age and earn more money—the relationship of their demographic characteristics to their earnings becomes more predictable. It may be only this variance that allows for the equality of pay in the youngest cohorts, and it fades away rapidly with

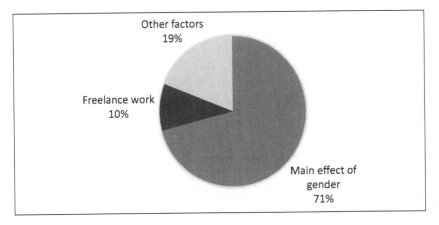

Figure 1.4 Proportion of gender wage gap explained

Note: Total gender wage gap = Average wage of boys ($737.57) – Average wage of girls ($606.76) = $130.81; Portion explained by main effect of gender = Dollar value attached to coefficient for gender = $93.01; Portion explained by freelance work = (Expected value of freelance for girls (0.4775) – Expected value of freelance for boys (0.4244)) × Dollar value attached to coefficient for freelance ($245.01) = $13.01; Portion explained by other factors = Total gender wage gap ($130.81) – Portion explained by main effect of gender ($93.01) – Portion explained by difference in likelihood of freelance work ($13.01) = $24.75.

increases in age and earnings. But, interestingly, a further analysis of the heteroskedasticity patterns shows an interesting clustering of older, higher-income youth—most of whom are boys, with the marked omission of girls.

So far, the analysis has identified the effect of gender on the earnings of youth, controlling for all possible explanations and demographic characteristics. However, it is important to show how these factors translate into the gender wage gap. While the maximum likelihood estimation identifies the direct effect of gender, it is also evident that the gender results in unequal earnings through the concentration of girls in freelance jobs. As presented in Figure 1.4, the total average gender wage gap in the youth sample is $130, 71 percent of which is accounted by the pure effect of gender. In addition to this, 10 percent of this difference is accounted for by the differential concentration of girls in freelance jobs. Therefore, we can say that overall, this model accounts for 81 percent of the gender wage gap.

What about Values?

The first model using the NLSY97 dataset tests a wide range of individual and occupational characteristics but does not include any variables on values and motives for working. Looking at values and motives are important because in the recent year, there has been an emergence of studies focusing on early work values and motives, in an effort to explain the unexplained portion of the wage gap (Fortin 2008; Gottfried 2013).

These early work experiences are especially important in understanding the transition to adulthood. The adolescent years have been referred to as a demographically dense life stage (Rindfuss 1991, 494), and many researchers have explored the effects of work on adolescents, including their aspirations, values, and motivations (see Fortin 2008) Research has shown that these early years and early work experiences are central in understanding later motivations and aspirations (even though these can change over time). When adolescents graduate from high school, which paths they take, whether they go to college, which college they go to, which occupational path they choose, and which area they want to specialize in all depend on their work values (Johnson 2002).

Some work values are associated with the importance of work rewards and how much adolescents emphasize the rewards associated with different kinds of work (Lindsay and Knox 1984; Herzog 1982; Marini et al. 1996; Mortimer and Lorence 1979). Margaret Marini and coauthors (1996) differentiate between the kinds of rewards that adolescents value in the workplace. Extrinsic rewards include instrumental and status attainment, as well as income and monetary gratifications, promotion opportunities, and occupational prestige. Others may value job security (Marini et al. 1996). Still others value intrinsic rewards, such as interest in the job, enjoyment of the topic, learning potential, opportunities to be creative, or enjoyment of being involved in decision making. Altruistic rewards come from helping others or contributing to societal advancement in any form. Social rewards are interpersonal and include the opportunity to make new friends, interact with people, and have positive relationships with coworkers. Finally, leisure rewards refer to the opportunity for free time, vacation, and freedom from direct supervision. Based on this schema, Marini and her research team (1996) find that young people tend to value a wide range of jobs, regardless of what will be available for them in their future careers in the adult labor market.

At these early stages, adolescents are not highly selective about the desirability of potential work rewards (Johnson 2001, 2002), and seem to have unrealistic expectations about jobs (Csikszentmihalyi and Schneider 2000; Schneider and Stevenson 1999). Because of such high expectations about future educational and occupational attainment, some researchers suggest that adolescents might be headed for disillusionment and disappointment when they are unable to realize these high expectations (Csikszentmihalyi and Schneider 2000). Arne Kalleberg (1977) finds that work values and job characteristics form the basis of job satisfaction: adolescents who fail to fulfill their high expectations and settle for less desirable jobs may feel less satisfied with their jobs and their lives and experience lower levels of satisfaction.

However, other research shows that these adolescents' values and aspirations, as well as their occupational aspirations, are not static but rather change considerably throughout their adolescent years and even during young adult years (Jacobs, Karen, and McClelland 1991; Johnson 2002; Rindfuss, Cooksey, and Sutterlin 1999). While the traditional research has treated adolescents as a uniform group when understanding their values, bourgeoning research calls for understanding inner differences, especially those based on race, class, and gender (Mortimer 2005).

Some research suggests that while the source of initial values about work are mysterious (Mortimer et al. 1996), they do tend originate from parents' and immediate families' socioeconomic backgrounds, as well as parents' jobs (Alexander, Eckland, and Griffin 1975; Gecas 1979; Mortimer and Kumka 1982; Mortimer, Lorence, and Kumka 1986). For example, workers in higher-social-class positions tend to put more emphasis on influence and intrinsic work values and less importance on extrinsic value and security. As Pierre Bourdieu writes, social origins and socioeconomic background are ongoing influences on young people's aspirations (Bourdieu 1973; Bourdieu and Passeron 1997). These goals are formed—both consciously and unconsciously—based on class positions along with perceptions of potentials of social mobility. These early class-based perceptions can heavily influence which jobs young people value and aspire to and which ones they think they can achieve (Girod, Fricker, and Korffy 1973; Mortimer, Lorence, and Kumka 1986).

In addition to class, race plays an important role. For example, African Americans place higher value on extrinsic rewards, such as higher income, and less importance on gaining a sense of accomplishment (Martin and Tuch 1993), which controls for many confounding factors such as class, occupational characteristics, and family background.

Finally, gender plays a role in the formation of work values, though these gendered work values have received scant attention, as research on gender differences in work values has been mixed with justifications of occupational segregation. Many early studies justified occupational choices through differences in work values; therefore, the study of work values in gender research has been deemphasized (Bielby and Bielby 1984; Fortin 2008; Rowe and Snizek 1995). In recent years, in an effort to reduce the unexplained portion of the wage gap, we have seen a renewed interest in gender research on work values (Fortin 2008). For an adult population, scientists have noted slight differences between men and women in their attitudes toward greed and altruism (Andreoni and Vesterlund 2001), leadership and competitiveness

(Gneezy, Niederle, and Rustichini 2003). While these studies have pointed to differences in values, not many studies have captured the effects of these differences on wages. Peter Kuhn and Catherine Weinberger (2005) show that for white men, leadership values translate to managerial positions, leading to higher pay.

Psychologists have also explored the role of external locus of control—the feeling of one's outcome controlled by forces outside one's realm of control—as well as self-esteem. They find differences in external locus of control and self-esteem between men and women, which might indirectly affect workplace outcomes. For example, scholars have argued that lower self-esteem results in lower investment in one's education, resulting in unequal labor market outcomes (Goldsmith, Veum, and Darity 1997; Heckman, Stixrud, and Urzua 2006; Manning and Swaffield 2008; Groves 2005; Waddell 2006), yet gender differences in self-esteem are very small, and there is little uniform support in the existing literature.

For an adult sample, researchers have also argued that valuing money and monetary gratifications, as opposed to other aspects of the job, could be important to understanding gender differences. They find that valuing money and the belief that money is an important aspect of the job results in more negotiation, more changes in jobs and other acts that can result in higher pay, and more promotions (Ajzen and Fishbein 1977; Tang, Kim, and Tang 2000). On the other hand, Lex Borghans, Bas ter Weel, and Bruce A. Weinberg (2006) show that women are more likely to value interpersonal skills and social aspects of the job, tend to volunteer more, and place a higher value on altruistic acts (Fortin 2008).

Studies based on youth and college students find that female students place higher emphasis on intrinsic, altruistic, and social rewards, whereas their male counterparts emphasize extrinsic job rewards and leisure (Bridges 1989; Herzog 1982; Lueptow 1980; Marini et al. 1996). Such findings seem to align with traditionally emphasized social roles for men and women. Nicole M. Fortin (2008) shows that these value differences in self-esteem and altruism have a very slight role in the gender wage gap. However, studies with more recent graduates and younger cohorts show that this gap is closing and a newer cohort of young women tend to value extrinsic rewards just as much as their male counterparts, though some gender differences remain (Marini et al. 1996). What is more interesting is the interaction effect of race and gender. Studies suggest that African American women and girls tend to value the monetary rewards of working more than their male counterparts (Martin and Tuch 1993; Thomas and Shields 1987).

The previous models have so far considered several sets of explanations for the wage gap among youth and successfully accounted for an overwhelming majority of the gender wage gap. However, some of the explanations, which may sound plausible when applied to the adult wage gap, are simply inapplicable to youth; other explanations were dispelled in the statistical analysis presented in this chapter. After all of this, there remains a pay differential of 19 percent that has yet to be accounted for. So far, the first two sets of explanations have been tested for, but the third set of explanations remains unknown. Could the reasons why boys and girls make different amounts of money be because they work for different reasons? To be certain of our findings, we turn to a final set of explanations: the differential values of boys and girls regarding the job market. We have yet to account for the possibility that boys and girls might be working for different reasons and value different aspects of work, which might be contributing to the gender wage gap. Even though there is early research to refute this argument for the adult labor markets (see Jacobs and Steinberg 1990), it is important to test whether differential values of youth could account for their differential earnings. First, we will test to see what values, if any, are important to the work decisions of youth, and second, we will see if these values differ substantially between boys and girls.

This analysis is based on the replication of similar studies measuring the differences in values in predicting labor-market-entry decisions in the adult labor market (Besen-Cassino 2014). The data employed for this analysis comes from the World Values Survey (WVS) (Abramson and Inglehart 1995), which provides reliable data on economic and social work-related factors on the population of interest. For our age group of interest, sixteen to nineteen, we focus on the differential reasons for working among boys and girls. I estimate a logistic regression model predicting the labor-market-entry decisions of youth. Then, I replicate the same model for boys and girls to capture the differential reasons for working. The advantage of the WVS is that it provides international, reliable, comparable data, which is nationally representative. It is one of the few studies that focuses on young people's values, aspirations, and motivations in detail. While the focus of this book is the United States, the international comparative data enable future comparative studies on the same topic.

Using the WVS, I estimate a logistic regression model, modeling the decision to work using a wide range of reasons to work—both social and economic—from the dataset. The dependent variable is the decision to work, and the independent variables include stated values of good pay, lack of pressure, pleasant coworkers, job security, promotions, respected job, good hours, ability to take initiative, useful work, good holidays, meeting new people, achievement, responsibility, interesting work, and work that aligns with abilities. These variables measure both economic benefits, such as pay and promotions, and social benefits, such as meeting people. These variables enable the researchers to compare and contrast different factors in the workplace. Overall, I see the work decisions of youth in the United States in the specified age group as dominated by social factors; however, when we control for gender and replicate the same logistic regression model for boys and girls separately, there are no clear differences in what boys and girls say that they value at work.

Traditional explanations associate women's work with social and noneconomic reasons and men's work with economic reasons, and they try to link these differential values in working with the gender wage gap. However, there is no statistical evidence to suggest that such a differential exists in the reasons why boys and girls work. Based on the 95 percent confidence intervals presented in Figure 1.5, I show that the coefficients attached to these variables in predicting work decisions can be safely said to be indistinguishable at any standard level of statistical significance. In short, there is no evidence to support differential reasons for working for boys and girls. Furthermore,

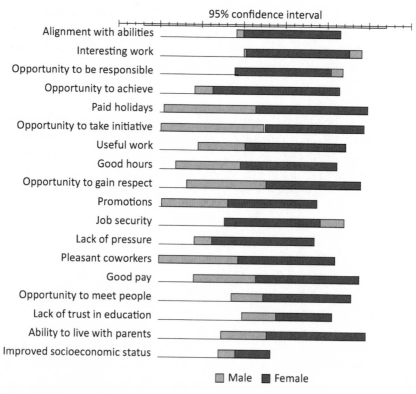

Figure 1.5 Gender values at work (95 percent confidence intervals)

these findings show that the gender interactions are not statistically significant, showing that there is no evidence that boys and girls work for different reasons or value different things about work. Therefore, differences in values, motives, and attitudes toward work do not result in differences in pay.

Overall, this chapter focuses on gender inequality in the youth labor force. My findings, based on NLSY97, show that when adolescents are twelve and thirteen years old, they are paid the same amount of money, but when they reach ages fourteen and fifteen, we see the emergence of the gender wage gap, which widens with age. Some demographic factors, such as race, exacerbate the gender wage gap; this topic are discussed in detail in Chapter 4. One of the major reasons for this wage inequality is the concentration of girls in freelance jobs: boys move to higher-paying employee-type jobs as they become available, while girls stay at freelance jobs longer. The concentration of girls in freelance jobs, especially babysitting, and the mechanisms through which they are asked to stay longer in freelance jobs are discussed in Chapter 2. However, even within freelance jobs and within employee-type jobs, there is still gender inequality. This chapter also shows that there is no evidence that boys and girls work for different reasons: boys and girls in this age group do not work for different reasons. The values, motives, and aspirations they bring to these first jobs are not the culprit of the gender wage gap, but it is important to study the gendered work values and gendered assumptions that boys and girls are socialized into at work.

Despite controlling for individual and occupational characteristics, there still seems to be gender-based discrimination. The mechanisms through which this discrimination is experienced in everyday lives are discussed in the next two chapters. In these chapters, I focus on the two sectors where young women work: freelance jobs—in particular, babysitting—and retail and service-sector jobs.

2

Babysitters

Pricing the Priceless Child (Care)

We Need You

It is 6:00 P.M., and I wait for Katie, at the coffee shop at the college campus where she is a full-time student, to talk about her experiences in babysitting. Katie is a twenty-one-year-old Latina majoring in sociology and minoring in family and child studies at a large state university and is scheduled to graduate at the end of the spring semester. She is excited to be the first in her family to go to college. She loves social issues and psychology, and she aspires to be a documentary filmmaker. When I meet her, she is in the midst of her applications to British universities for a master's degree. Even though she is almost done with her classes, she still babysits—something she has been doing since her early teens.

Around 6:30, I see Katie hurrying—almost running—into the coffee shop, and she apologizes for being half an hour late to our appointment. As she sits, she puts down her large tote bag, which is full of art supplies for the children, and tells me she is so late because the mother of the two children that she babysits arrived late from work and wanted to chat about the children's playdates and activity schedules for half an hour after Katie was off the clock. "She needs to vent sometimes. I am like a wife to her," she says. The parents work so much and the children have such busy lives that, according to Katie, she almost never leaves her shift on time, even though she still gets paid the same amount. The bus is always late, there is always tunnel traffic, and the parents—usually the mother—almost always want to chat about something.

Katie has been working as a babysitter for a long time. Both her parents work to put Katie and her younger sister through college, but she needs to work as well, to help with her school expenses. These days, it is even more important, because of all the graduate school application fees. She has been babysitting for the same family for years. It all started as a part-time job when she was in high school. She liked the extra bit of cash to pay for new clothes, movies, makeup, and accessories. She knew some of her friends were working, and she wanted to work, too. She did not directly know the family, but her friend was babysitting for a woman whose coworker had just had a baby. The fact that she "knew" the family was important to Katie, as she did not feel safe in just anyone's house. She describes the family she works for as "nice" and says that they are genuinely good people with "cute kids." When she started, the parents had a newborn and needed occasional babysitting on date nights. Some Friday and Saturday nights, she would go over to their place, which was relatively close to her house. The proximity to her home was a big advantage, and the job itself was not that challenging. The baby would often be asleep, so she could watch television, read a book, or do homework. When the mother went back to work full time, she had a more structured schedule, and soon, the family had another child. Now, they have two school-age children with numerous scheduled activities. Her job is to pick them up—from two different schools—drive them to different activities (swimming and gymnastics), bring them home, give them snacks, and help them with their homework.

She thought by the time she was in college, she would not be babysitting anymore, but now she finds it very difficult to leave. She constantly feels guilty, like she is missing out on something. Her friends who used to babysit as teenagers have moved on to working for corporations, oftentimes working in retail and service-sector jobs. Many of her friends have even moved on from retail and service-sector jobs to jobs related to their future careers, in internships and entry-level positions. "I have a friend who is a political science major, and he has been working for a [local mayor's] office, and another friend has an internship at a company that does market research," Katie says. She feels like she is falling behind.

In high school and college, many of her friends were working retail and service-sector jobs, getting discounts from clothing stores. Even though working retail and service positions would have been easier, Katie continued babysitting. "It's not like working at a coffee shop," she tells me as we sit at the university's café, pointing to the baristas. "Try looking after kids." But despite the challenges of looking after children, she has found it difficult to quit her job. She thought about it when she started college, but every time she tried to quit, she felt like she had a personal responsibility to the children and to the parents, and every time she told them she is thinking about quitting, they told her they *needed* her. She says she should have quit the family a long time ago. The family is very hard to turn down, according to Katie. "They need me," she says. Without her, the family could not function. The dual-earner couple she describes lives in a four-bedroom house in an affluent nearby suburb and is overscheduled. For the past few years, she got into the habit of scheduling her classes in the mornings and mostly Monday and Wednesdays just so she could accommodate the children's school schedules. She says that because the two children have hectic schedules, packed with playdates, extra lessons, and extracurricular activities, making her school schedule is a challenge, and she finds herself in a quandary every semester.

Since she started working for the family, the terms of her employment have changed substantially. Her job went from caring for one small baby to two school-age children, from essentially being at home with a child in a crib, doing some of her homework, watching television, and even talking to her friends when the baby was asleep, to picking up children from school and driving them to different activities, arranging playdates, scheduling activities, and preparing arts-and-crafts projects to entertain them. She puts in a load of laundry sometimes, as the younger child might need to wear a green shirt tomorrow for "Grinch Day" at school, she makes snacks for them and helps them with homework everyday, and sometimes she makes them dinner when the parents are late from work. There are also last-minute calls: the past winter was especially challenging because there were many snow days, with school cancellations and late starts. To accommodate the family on these days, she had to juggle her own school schedule so that she could pick up the children, entertain them, and help out the family. Especially during these winter months, unpredictability is built into her schedule. Even if the winter is milder, the children often get sick, and she has to stay home with the children.

Despite this vast change in her job description, her hourly rate has not changed much since she was hired. At the end of each shift, she says she is exhausted physically and emotionally. Her work also does not end at the end of the shift. Many days, the family wants to chat with her after her shift, just to be on the same page. One time it was about the children's diet and the snacks she was allowed to prepare, many times it is about the playdates, activities, and after-school events, and once it was the head-lice outbreak in school. These "brief chats" are usually not part of her paid work, but she has to be there, sometimes even listening as the mother of the family vents about the challenges of work-life balance.

Katie is one of many babysitters in the United States. According to the International Nanny Association, there are 1.2 million in-home child-care providers and countless more babysitters in the informal economy (Sullivan 2015). On March 20, 2012, the *New York Times* published an article titled "The Best Nanny Money Can Buy," which highlights elite nannies who make approximately $180,000 per year, as well as a Christmas bonus and a $3,000 monthly allowance for a Central Park West apartment (Davidson 2012). While the media depictions of babysitters focus on these glamorous and high-paid cases, they do not reflect the everyday reality of babysitters. According to the International Nanny Association, the average pay is $12 to $15 an hour, with many younger students getting paid much less per hour (Sullivan 2015). According to a 2015 report by the Economic Policy Institute, the median wage of child-care workers is $10.31 an hour. For such an important job—taking care of children—this is a low figure, but the report also shows that these wages are approximately 23 percent lower than what these same workers could make in other sectors, controlling for gender, race, education, age, and geography, as well as many other background factors (Gould 2015).

Katie makes $12 an hour, which she considers to be good pay, as compared to the pay of her friends who babysit. Many of her friends make somewhere between $8 and $12 an hour, so she is at the high end of that spectrum. Unfortunately, there are also many tasks and many portions of her time that are not paid. In her own time, she says she looks for activities to do with the children, sometimes buying little toys or art supplies out of her own pocket.

In the United States, the Fair Labor Standards Act of 1938 sets the minimum age of nonagricultural work as sixteen, but work starts much earlier than sixteen. It is legal for fourteen- and fifteen-year-olds to be employed in nonmining and nonmanufacturing jobs, during times that will not interfere with their school schedules and under conditions that will not undermine their health or their emotional development. Children younger than fourteen are typically considered too young to be employed in the formal sector, but many people as young as twelve enter the informal economy. In the Department of Labor's "Report on the Youth Labor Force," using National Longitudinal Survey of Youth (NLSY97) data, over half of the thirteen-year-olds interviewed said they had worked as twelve-year-olds, with the majority of early jobs being in either babysitting or yard work (Herman 2000). Among twelve-year-old boys, approximately 25 percent reported doing babysitting, and two thirds did yard work. Among the female twelve-year-olds, 85 percent reported babysitting, but only 14 percent had done yard work. By the time they were fourteen, more than 90 percent of the girls had done some babysitting in the past. Despite such differences, around ages twelve and thirteen, both boys and girls start out in freelance jobs, but as more and more employee-type jobs become available, boys move into employee-type jobs, whereas girls are more likely to stay in babysitting jobs (see Herman 2000 for a more detailed overview).

Babysitting is the first entry into the workforce for many women. It is the first time many girls as young as twelve start earning money, interview for a position, and learn to work with employers. In this chapter, based on in-depth, qualitative interviews, I explain the mechanisms through which young women are kept in babysitting jobs and the everyday mechanisms through which gender inequality in pay is reinforced.

You Are a Natural

Many babysitters I talked to emphasized that they were told they were "naturals" by the parents they work for at some point. Katie told me the mother of the family she works for said to her that she was "a natural," that she was just "good with children." She thought it might have something to do with the countless hours she spent babysitting her own sister and baby cousins growing up.

Similarly, Holly has been a babysitter since she was a teenager. She said she would like to work in education, but she does not believe that it comes naturally to her. In fact, when parents tell her she is a natural, she is offended. She told me about one time, when she was interviewing for a job, the four-year-old started fussing, so Holly pulled out a bag of stickers from her purse and gave them to the child to distract him. The parents commented on what a natural she was and asked if she had siblings or if she grew up with children around. She found this comment offensive because it made it sound like she was born with this skill; in fact, she said, she was professional and prepared. Based on her previous experiences in babysitting and her part-time work at a co-op day care's summer camp, she always brings something to the interviews to keep children occupied. The interviews are usually challenging because the babysitter needs to keep up a conversation with the prospective employers and connect with the children at the same time. Holly always keeps a bag of stickers and crayons with her and gives them to the children to keep them occupied; she said that this gesture also signals to the employers that she knows how to connect with children.

Such planning is reflected in the narratives of many babysitters. Lily is a college student in her first year at a large public university, where she has just transferred to the psychology department from a community college. She has been working as a babysitter since she was a teenager. Before every interview, she makes sure she has a small plastic ball and a bag of small squishy animals

with her to give to the children when they fuss. It may look like a spontane-
ous reaction, but it also makes her look prepared.

In these cases, the babysitters thought about the interviews and prepared
exclusively for the events based on their past experience with children and
parents. However, such efforts are not acknowledged as experience or knowl-
edge-based but, rather, are seen as natural or instinctual.

In addition, while many parents praise such "natural" characteristics, in
reality, many of them require babysitters to have considerable certifications
and credentials. Katie, for example, took CPR courses, as well as babysitting
classes at the YMCA, before she started babysitting as a young teen. Emma,
who just turned twenty-two, has been working as a babysitter for almost ten
years, babysitting for as many as five children at a time. Her job search for her
current position of babysitting up to ten hours per week did not take long: she
said she was hired immediately, but she said credentials like CPR and babysitting classes are desired by the parents. She took a similar babysitting class
as a part of her time in the Girl Scouts, and this year alone, she spent close
to $200 on similar classes. More recently, Katie has been taking family and
child studies classes at the university, even though they are not in her major
field of study. Similarly, some of the babysitters told me that parents who
request that babysitters drive the children have requested that they complete
defensive-driving courses, in addition to having a clean driving record.

Lily mentioned her child psychology classes being important in the hiring process. As a psychology major, she was not necessarily interested in
developmental psychology, but she has taken a few classes just to put on her
résumé. When she goes to interviews, parents have consistently mentioned
these classes. Lily also worked at the day-care center at the university where
she studies, even though she did not necessarily want to, because that particular day care had a good reputation locally. She found that it was a good
credential in the parents' eyes, and it distinguished her among a pool of applicants.

Deniz, an eighteen-year-old Turkish-born college student, works as a
babysitter in addition to working as a math tutor at her university. She used
her experience as a tutor as a sign that she would be able to work with children and help with their homework. Similarly, Jenna has kept her job as a
lifeguard at the local pool in the summers. Because she worked as a lifeguard,
parents trusted her to take the children she was babysitting to the munici-
pal pool during the summer. This is something many babysitters reported
doing: using classes they take and other school experience to find and keep
babysitting jobs.

The existing literature on labor markets and nannies describes the baby-
sitter-finding process based on the queuing theory (Reskin and Roos 2002;

Thurow 1969). Queuing theory argues that babysitters and nannies rank potential employers based on pay and work conditions. Simultaneously, employers rank potential babysitters and nannies based on education, job skills, gender, and race (Macdonald 2015). According to Cameron Macdonald, "The ordering of these two queues varies according to worker supply, changes in the relative composition of a given occupation, and changes in customers' needs and expectations." (2015, 154). Since nannies and babysitters, culturally, are mother substitutes, caregiving—providing care and love while not directly substituting for the mother (Macdonald 2010)—is assumed to be the realm of mothering (Duffy 2011). Despite the professionalization of babysitting, research has found that outside institutionalized day-care settings, education and credentials do not play a role in hiring (Macdonald 2015). Yet in the in-depth interviews, my sample showed that female babysitters valued credentials such as CPR (especially infant CPR) certification, babysitting classes, and college-level courses in child psychology and family and child studies. In my surveys, 92 percent of the babysitters said that they had taken a CPR class, and more than 90 percent reported taking defensive-driving classes. One participant, who typically babysits in the summer and takes an elementary-school-age boy to the town pool, has a lifeguard certification and has worked as a lifeguard before, which made her appealing to the boy's parents.

In addition to specific certifications, fluency in a foreign language is an important asset in the babysitting job market. Francesca, a nineteen-year-old undergraduate at a community college, is originally from Italy, and in this competitive market, her foreign-language skills have been an asset. She said that many parents ask her to speak to younger children in her native tongue. It makes the babysitting jobs more challenging for her, but she said that it makes finding jobs much easier Even though babysitters point to a wide range of certifications and skills that parents are looking for, and despite extensive, time-consuming, and unpaid credentialing processes, the skills desired by parents are assumed to be "natural," and babysitters are consistently told they are naturally good with children.

Aesthetic Labor and Emotion Labor in Babysitting

Today, research shows that aesthetic labor—looking good and sounding right for a job—is central to securing employment (Besen-Cassino 2014; Gatta 2011; Misra and Walters 2016; Pettinger 2004; Williams and Connell 2010). New research by Child Trends shows that for fifteen- to twenty-nine-year-old workers, having soft skills and communication tools are central in finding a job (Lippman et al. 2015). Recent work has also identified the role of aesthetic labor and soft skills in retail and service-sector jobs (Besen-Cassino 2014; Gatta 2011; Grugulis and Bozkurt 2011; Nickson, Warhurst, and Dutton 2004), which are discussed in more detail in Chapter 3. However, the role of aesthetic labor and soft skills remains relatively unexplored in freelance jobs because of the informal nature of the work. Despite limited prior work, most babysitters and nannies I interviewed pointed to the importance of looking good, sounding right, and having soft skills. Many students who worked at retail and service jobs mentioned the importance of aesthetic labor and soft skills. Jules, who has worked at a high-end clothing store targeting young people, Seymour and Smith, mentioned that looking like the brand and projecting the right image was the most important component of her work, more important than the actual job she was supposed to be performing. However, Katie told me that the soft skills needed for babysitting are much more complicated. When I asked her how soft skills in retail and babysitting are different, she told me that in babysitting, it is not one type of persona she has to project. Instead of projecting an Abercrombie and Fitch persona or a Starbucks persona, she has to maintain different images for different people in the family. She needs different skills to talk to the parents than the ones she needs to talk to the children. She said she acts differently with the other babysitters than with mothers and uses different tools and skills to deal with even the older and younger children, not to mention children of different genders.

Lily, the psychology major, told me that when she is interviewing, she not only brings toys and snacks to engage the children but also has engaging conversations with the parents about how responsible she is. I observed her during an interview, when she made sure to look as upbeat as possible and pulled out a tennis ball from her bag to give to a fussing infant. Katie also pointed to these often-clashing expectations to appear polished, responsible, and dependable for the parents and fun and cool for the children.

In addition to aesthetic labor, another important component of babysitting is emotion work. In *The Managed Heart* (1983), Arlie Russell Hochschild focuses on the concept of managing one's emotions and the way in which they are displayed, with the intent to influence the feelings and actions of others. She introduces two new concepts: emotion labor, which refers to employers' demands that employees display a certain set of acceptable emotions in the workplace, and emotion work, which refers to the set of emotions women display at home, especially when balancing work and family needs (Hochschild 1979, 1983; Lively 2000; see also DeVault 1999; Wharton and Erickson 1995).

Extensive research on the organizational behavior literature has explored the role of emotional labor, focusing on how emotions are expressed and experienced (Ashforth and Humphrey 1993; Parkinson 1991; Rafaeli and Sutton 1987, 1989; Schaubroeck and Jones 2000; Van Maanen and Kunda 1989; Wharton and Erickson 1993; Zerbe and Falkenberg 1989), but Hochschild focuses on the experience of emotions during service transactions. She shows that service-sector workers are expected to experience and express certain feelings and emotions during service interactions.

Katie remembers many occasions when she was frustrated with the children because they not only misbehaved but also were rude to her, but she had trouble expressing her frustration and her disappointment. During some shifts, she feels physically exhausted, but expressing her physical exhaustion would not be acceptable; her physical exhaustion, especially, made the family uncomfortable. Ruthie, an eighteen-year-old full-time student, started working as a babysitter three months before I interviewed her. At the time of the interview, she was working for three different families, often looking after the children overnight and on weekends. She remembers a weekend when she was supposed to babysitting the two siblings, but the parents dropped off the children's two cousins as well: "The children started acting up and stopped listening to me," she said. The shift took longer than she expected, and the parents called to ask if she could give snacks to the children, give them dinner, tidy up the house, and start working on an art project. However, despite the extra work, she was paid her typical $10 per hour.

Ruthie was frustrated and exhausted, but she felt she could not talk to the parents. "I heard them casually mention how expensive child care is and how they are always on a budget," she said. Ruthie also notes that the parents talk about how fun and nice spending time with the children is, limiting her expressions of frustration, exhaustion, and other similar emotions. Madison, a nineteen-year-old full-time college student, has also felt that expressions of her emotions were limited. During the summer months, she looks after five-year-old Noah and takes him to the local pool. One time at the pool, Noah let go of her hand, ran around the pool, and dived into the pool without his floaties. Madison was genuinely scared and upset, but she was not able to express her emotions: she felt the parents would not really understand or care.

Many organizations demand that their employees express positive emotions and suppress their negative emotions (Schaubroeck and Jones 2000), beginning as early as the interview process (Fox and Spector 2000). Past research has found that such requirements to suppress real emotions and, at the same time, display emotions other than the ones individuals are feeling results in emotional dissonance, negatively affecting physical and psychological health (Ashforth and Humphrey 1993; Hochschild 1983; King and Emmons 1990; Morris and Feldman 1996; Rafaeli and Sutton 1987; Wharton and Erickson 1993), as well as diminished job satisfaction (Fisher 2000). The emotions that the employees are required to display also differ widely based on the position held and the class, gender, and race of the employee.

The gender of employees in leadership positions is important because employees respond differently to the negative emotional expressions of male and female leaders (Lewis 2000). In her laboratory-based study, Kristi M. Lewis finds a significant negative effect of the interaction of gender and emotional displays. Female leaders in her study received lower ratings when expressing either sadness or anger (Lewis 2000), while male leaders did not. The expression of the same emotion has differential meaning for the perceptions of leader effectiveness for men and women. Lewis argues:

> One might expect that either anger or neutrality expressed by a male leader would lead to high ratings of integrity, confidence, and assertiveness (all associated with strong leadership), while anger from a female leader may lead to perception of instability, aggressiveness, or other negative traits. (2000, 232)

Jennifer Pierce (1995), similarly, in "Rambo Litigators: Emotional Labor in a Male Dominated Job," her study of litigators in her book *Gender Trials: Emotional Lives in Contemporary Law Firms*, finds that women litigators are penalized harshly for their displays of anger and aggression, while their male counterparts are encouraged to display anger and aggression as part of their job. Such gender inequality in emotional labor is not limited to women in leadership positions. Pierce also documents unequal expectations of emotional labor for male and female paralegals: male paralegals are actively discouraged from doing deference and emotional caretaking at the workplace, while such emotion labor is expected from women paralegals (Pierce 1995; see also Lively 2000).

In the context of babysitters, gender is a very important factor in the expression of emotions. The young women I interviewed pointed to the limited range of emotions they were allowed to express. Tiredness, anger, physical pain, and frustration with the children were off-limits. "Some shifts are better than others," Emma said. During some shifts, the children would act out, misbehave, or would be disrespectful to her, but she found it challenging to try to discipline the children, express frustration, or even tell the parents.

For Rachel, however, the hardest part of babysitting was dealing with the emotions of the children. Rachel, a sociology major at a large state university, has been working as a babysitter since she was a tween. One day, she remembers, the parents were going out on a Friday night, and in order to avoid making a scene, they snuck out while the little girl she was babysitting was watching television. However, an hour into her shift, the little girl started crying and asking for her parents. After the little girl screamed and cried for hours because her parents were not there, Rachel gave the little girl a treat. By the time the parents came back, the girl was asleep, and they did not comprehend how difficult her night had been. "The mother was very upset that I gave her a treat," Rachel said, but the mother did not really want to listen to how difficult and frustrating it was for her.

Emily said she had moments when she genuinely experienced fear. "When children do not want to do something—ugh. I had a kid [eight years old] threaten me once, . . . and it was very manipulative. Where is this coming from? I was telling her to do her homework. I said, 'You have to.' Then she said, 'I'll tell my mom you hit me.' I was like—I actually called my mom. What do I do? [My mom said,] 'The moment the mother comes home, tell her. Do not ignore it because she needs to be told.' That was really scary. It was this creepy feeling; there were the crazy stories you hear about." When she told the child's mother about the threat, Emily was surprised that the mother was upset at her child's behavior but did not even ask Emily how she was feeling.

Katie, similarly, was in a car accident driving the children home from swim class. Even though she has an excellent driving record—which the parents inquired about during the interview—as she took the exit for the town, their car was rear-ended by a large car. Luckily, none of the passengers were hurt, but Katie was devastated and did not want to drive for a while. She was disappointed that the parents did not ask her about how she was feeling.

Overall, the interviews demonstrate that babysitters have emotion-labor restrictions: they are discouraged from expressing physical exhaustion, tiredness, emotional frustration, and fear. It is important to acknowledge that there are differences based on race and socioeconomic status in expressing emotions, which are discussed at length in Chapter 4.

Care Work

In addition to emotion work, a central component of babysitting is care work. Care work broadly refers to any paid work involving caring for children, the elderly, and the sick, usually by workers in health care, education, child care, mental health, and social services (Duffy 2005). Mignon Duffy, Randy Albelda, and Clare Hammonds (2013, 147; see also Duffy, Armenia, and Stacey 2015) describe care work as follows:

1. The activity (of the industry) contributes to physical, mental, social, and/or emotional well-being.
2. The primary labor process (in the industry) involves face-to-face relationships with those cared for.

3. Those receiving care are members of groups that by normal social standards cannot provide for all of their own care because of age, illness, or disability.

4. Care work builds and maintains human infrastructure that cannot be adequately produced through unpaid work or unsubsidized markets, necessitating public investment.

Mignon Duffy (2005) further categorizes care-work jobs into two distinct groups: nurturant and nonnurturant. Nurturant care work, performed by workers such as babysitters, nannies, teachers, and nursing home aids, involves more face-to-face interaction and direct relationships with the people being cared for, while nonnurturant care work, performed by those such as janitors, care-work administrators, and lunch aides, does not have such an interactive component. In this chapter, I focus primarily on the nurturant care workers as defined by Duffy (2005).

Many scholars of care work point to the overwhelming dominance of women in nurturant care-work jobs. Nationally, approximately 24 percent of our labor force is employed in care-work industries, and 15 percent of all workers are employed in nurturant care work (Folbre 2002, 66). According to Duffy, the number of nurturant care workers, such as career child-care workers, expanded six-fold between 1950 and 2007 (2011, 78). This growth in the nurturant care-work sector is unprecedented and outpaces the growth in all other industries in our economy (Duffy 2011). Therefore, it is imperative to focus on nurturant care workers, such as child-care workers, as an important component of our economy.

Frederick Engels ([1884] 1972) coined the term "reproductive labor" to refer to jobs that reproduce and maintain the labor force. Such jobs include cooking, cleaning, and child care—tasks traditionally performed by women for free. Because they were performed for no monetary gain, they were rendered invisible in the economy and were not considered work (Crittenden 2001; Duffy, Armenia, and Stacey 2015). Even after these tasks started to be performed for economic rewards, they were undervalued economically. With women's increasing labor-force participation and the commensurate proliferation of paid care work, feminist scholars have called for economic and social recognition of the value of care work. Ann Crittenden (2001), for example, has called attention to the moral and social value that society attributes to care work, especially child care, and the mismatch between the stated value and the economic value given to it. Starting with the feminist scholarship of the 1970s, research on care work expanded from unpaid care work to include both paid and unpaid work (Hansen and Philipson 1990; Laslett and Brenner 1989). Barbara Laslett and Johanna Brenner (1989), in particular, call attention to the social responsibility component of care work: it has the important role of reproducing the basic economic and social well-being of any society.

Today, scholars refer to this concept as human infrastructure (Duffy, Albelda, and Hammonds 2013). Just as physical infrastructure, like roads and bridges, support our society physically and ensure its smooth function, social infrastructure such as care work—that is, child care, elder care, sick care—ensures that our society and economy run smoothly. Human infrastructure provides our society with the help it needs by addressing care-work needs so the rest of the population can function economically and socially. Despite the growing literature on the social and economic importance of care work, care workers, especially babysitters, still have low pay and poor work conditions.

In addition to the low pay, care work typically involves an important emotion-labor component. Emotion labor refers to the demands of jobs to "induce or suppress feelings" to produce a certain state of mind or feelings in the customers (Hochschild 1983, 7). Such emotion labor is an inherent component of care work and is often detrimental to emotional, psychological, and even physiological health (Garey and Hansen 2011; Hochschild 1983). While emotion labor is a central component of other jobs, such as retail and service-sector jobs, some care-work scholars argue that the emotion-labor component of care work is vastly different. They point to the relationality of care-work jobs, referring to the "sustained emotional connection that may or may not take place in the context of paid work and that does not necessarily result in negative outcome(s) for the persons engaged in the emotional exchange" (Duffy, Armenia, and Stacey 2015, 8). The concept of relational work is not new: it is based on early feminist psychoanalytical and care-work scholarship (Chodorow 1978; Parks 2003; Tronto 1993) and is defined as work that involves "sustained, reciprocal, emotional connections between two people" (Parks 2003, quoted in Duffy, Armenia, and Stacey 2015, 8). While retail and service-sector workers can have sustained relationships with customers as they pour their coffees, work cash registers, fold their sweaters, and give them change, the nature of the human interaction is different with nurturant care workers. A child-care professional, for example, spends long hours with a child, knows his favorite blankets and favorite toys, and may feel like a member of the family rather than an employee (Dodson and Zincavage 2015; Stacey 2011a). While such relational linkages can be rewarding and personally gratifying, they may also result in expectations that care workers will put in unpaid hours and perform extra tasks (Duffy, Armenia, and Stacey 2015), in the way that family members would.

Of the babysitters I spoke to, almost all of them mentioned their connection the children: "I love the children," "I love kids," "Playing with the children is the best," "I have lots of fun with the children," and "I love spending time with kids" were some of the responses to the question of what they most liked about their jobs. Many of them talked about how they had a genuine connection to the children, including specific knowledge of what toys the children like, which foods they dislike, or which television shows they watch. Shannon, a twenty-year-old student, has been babysitting for the past four years. She knows that Celine, the four-year-old, loves Princess Sofia and Doc McStuffins, only wears pink princess dresses, and loves drinkable yogurts in strawberry-banana flavor. Sometimes before Shannon goes over to Celine's house, she downloads episodes of cartoons on her tablet, and she brings over Celine's favorite flavor of yogurts.

Because of the nature of the work, care workers are also asked to care, or at least pretend to do so (Folbre 2002). In the United States, especially, care of family is seen as a private, personal matter: something you do out of love and care and not obligation (DeVault 1991; Folbre 2002; Kittay 1999; Uttal and Tuominen 1999). As American workplaces, governments, and existing policies fail to fund and acknowledge—socially or economically—the value of family caregivers, much of the care work is paid by families, who often struggle financially and emotionally to provide it (Chorn-Dunham and Dietz 2003; Gallagher et al. 1989; George and Gwyther 1986; Meyer 2000). According to Clare Stacey and Lindsey Ayers (2015), despite the lack of institutional support, the idea that care work is personal and familial is deep set. Viviana Zelizer (2005) has illuminated the ways in which the worlds of money and love often clash. Zelizer argues that "contact between the personal and economic spheres corrupts both of them" (2005, 207). Especially in the case of paid family care workers, the concept of paying for care "stirs acute political and moral debates, often with hostile worlds warnings about the contamination and undermining of moral obligation" (2005, 171). Home child-care workers lie at the intersection of this conflict of two hostile worlds: money and care (Folbre and Nelson 2000; Himmelweit 1999; Zelizer 2005). In their everyday lives, many home-care workers have to walk that delicate line between love and money. This clash of work and love is reflected in confusion over which set of rules should apply in each individual case: rules of work or rules of family/kinship? (Hochschild 2003). Many scholars have pointed to this confusion over work and family/kinship rules, especially in the context of telecommuters (Mirchandani 2000), domestic workers (Hondagneu-Sotelo 2007), nursing and personal care (Stacey 2011b), home-based child care (Tuominen 2003) and personal concierge services (Sherman 2010). Mary Tuominen (2003) refers to the "golden rule" of babysitters and nannies: the obligation to care for the children as if they were their own kin.

The babysitters are aware of the intersection of the fine line between money and care, and therefore they go through visible expressions of care. Katie, for example, genuinely cares about the children, but simply caring is not enough: she has to show the parents how much she cares. Often times, displays of care are denials of money. For example, her university had a family and alumni day, and she told the parents that she would take the children there for free rides and bouncy castles. "The children had a fantastic time," she told me, but she ended up paying for all the food, and she bought T-shirts and small toys for them because they asked for them. Francesca says she always compliments the parents on how well behaved or nice their child is. She also mentions how much she loves children and that she wishes to have children one day. Almost every babysitter I interviewed used a similar technique to signal that this is not just a job but that they genuinely care. Francesca says she never gets paid for the first session; she tells the parents it is a trial session for the children to get comfortable with her. These expressions of showing care over money are not simply displays at the beginning of the work process but are sustained throughout.

Emily, for example, regularly takes the children to her own parents' house, which has a pool, showing that she treats the children she's being paid to care for as if they were her own family. Sometimes the children come over to her pool, and she ends up watching them, even though she does not get paid for it. Madison, who was asked to babysit the five-year-old at the pool, had to pay for her own pool membership. Her parents reside in a predominantly white, affluent suburb and had a family membership to the pool, which was an important factor in Noah's parents hiring her, because they wanted a babysitter who could take Noah to the pool. She ended up renewing her membership and paying for her portion herself. Many babysitters I spoke to had similar unpaid expenses.

In almost all cases, the babysitters experience a clash or confusion over whether rules of work or rules of kinship should apply (DeVault 1991; Hondagneu-Sotelo 2007; Romero 1992). In almost every case, they have stories or individual accounts to help rationalize their choices, make sense of their everyday lives, and make their behavior more morally acceptable (Shotter 1984; for an overview see Duffy, Armenia, and Stacey 2015).

As Mignon Duffy, Amy Armenia, and Clare Stacey observe:

> Caregivers offer their accounts in two broad ways: by emphasizing caregiving as a "real" set of tasks worthy of renumeration and by framing their labor as a public good that benefits the broader community. In both cases, these accounts serve to remind caregivers—as

well as "generalized others"—that their labor is worthy of respect. (2015, 203)

It is important to focus on these individual accounts and the lived experience of care work from the perspectives of the central actors. Unlike other jobs that involve emotional labor, such as retail and service-sector jobs, the emotion-labor component in care-work jobs often involves projecting the image of caring. While a typical barista is just expected to serve with a smile, a typical child-care worker is expected not only to serve with a smile but also to project the image of genuinely caring for the children. Because of that, recent studies call for a new theoretical lens and argue that emotion-labor looks very different for care workers (Erikson and Stacey 2013). As care workers are expected to care as a part of their emotion labor, they report feeling conflicted and confused about which rules apply—ones of friendship and family or ones of employment. Should a child-care worker stay longer hours because a child is scared? What should a child-care worker do if the parents would like to chat about the child after the shift? Such decisions are emotionally fraught but also carry economic consequences (Dodson and Zincavage 2015; D. Stone 2000). Similarly, research has focused on the disadvantages of low-income women working in child care (Dill 1994; Hondagneu-Sotelo 2007; Rollins 1985; Romero 2011), but student babysitters have not received systematic attention. This chapter focuses on the economic costs of such conflicts in the context of child-care workers—in particular, the pay and the resulting pay gap.

Money or Care?

Monetary gratifications are often defined in direct opposition to genuine care: if someone really loves their work, they would do it for free. Therefore, caring about the money is seen as being diametrically opposed to caring for the children. To counter that, many babysitters I interviewed pointed to strategies they use to show the parents they do not care about the money. Deniz, for example, in her negotiations with the parents, asked for an extra allowance to help with transportation costs. She babysits an elementary-school-age girl, whom she also helps with her homework. Even though she was granted the transportation allowance, on Deniz's first day, she did not take the transportation money and told the parents that her father gave her a ride because she was not sure about the address. Katie mentioned over and over how much she cares about children and how much she genuinely likes the two she babysits, in particular. Lily mentioned that she schedules a free first session with the parents present, almost like a mother's helper, to acclimate the children. Gestures like these signal to parents how much the babysitters genuinely care about the children and not just about the money. Even when they genuinely do care, these babysitters feel the need to come up with concrete, tangible signals to demonstrate that concern.

Work-Nonwork Boundaries

One of the most important common characteristics in these young women's lives is the work-nonwork boundary. Stephanie is a twenty-year-old college student studying sociology. She has been working as a babysitter for one year now, for the same family, looking after their two boys. She says she just babysits, but her actual job description includes transporting the two boys to and from school, driving them to activities, making snacks for them, helping them with their homework, and playing with them. Her responsibilities do not end there. On many nights, she cooks for the whole family, does the children's laundry, and does some light housework, as well as running errands for the family. Most days, she says, her work does not end. Her least favorite part of the job is "parents not coming home on time." She works approximately thirty to thirty-five hours per week, and she said that it was one of the most difficult jobs she has had, often involving nights and weekends.

For Emily, work crosses over into her nonwork time when she does extra math in her free time so she can help the children with their homework. She asked me, "Do you know about the whole Everyday Math? The whole thing they switched to? When I was in school, we learned math a certain way. Then, when my sister was in school, they changed the way they teach math. It's shapes and stuff. I did not understand it. I had to really learn this stuff. I went on Wikipedia—I was in high school—[and] I had to teach myself the whole thing." After all, she was expected to help the children with homework. The parents had a difficult time helping the children with their math homework, so Emily felt it was expected that she knew not just the math but the way it was taught, so she could be more useful.

Overall, most of the young women I spoke to pointed out having long hours of unpaid time.

Asking for Money

The perception that caring and money are opposed makes asking for money tricky. Emma told me that she found asking for money almost impossible. She was babysitting for a summer for two girls, age six and four. She had to run certain errands for the parents. The parents cooked the children's food, but she had to heat it up and give snacks to the kids, and the worst part was that her shifts would be approximately five hours. Unlike Rachel, who ended up watching *Rapunzel* several times, Emma had to entertain the children herself. For Rachel, the family's dogs were the worst part of her shifts. They chewed on everything, and when she was babysitting the two girls mostly on Friday nights, she also had to take care of the dogs.

However, despite the challenging nature of the jobs, which often involved juggling multiple activities together, some of the families did not fully inform the workers about tasks such as dog sitting and running errands. Rachel said that despite these difficulties and the increasing demands and changing job descriptions, she would never ask for more money because it would come across as though she did not like the children or the dog. When I asked Emma if she ever negotiated or asked for money, she said she was not in a position to do so. "I am bad with that stuff," she said. "They asked me how much I wanted. It was hard. The parents did not [ask me,] 'Is this okay?' I guess you kind of base it on what they offer."

Rachel agreed that she found it difficult to ask for money or negotiate. One of the factors that made it difficult to ask for more money was that she knew the people she was babysitting for. One of the families she worked for was a cousin, and the other one was a neighbor, so asking for money or complaining about their dog would have been awkward. "Strangers might be easier," she said. "Because they were my cousins, I started as a favor, and it turned into a regular job."

For Emma, her employer was her godmother's daughter, so she had the same problem: she did not feel comfortable asking for more money or complaining about the length of her shift or all the extra work she had to do running errands for the family. "It's awkward," she said. She reasoned that at least her work babysitting was useful in getting a job at a day care, but the job does not pay more than babysitting.

Parents are looking for babysitters who have a long history of experience, even just to pick their kids up from school, and they ask applicants to point out such experience on their résumés. Full résumés, references, lengthy babysitting experience, and certifications like CPR are big plusses. Emma was surprised that her interview with the family for the babysitting job was more rigorous than her interview for the job at the day-care center later. At the day-care center, she makes $8.50 per hour and takes care of fourteen children, infants through age four. She changes the babies, gives them bottles, feeds them, teaches them, and plays with them during her four- to five-hour shifts. However, she told me that her interview was much shorter than when she interviewed to babysit Abby, six, and Nya, four. The parents were much more rigorous, asking for many qualifications and certifications. About the terms of payment, Emma said, the "parents did not give me the option. I think I was underpaid, and I am still underpaid. [There were] no negotiations."

"It would have been easier to talk and negotiate with strangers. Because I knew them, it was much more challenging to talk about money; it was awkward," said Emma. But even when the parents were either relations or acquaintances of the babysitters, their interviews were long and detailed. Abby and Nya's parents asked Emma about her work experience, her classes and certifications related to babysitting, her babysitting philosophy, her experience with children, and her driving record.

Like Emma, Emily had a challenging time asking for more money. When she was babysitting for the four children of her next-door neighbors, becoming employed was a very informal process:

> I started when I was twelve and the neighbors only had one kid. I have always loved children, and my neighbor brought it up to my mom. "Hey, would she be able to watch Ashley?" She had, like, a work function one night, and we tried, and I loved it. She has four kids now, and I have babysat them throughout their lives—sometimes all four at the same time, especially over the summer. Monday to Friday, [from] 6 A.M. to 3 P.M., [I] take them to school things [and] camps. . . . I take them to pools and discovery zones. Because the parents work full time, I cooked for the family. I cook for my family, anyway—I love to bake, too—so it was something I did with the kids: cakes, cookies [*pauses*] and homework, too.

Despite the intense nature of the job, Emily did not feel comfortable asking for money. After all, they were the neighbors, and the mother of the family was close to Emily's mother. While these informal ties are influential in finding jobs, they are also the barriers against asking for more money. During the time she babysat, Emily's job description changed immensely. It started with babysitting infant Ashley on a Friday night, when the parents went out for a work function, and then it was babysitting four children for the whole summer, Monday through Friday from 6:00 A.M. until 3:00 P.M.

However, despite the change in the job description, Emily never asked for more money. "The interview was visiting with the mom; the dad wasn't really there. I played with the kid a little. Basically, I think they wanted to meet me to make sure I wasn't a serial killer. I would reassure them [that] I am in school, and I'm not crazy. Also, they knew my mother." She said that she never tried to negotiate her pay. "It was something my mother brought up with me. She was a recruiter before she was a teacher, [and] she said you need to go in and negotiate, but I didn't. I was so happy they picked me. I was so nervous [that I would have taken whatever they offered me]. Knowing them made it much worse."

This is not to say that the babysitters were not professionally oriented in other areas of their work. "I was very professional," Emily said. "I had pamphlets printed—this is so embarrassing. There were a lot of kids being born, [and] I [was] going to take advantage of it. I printed [and] put fliers in mailboxes. I was certified in CPR—that was a big selling point." But even though she was very proactive in her marketing approach, when it came to asking for more money, she did not feel comfortable. Even though the job description and the conditions, including the number of children, changed, she kept getting the same amount of money.

For Emily, the monetary issue went beyond the absence of negotiation. She also told me that she was not paid for her last week of work.

> The ones next door were not really that well off. Like I said, four children, [and] they had to be at camp at the same time. I was really spread thin. She was paying me $15. I brought it up with her that I [would] need more money; with all the gas [money] I was spending, I was breaking even. She was much more receptive than I thought she would be, but she did not pay me: that's how we fell out. She didn't pay me for an entire week. I decided—I mean, I never confronted her about it; I felt so awkward. I provided the service; I felt so bad for her, poor woman. She comes to our house for dinner. I was seventeen and really mad at the time.

Despite these problems, Emily said she still loves babysitting. "I never got sick of it. I love the freedom attached to babysitting. I was in charge. It was my first job; it was the first time of being paid, dealing with money. You open your bank account." Emily also said that babysitting was how she learned about work. "It taught me, like, responsibility. You have to do what the parent says; there's consequences. You learn to be an employee." However, even though she learned about working relationships, the nature of her relationship with the parents was unclear.

Emily recalled, "Lines are blurred. You are an employee; you have to run everything by her. We had this pond in our backyard [where] the children could feed the fish, [and] I had to run it by her, you know. I would check with the mother a lot. After a while she told me, 'I trust you.' With kids, that's big." For Emily, the fact that she was being respected, that she was being treated as a responsible adult, complicated the employee-employer portion of the relationship.

The Strength (and Weakness) of Weak Ties

Mark Granovetter (1973), in his analysis of finding jobs, coined the term "strength of weak ties" to emphasize the importance and centrality of not immediate, close relatives and acquaintances but weaker, second-degree acquaintances. Counter to conventional wisdom, he points to the importance and the significance of weak ties—distant acquaintances, friends of friends, or casual acquaintances—in securing a job. He defines the strength of a tie by the amount of time spent together, the emotional intensity, and the intimacy of the relationship (1361). Similarly, he stresses the importance of these seemingly unimportant and tenuous linkages, or weak ties.

This was certainly true in the case of the babysitters: almost every babysitter I interviewed said that they had found their jobs through informal networks. While almost none of them worked for money for immediate family and friends (though they reported volunteering their time to babysitting the children of their immediate family and friends), almost all found their jobs through weak ties. They work for their distant cousins, cousin's neighbors, godmother's daughter, family friends, parents' old neighbors, and friends' friends. Granovetter, along with other network scholars, focuses on the positive aspects of weak ties: they let you find jobs through connections. However, in the case of the babysitters, weak ties also had negative effects. Just as weak ties were instrumental in finding jobs, they were one of the reasons for not asking for more money.

Emma and Rachel agreed that the reason they did not negotiate their pay was because they were connected to the people they were working for. Similarly, Rachel remembered that she started babysitting for a much older cousin as a favor on Valentine's Day, so her cousin and her husband could go out for dinner, but that occasional favor turned into a job. Because she was weakly related to her employer, she found it difficult to negotiate her pay, while she feels that she would have had an easier time doing so with strangers.

The weak ties that bound the babysitters to their employers both made it possible for them to find work and stopped them from asking for more money, renegotiating pay or even asking for a raise after working for a substantial length of time. Emma said that these informal, weak ties—in her case, her godmother's grandchildren—still constituted a close in-group, which prevented them from talking about money.

Complex Web of Ties

Many babysitters also keep secondary jobs to find and keep babysitting jobs. Alexandra is a full-time college student who has been working as a babysitter since the eighth grade. Her first job was babysitting her neighbor's two-year-old, and then it was her cousins. As she got older, finding and keeping babysitting jobs became more challenging, as there were so many neighbors and family friends. One of the problems with babysitting is that children grow up, and babysitters need to frequently find new children to babysit.

Currently, Alexandra is working at a camp, teaching children ages four to fourteen how to play lacrosse. The organization, which is located in one of the most affluent suburbs of a major metropolitan area, offers weekend and summer camps in lacrosse, as well as courses. The hours are 8:45 A.M. to 3:00 P.M., and the pay is "great," she said, at $20 an hour. However, the courses are only for three to six weeks over the summer, and she describes the experience as quite intense. Usually in very hot and humid weather, she is responsible for teaching outside during long shifts of physical activity. Sometimes the children throw tantrums, and some do not want to be there: "Their parents sign them up," she said, "and they don't even want to play lacrosse." Sometimes, she has to deal with what she refers to as "bratty kids." One time, she remembered, one of the students refused to do what Alexandra asked her to do, because the child was wearing a Lululemon jacket. The child asked Alexandra if she knew how much Lululemon clothing costs and told Alexandra that she could not risk getting grass stains on her designer outfit. "Sometimes," Alexandra said, "this job requires a lot of patience." She is always expected to smile and be upbeat for the duration of her shift. Despite the hot weather, she has to wear a uniform, and she is not allowed to even wear sunglasses. Even when the children misbehave—and they often do—she still has to be nice and act happy and upbeat.

The job is a challenge, according to Alexandra, and while she might prefer to take on easier work, she feels that she needs to keep the lacrosse job in order to find babysitting jobs. She has been babysitting two girls, age eight and five, since September. They attended the lacrosse camp, and she was their coach last summer. As Alexandra was chatting with the mother and helping her load the girls and their equipment into her van last summer, the mother casually asked her if she would be interested in babysitting. It is very typical for parents, especially mothers, to recruit babysitters from the camp. The other coaches, too, all have babysitting jobs, and they keep their coaching jobs in order to find babysitting jobs for the fall semester. Every day, she babysits them for three to four hours, but there was not even a formal interview. It was replaced, Alexandra said, by the mother watching her interact with the two girls throughout the camp. Because it was so casual, walking from the camp to the mother's van and chatting as they were loading the van, she did not feel like she could negotiate or ask for more money. Currently, she is paid $15 an hour for babysitting the two girls. Mostly, she plays with them, takes them to the park, and plays sports with them. She is supposed to keep them active, help them with homework, and drive them to activities. She is also expected to coordinate playdates and cook organic snacks, and she is required to keep the girls from sharing food and consuming nuts.

Despite the formal separation between her two positions, Alexandra feels that they are closely intertwined. She told me that she often would like to quit babysitting, but she worries that the mother will complain to the camp. Similarly, despite the intensive conditions, she feels that she cannot quit the camp because that is where she recruits her babysitting gigs. The weak ties she creates at the camps are essential to finding jobs, but they hinder pay negotiations and stop her from quitting a job she is unhappy with. Many of the women I interviewed shared stories of similar situations.

What about Male Babysitters?

Even though the focus of this study is on female babysitters, I have wondered about what it might be like to be a male babysitter. According to the "Report on the Youth Labor Force," almost no boys babysit, perhaps because of the gendered perception of the work (Herman 2000), but it is possible that male babysitters would not feel the same pressures felt by the young women I spoke to.

Of course, there has been extensive research on men in stereotypically feminine jobs, based on Rosabeth Moss Kanter's ([1977] 1993) landmark work on professional women in predominantly male jobs. Based on her study of female doctors and professionals, she found that being in the minority gave women extra visibility, as the "woman doctor" or "woman lawyer," but that such a visibility resulted in negative attention. Women's minority status attracted scrutiny from managers and coworkers, and Kanter argues that minority status in the workplace resulted in tokenism for women in traditionally male jobs: because of their gender, they attracted negative attention with their mistakes, and such mistakes were attributed not to individual error but to their entire gender. This combination of negative attention and visibility resulted in a hostile work environment for these women. Kanter also argued that women in men's jobs such as doctors, lawyers and professionals, experience the glass ceiling, an invisible barrier that women experience in promotions and raises as they move up the ranks.

Based on these findings, later researchers studied the experiences of men in traditionally feminine jobs. For example, Christine Williams (1992) focused on the experiences of male nurses in the 1990s. She finds that, unlike the women in traditionally male jobs, such as doctors and lawyers, that Kanter studied, male nurses do not experience tokenism or the glass ceiling.

They do receive visibility and are seen as "the male nurse," but the visibility works to their advantage. Because male nurses are rare, they are requested by the patients and noticed by their supervisors. Based on ethnographic research and in-depth interviews, Williams finds that male nurses experience what she refers to as the glass escalator effect, in which they are promoted quickly by invisible forces. They are kicked upstairs: promoted to better jobs, higher pay, and more prestige, because nursing does not seem appropriate for their gender.

In addition, their gender results in stronger networks with supervisors and doctors: for example, because of their gender, they eat lunch or go golfing with the doctors. Unlike the male colleagues who created a hostile work environment for the women, male nurses experience a supportive and nurturing environment. The female nurses mentored them and helped them greatly on the job. Their everyday experience at the job was an overall pleasant work environment, not a toxic environment of hostility. While their outside friends and family were less enthusiastic about men working in traditionally feminine jobs such as nursing, their coworkers and employers were highly supportive and encouraging. One of the explanations for the nurturing and mentoring work environment could be that the women in nursing would want their profession to be seen as a more masculine profession. Existing research on occupational segregation shows that when a profession is predominantly female, it is considered a "feminine job," and the overall pay of the sector goes down. For example, clerical work was considered mostly a masculine job historically, but when women started doing clerical or secretarial work, the overall pay of the sector went down because it came to be considered a woman's job (C. Williams 1992). Similarly, Williams shows that as men started moving into nursing, which was a predominantly female profession, the overall pay and prestige increased. Therefore, it would be rational for the existing female nurses to encourage and mentor male coworkers in hopes for higher wages for the entire profession. More recent studies also confirm this finding on men in predominantly female-dominated—and mostly care-work—positions (Baughman and Smith 2011; Price-Glynn and Rakovski 2012; Ribas, Dill, and Cohen 2012). While the overall wages of the female-dominated, care-work positions are lower (Budig 2002; Cohen and Huffman 2003; England, Budig, and Folbre 2002; Gauchat, Kelly, and Wallace 2012), the glass escalator effect is in effect for men in female-dominated positions, as they experience higher wages and higher promotion rates (Baughman and Smith 2011; Price-Glynn and Rakovski 2012; Ribas, Dill, and Cohen 2012) and experience higher prestige (Snyder and Green 2008).

Little has changed from these early landmark studies. When we look at men and women in occupations, a large body of recent studies confirms the gendered nature of organizations (Acker 1990; Brumley 2014). Despite structural and technological changes (Caraway 2007; Pozas 2002), these gendered inequalities persist in the new economy (Brumley 2014; J. Williams 2000; Williams, Muller, and Kilanski 2012). Recent research shows that employers still expect the ideal worker to be a male worker without dependents (J. Williams 2000), and these gendered, biased expectations and assumptions heavily influence hiring, promotion, and other personnel decisions, keeping women in lower-paid positions and excluded from authority positions (Bank Muñoz 2008; Brumley 2014; Caraway 2007; Plankey-Videla 2012; Salzinger 2003). Therefore, despite changes over time, an overwhelming number of studies point to the persistence of tokenism and gendered assumptions in the workplace, which hurt women (Maxfield 2005; Radhakrishnan 2011; Zabludovsky 2004).

While Christine Williams (1992) shows that men in predominantly female jobs experience social and economic benefits of their gender, later studies have pointed to mixed results based on an intersectional approach. Adia Harvey Wingfield (2009) shows that the social and economic benefits of being in feminine jobs are not equal for all men but are rather enjoyed by white men. In her qualitative study of seventeen African American male nurses, Wingfield finds that African American male nurses do not experience any benefits. In fact, Wingfield writes, "For Black men nurses, gendered racist images may have particular consequences for their relationships with women and colleagues, who may view Black men nurses through the lens of controlling images and gendered racist stereotypes that emphasize the danger they pose to women" (2009, 10). As a consequence of such gendered racist perceptions, their coworkers do not offer friendship or mentorship, so African American male nurses do not enjoy the same social benefits their counterparts enjoy. Similarly, their employers are also influenced by the gendered, racist stereotypes: supervisors view African American male nurses as less qualified for promotion and less capable. This is parallel to the existing research showing whites often perceive blacks (regardless of gender) as less intelligent, less hardworking, less ethical, and less hardworking than all the other racial groups (Feagin 2006), making such perceptions critical in understanding the actions of the supervisors, who are mostly white. Wingfield shows that the glass escalator effect is not just a gendered term but also a racialized one. Similarly, she finds that sexual orientation plays an important role in the experience of the glass escalator effect. For example, she argues that gay black men experience additional difficulties on the job and face discrimination by their supervisors as well as their coworkers.

Similarly, Kevin Henson and Jackie Krasas Rogers, in their article "Why Marcia You've Changed!" (2001), look at the case of male temporary secretaries to show that glass escalator effects are not experienced by all men in all professions. Based on their ethnographic, qualitative work on temporary secretaries, the authors compare the two dominant theories: Kanter's theory of tokenism (the position that any token, male or female, who is in the minority in the workplace will experience negative experiences socially and economically) and Williams's glass escalator theory (the position that some men will receive social and economic benefits from their token status, being promoted more quickly, receiving higher pay, and moving to more prestigious and higher-paying jobs [Maume 1999; Pierce 1995; C. Williams 1995]). Within the context of temporary clerical work, Henson and Rogers (2001) find that men in this group experience the negative effects of tokenism, like the women Kanter initially studied. Because secretarial work was seen as a quintessentially woman's job in support of a male manager (MacKinnon 1979), male temporary secretaries were viewed as out of place and lacking in certain emotional and relational skills (Hochschild 1989; Leidner 1993; Pierce 1995). These men who worked as temporary secretaries were criticized for "not having a real job," because men are expected to be breadwinners and providers (Cheng 1996; Connell 1987, 1995; Kimmel 1994), as a core component of hegemonic masculinity (Connell 1987). The mere fact of their part-time work was perceived as less manly or less masculine (Epstein et al. 1999; Henson and Rogers 2001). While women's part-time work is seen as appropriate to accommodate housework or child care, for men it is perceived as inferior, and thus men employed part time are thought to have lower aspirations or qualifications. As a result, these male temporary secretaries have experienced not only discrimination in hiring but extensive social and economic hardships on the job.

For me, the question was whether male babysitters would experience the positive side of tokenism or the negative consequences of being male in a predominately female occupation. While it was challenging to find boys who babysat, I interviewed three male babysitters as case studies. Benjamin, a twenty-year-old male college student, briefly babysat three boys a few years ago. He said he did not understand why people babysit and that it was one of the most challenging jobs he ever had. When I asked him how difficult it was on a scale from zero to ten, he says no scale can capture how difficult it was. He quickly moved to the retail sector, where he works directly with customers. He said, "I do not like the nasty attitudes from customers and the disrespect," but he still thinks retail is much easier than babysitting.

Benjamin remembers being hired very quickly, without the intensive inspection of qualifications reported by the female babysitters. Male babysitters do not have a universal appeal, but, he said, there are families, especially ones with boys, who seek out male babysitters. Benjamin told me that he was especially in demand because he is a student athlete, and the parents of the three boys were looking for someone who would play sports with the boys. He did not take any babysitting classes and did not have any related experience. He did not have a CPR certification. His main qualification was his athletics background.

One of the most interesting differences between him and the female babysitters I interviewed was the difference in their job descriptions. Even though they all described their jobs as babysitting, Benjamin said he only took care of the children, mostly playing sports with them, and the family never asked him to run errands or expected other extra services. This is in sharp contrast to the experiences of almost all of the female babysitters I interviewed, who talked about extra expectations, including tutoring, cooking, preparing snacks, driving the children to and from activities, arranging and coordinating playdates with the children's friends, and even unrelated errands such as picking up dry cleaning, cooking for the family, grocery shopping for the family, and dog sitting.

Similarly, Christopher, a twenty-year-old gender studies major, worked as a babysitter for three years when he was in high school, babysitting for three families. He said that in high school, he really enjoyed the money, which he described as a lot for high school. However, after babysitting for three years, he moved on to the service sector. The service sector is not without its problems, according to Christopher, who said that angry customers are the biggest challenges. However, he said that such challenges are minor compared to the challenges of babysitting, which he described as his most challenging job; getting the children to bed was a big struggle for him. The minute he could get another job and move out of babysitting, he did. He said that it did not come as a surprise to the three families he worked for: by the time he graduated from high school, they expected him to move on to service sector jobs. Just as with Benjamin, Christopher told me that the families he worked for never asked him to run errands for the family, cook, or do light housework. In fact, he was surprised when I asked him about those tasks; he clearly thought they were outside the realm of his job description.

Richard is a nineteen-year-old full-time college student on a sports scholarship. Richard, similarly, remembers working as a babysitter for a very short time: only for a few months and for one family. However, babysitting three children was very challenging, and he, too, moved on to the retail sector soon after. His experience in sports was a big selling point for the family, and he was expected to play sports and teach the three children about different sports. Just like Benjamin and Christopher, Richard was never asked to do extras such as cooking, cleaning, or errands. While the young women were asked to carry out any number of jobs not related to child care, the young men all said that their job descriptions were strictly limited to taking care of the children, and they were never asked to do more. In addition, they remember the parents coming home on time, while many female babysitters remember either parents being later or parents chatting with them when they got home. These male babysitters also typically left their shifts when they were done, rather than sticking around to talk to the parents.

Another striking difference was the fact that none of the male babysitters knew CPR or spoke a different language. None of them pointed to requirements of extra certification or credentials to find or keep jobs. While the female babysitters pointed to taking classes on babysitting, taking family- and child-related courses at their universities, working at their college's child-care center, and keeping art classes or jobs at summer camps or sports camps to recruit or keep babysitting jobs, male babysitters seemingly just showed up.

Finally, an important difference was in the way parents negotiated pay with male and female babysitters. Female babysitters reported being unable to negotiate because parents simply told them what they pay was; male babysitters, on the other hand, were asked how much they charged and what they expected to make. Both male and female babysitters reported the importance of weak ties: many worked for family friends, neighbors, and acquaintances, but these networks treated boys and girls differently. The male babysitters did not remember the parents ever referring to love or care for the child. For the male babysitters, the relationships with the children were always more professional and distant. Respect and admiration were mentioned—for example, "He looks up to you," or "He wants to play football like you when he grows up."

Parents' Perspectives: Love or Money?

The conflict and confusion over the dichotomies of love or money and rules of work versus rules of family or kinship are well documented in the literature. Care and love have become central components of care work, especially babysitting. Almost all the female babysitters I spoke to as part of this survey pointed to the importance the parents placed on care and love in their hiring process. Loving children, showing care, and caring about the child and not money is often a prerequisite for getting and keeping the job, but the very act of caring becomes the impediment to asking for pay raises. While this chapter focuses on the experiences of the babysitters, in order to capture the perspectives of the parents, I designed an experimental study, with participants recruited through Amazon's Mechanical Turk service (MTurk). MTurk is often criticized for offering convenience sampling; however, the point of this study is to offer not a generalizable dataset but, rather, an experimental one. Typical experimental studies recruit subjects through departmental subject pools, relying extensively on students. The recruitment method employed in this experiment is similar to typical experimental designs, but it has one advantage of including older participants, especially parents. As typical experimental research pools recruit on college campuses, the samples in typical experimental designs are convenience samples based a predominantly younger, college-educated pool. One of the disadvantages of such a design would be to focus exclusively on young people, many of whom are not parents. In contrast, MTurk allows researchers to access desired demographics and offers comparable convenience sample. In recent years, the use of MTurk has gained popularity among researchers and is considered a standard method for experimental design, with most of the concerns about its use coming from criticisms of its generalizability and the ethics of the low pay offered by many researchers (Berinsky, Huber, and Lenz 2010; Berinsky, Margolis, and Sances 2014; Buhrmester, Kwang, and Gosling 2011; Horton, Rand, and Zeckhauser 2011; Paolacci and Chandler 2014).

An experimental design is especially important to capture the perspectives of the parents and potential employers. While the focus of this study lies on the employees, it is important to capture the perspectives of the parents to better understand the nature and mechanisms of bias in pay. My in-depth interviews show that many female babysitters are hesitant about asking for a raise because they feel they will be turned down and viewed negatively by the employers. I wanted to test if this was actually true or if this is simply a false perception on the part of the employee. In either case, it would result in the employee not asking for a raise, but the mechanisms leading to the inequality are different, and therefore the tools we should use to address these social problems would differ, as well. In addition, I also wanted to test the effects of the gender of the employee in considering a raise: Are parents equally likely to give a raise to boys and girls?

Similar experimental research designs are ubiquitous in the study of inequality. Researchers have provided employers with different résumés and have asked participants to rate potential employees on their competence, work ethic, and other characteristics to determine whether different demographic characteristics play a role in hiring and promotion processes. With experimental designs and offering different vignettes to participants, different researchers have unraveled gender penalty in the job market (Correll, Benard, and Paik 2007; Cuddy, Fiske and Glick 2004), a gay penalty (Tilcsik 2011) in the workforce, and race penalty in hiring. The experimental vignette design (Rossi and Anderson 1982) is especially important because it creates the circumstances of employment to see what the reactions of the employers are going to be. While employers would undoubtedly deny having any bias on surveys, experimental designs allow the researchers to eliminate such bias.

In the experiment, 102 respondents reviewed a vignette about a babysitter asking for a raise, and then they were asked how likely they would be to give the raise. They were also asked to rate their views of the babysitter. The respondents were 43 percent female, 79 percent white, and 11 percent African American. Almost half of the sample (47 percent) was twenty-one to twenty-nine years old, 25 percent were thirty to thirty-nine, 13 percent were forty to forty-nine, 10 percent fifty to fifty-nine, and 5 percent were sixty or older. Of all the respondents, 42 percent said that they currently had children under the age of eighteen living with them at home, 25 percent said that they regularly used a babysitter, and 31 percent said that they had used a babysitter regularly in the past.

There were four versions of the vignette. Half of the respondents (49 percent) were asked to evaluate a male babysitter (Jake), and the other half a female babysitter (Molly). The names of the babysitters were the demographically "whitest" names in American in 2015, to avoid any racial confounds. The versions of the vignette also differed in the emotional investment the babysitter showed in the child. In one version, the babysitter says that he or she has "formed a strong emotional connection to the child" and brings homemade snacks (50 percent). In the other, the babysitter says that they would "like to continue in the position" and brings store-bought snacks. Following is the text of the vignette:

A few months ago, you hired (Molly/Jake) for a regular babysitting job. You've heard nothing but good things from the child, and (Molly/Jake) has said that (he/she) very much enjoys the job, and (has formed a strong emotional connection to the child/would like to continue in the position). The child especially likes the way that (Molly/Jake) frequently brings (homemade/store-bought) snacks to babysitting sessions. After six months of regular work, (Molly/Jake) asks for a significant increase in (his/her) hourly rate. You can afford the extra expense, but believe that you could find someone else to do the babysitting for what you were originally paying.

There are two experimental conditions. The first one is gender: the participants are given either the male babysitter, Jake, or the female babysitter, Molly. The need to compare male and female babysitters is another reason for using an experimental methodology, given the relative scarcity of male babysitters in the outside world. The second experimental condition involves emotional labor. Prior research points to the central importance of emotional labor in hiring (Tuominen 2003), so the aim is to test whether emotional labor is also central to the understanding of pay increases. That is, would parents reward babysitters who show an attachment to the children and display genuine care?

According to Virginia Valian, who coined the term, gender schemas refer to "our intuitive hypotheses about the behaviors, traits, and preferences of men and women, boys and girls" (1999, 11). Gender schemas refer to the gendered evaluations and gendered double standards of women's and men's evaluations in the workplace (Valian 1999). These gender schemas reflect biases in our society and social expectations and cultural assumptions about how each gender should behave. For example, they reflect hegemonic masculinity (Connell 1995) and ideas of what a man should be like. Pascoe (2007) finds that hegemonic masculinity is often related to what we expect from leaders: assertiveness, rationality, no emotions, authority, and competitiveness (Blair-Loy 2005; Eagly 2007; Haveman and Beresford 2012).

Similarly, "hegemonic femininity" (Pyke and Johnson 2003; Schippers 2007) defines what femininity is. Hegemonic feminine traits are defined by emotional sensitivity, sociability, and nurturance (Blair-Loy 2005). Gender schemas are important for social scientists because people tend to rely on them in their everyday thinking and decision making, even unconsciously, despite an increasing number saying that there are no natural differences between men and women (Pager and Quillian 2005; Valian 1999). These gender schemas are based on our preconceived notions and cultural assumptions of what men and women are really like. Therefore, they are based on hegemonic masculinities and femininities of a certain time, place, and culture. Because of that, they can change, and once actors are aware of the gender schemas, they can actively resist them (Bridges and Pascoe 2014). Prior research has documented that these hegemonic masculinities and femininities influence men's and women's evaluations in the workplace (Blair-Loy 2005; Correll, Benard, and Paik 2007; Eagly 2007). For example, employers have reported not hiring women during childbearing years because they assume these women would prioritize motherhood over demanding careers (Browne and Kennelly 2006). This results in men dominating leadership positions in many male-dominated as well as female-dominated areas (Budig 2002), lower salaries for women, and fewer promotions (Blau and Kahn 2000; Budig 2002). Similarly, women have received lower evaluations and been seen as less effective leaders than equally qualified men (Blair-Loy 2005; Haveman and Beresford 2012), and their potential for leadership has been questioned (Blair-Loy 2005; Correll, Bard, and Paik 2007; Merluzzi and Dobrev 2015).

To test these biases and capture their direction and magnitude, the described vignettes were presented to the respondents. After reading the vignette, respondents were asked to decide if they were very unlikely (8 percent), somewhat unlikely (15 percent), somewhat likely (58 percent) or very likely (20 percent) to give the babysitter the requested pay raise. They were also asked to rate the babysitter on seven traits, identifying whether each trait described the babysitter "not at all," "not very well," "somewhat well," or "very well." The list included three negative traits (manipulative, disloyal, and greedy) and four positive traits (caring, competent, honest, and assertive). For the purposes of the analysis, each variable is rated from 1 to 4, where 1 is "not at all" (or "very unlikely" for the pay-raise scale) and 4 is "very well" (or "very likely").

Respondents gave the babysitters the highest scores on "caring," with 61 percent saying that the statement described the babysitter "very well" and none of the respondents indicating that it described the babysitter "not at all." Respondents were least likely to characterize the babysitters as "disloyal," with 40 percent indicating that it did not describe the babysitter at all, and only 3 percent saying that it described the babysitter "very well."

To correct for agreement/positivity bias, the responses for each respondent were subtracted from their mean rating (so, if a respondent's mean rating on all of the scales was 2 [out of 4], a rating of 1 would be counted as –1, a rating of 2 would be counted as 0, and a rating of 4 would be counted as 2). After this correction, the mean values for each experimental condition were calculated for whether or not the respondents would give the raise and for the sum of all of the positive and negative traits. The correction essentially accounts for the fact that respondents answering these online surveys start at one place on the screen and mostly move the mouse left or right to register their responses; the correction means that we are looking at how *far* left or right they are moving to register their approval or disapproval.

Overall, as shown in Table 2.1, respondents who read about the male babysitter (Jake) who expressed no emotional connection to the child had the most positive impression of the babysitter who asked for a raise; he was viewed much more positively (an average of one point higher on each of the positive traits) than the version of Jake who had an emotional connection with the child. For respondents who read about the female babysitter (Molly), the version who expressed no emotional connection was viewed more positively than the version who did, by a margin of 0.7 points per positive trait.

This is not to say that respondents did not like Molly when she had an emotional connection with the child; that version of the babysitter had the lowest level of negative traits, by far (the male babysitter without an emotional connection was rated the most negatively). The version of Molly who had an emotional connection with the child was also the *least* likely to get the raise, by a narrower margin. The male babysitter without an emotional connection was the most likely to get the raise, followed by the female babysitter without an emotional connection. In both cases, the babysitter with the

TABLE 2.1 RESULTS OF EXPERIMENT ON HIRING BABYSITTERS

	Overall positive	Overall negative	Give raise
Molly, emotional connection	1.2	−3.3	0.0
Jake, emotional connection	3.3	−0.3	0.4
Molly, no emotional connection	4.0	0.8	0.7
Jake, no emotional connection	7.1	2.4	1.8

TABLE 2.2 EVALUATIONS OF BABYSITTERS: POSITIVE ASSOCIATIONS

	Caring	Honest	Competent	Assertive
Molly, emotional connection	0.5	0.3	0.5	0.3
Jake, emotional connection	1.2	0.9	1.2	0.9
Molly, no emotional connection	1.4	1.1	1.6	1.4
Jake, no emotional connection	2.5	2.2	2.5	1.9

TABLE 2.3 EVALUATIONS OF BABYSITTERS: NEGATIVE ASSOCIATIONS

	Manipulative	Disloyal	Greedy
Molly, emotional connection	−0.7	−1.5	−1.0
Jake, emotional connection	0.0	−0.4	0.1
Molly, no emotional connection	0.4	−0.1	0.5
Jake, no emotional connection	0.9	0.5	0.9

emotional connection was less likely to get the raise, but the male babysitter was punished more for having an emotional connection than the female babysitter.

The female babysitter with the emotional connection was the least likely to get the raise, and she was the least positively evaluated of the four conditions, while the male babysitter without the emotional connection was the most positively evaluated on all of the dimensions. The results are presented in Table 2.2.

Interestingly, while the female babysitter with the emotional connection to the child was not viewed positively, she was the least likely to be viewed negatively. She received lower ratings on all of the negative traits—by a large margin—than the babysitters in the other conditions. The most positively viewed babysitter, the version of Jake without an emotional connection, received the highest ratings on the negative traits (Table 2.3).

Overall, the story seems to be that respondents were ambivalent about the male babysitter with the emotional connection, but they gave him the raise anyway. When Molly had an emotional connection with the child, she was not viewed negatively, but she was not viewed positively, either. Respondents did not think she was greedy or manipulative—but they did not think she was competent or honest, either. More importantly, that ambivalence—for her, and not for him—meant that she did not get the raise she asked for.

The overall accounts and personal narratives of young women show that babysitting is indeed a physically and an emotionally challenging job. In original surveys, I asked young men and women to rate the difficulty of babysitting; they described babysitting as a predominantly easy job, rating it on average at 2 on a 0–10 scale, much easier than traditionally male jobs such as snow removal or yard work. While the perceptions of babysitting were that it is relatively easy, the actual lived experiences, from the perspectives of young women (and the few men) who perform this task, are remarkably different. Many pointed to physical and emotional exhaustion as a result of working as a babysitter. They also pointed to the emotional challenges: fear that children will say they were mistreated, apprehension about parental jealousies, and challenges of disciplining children. They noted the fluid definition of the work, where work and free time often blend together, with parents chatting with the babysitters for long periods of time after their shifts are over. They also pointed to the fluid definition of their work as supporting the mother, as mother's helper, or as the wife of the wife, often performing tasks that are unrelated to child care, such as cooking, cleaning, and laundry. However, many acknowledged their attachment to the children and their genuine care for the children they babysit.

However, their genuine love and care is rarely enough. Many perform extra aesthetic labor as well as emotion labor, demonstrating their care and love for the children, as well as presenting themselves as fun companions and older-sibling figures to the kids while presenting themselves as reliable figures to the parents. Such a task involves spending their own money and investing their own free time for classes, certifications, and credentials. They also invest a substantial amount of time planning activities, crafts, and games, and they buy new toys and trinkets, and download music and videos, to reward the children and pass the time.

Many also keep additional jobs, working at day-care centers, summer camps, and additional jobs to find and keep their babysitting jobs. Informal networks and ties help young women find babysitting jobs easily. However, these informal networks also become the reason why the pay remains so low. Since the majority of the employers are distant connections, female babysitters reported finding it challenging to ask for a raise or negotiate pay. While these informal networks are influential for male babysitters, as well, males report using these networks in finding jobs but do not suffer the negative effects. In addition, for female babysitters, relative to their male counterparts, work boundaries were not as rigid. Many reported that their shift would not start or end promptly, forcing them to come in early or stay late, talk with the parents, strategizing for the next shift, and often offer companionship and emotional support to the parents.

Furthermore, another difference in male and female babysitters' definitions of work was the content of babysitting itself. While both male and female babysitters technically do "babysitting," the lived experience and the content of babysitting was not the same. Male babysitters reported just being responsible for taking care of children and performing child care, whereas almost all the female babysitters reported that their job description included a wide range of activities, including cooking for the children or for the entire family, cleaning, laundry, preparing snacks, driving, arranging play dates, picking up dry cleaning, dropping off Netflix envelopes, and so on. Adding these activities to the definition of babysitting often changes the lived experience of jobs and the intensity of the shifts, and it creates an unequal work experience based on the gender of the babysitters.

Finally, female babysitters were more likely to stay in babysitting jobs for longer because of the previously mentioned informal links. They were told that they were too valuable to the family, that the family could not survive without them, that the mother needed them, and that they were essential to the emotional well-being of the children. While majority of the female babysitters wanted to quit babysitting and move on to other jobs or activities, they were asked by the family to stay on longer or even to come back after they had left babysitting. Female babysitters pointed to this dilemma of being asked to stay; they ended up staying in babysitting positions longer than they wanted to because it was difficult to refuse families and children to whom they are connected.

Overall, female babysitters I interviewed pointed to the general difficulty of asking for money, negotiating on hire, and asking for a raise. While many pointed to their rising demands and changes in job description, often including babysitting more children and taking on more tasks as the children get older, such as driving to activities, cooking, arranging play dates, helping with homework, and making snacks, they report that they do not feel comfortable asking for more money and feel they will be faced with animosity if they do.

Given the gender imbalance of these freelance jobs, this chapter also captures the perspectives of the parents. Are the perceptions of the babysitters really true? Will they, in fact, be faced with animosity? Will they receive higher pay if they ask for more money? Based on the results of the experiment, I can confirm that the reluctance to ask for raise I find in the interviews was not simply the perception of the babysitters; female babysitters do face a serious bias in evaluation. When male babysitters ask for more money, they are seen as more assertive and competent and are given the raise. Interestingly, employers are suspicious of men only when they form an emotional connection and add personal touches, such as bringing home-baked goods. Such acts, coming from a male babysitter, are seen as manipulative and not genuine.

While emotional labor is not celebrated and often met with suspicion among men, for female babysitters it is a central component to the job, often referred to as the golden rule in the care-work and child-care literature. Caring, showing care, and emotion labor are prerequisites to getting and keeping babysitting jobs; however, caring does not make it easier for female babysitters to talk with their employers about money. Female babysitters who do not show care are heavily chastised by potential employers. If they fail to show care, they do not deserve a raise, and they receive some of the lowest ratings by the employers. However, the alternative is not much better for the female babysitters. When they show care and ask for money, they are rated as caring but also as manipulative, and the employers like them less for asking for a raise. On top of it, they are less likely to get the raise. As a consequence, there are no good options for female babysitters: when they do not show care, they are disliked because they are not caring, and they do not get the raise, but when they care and ask for the raise, they are perceived as manipulative—using their care to ask for more money—and they still do not get a raise. Men who do not show care not only are more likely to get a raise but are seen as more assertive and more competent. Either way, young women are in a restrictive bind. This chapter focuses on the experiences of babysitters, who are unable to negotiate and are kept in lower-paying babysitting jobs through informal networks. In the next chapter, I explore the everyday experiences of young women who, like the male babysitters I spoke with, move from babysitting into the retail and service sectors.

3

Shop Girls

Gender Inequality in Retail and Service-Sector Jobs

Heather explains, "I work at this place called Fresh. Have you heard of it? It's awesome; it's the best job ever. I went into a Fresh for the first time maybe like five years ago. I got the whole treatment, like demo and everything. It's really awesome. You can go in, and the employees will give you a tour of the store and show you how everything feels on your hands. It's awesome, so I got that with my mom. We were at the [nearby high-end mall], and I walked out thinking, 'I would love to work here.'" Heather is a twenty-year-old senior at a public university, where she studies social science. When I meet her for our interview, she rushes to our meeting carrying a large Fresh bag that she proudly carries everywhere, holding her books and bottled water. She has been working at Fresh, a cosmetics store that specializes in natural skin-care products, for two years, and it is the only place where she would even consider working.

She describes the store as being "laid back and really friendly. So much fun." When it opened at a nearby mall, minutes from her house, she was so excited that she immediately rushed there to inquire about job openings. She even considered the hour-long commute each way to another mall before a local branch opened, but her mother discouraged it. She still remembers her interview: "It started as a group interview and broke into smaller individual groups." After the numerous interviews, she was discouraged that she did not get a call for four months. "I didn't think I got it," she says. She loves the products and the brand so much that she would not even consider working anywhere else. The brand was very important in her choice of where to work, leading her to wait four months for even the possibility of working there. But after the lengthy wait, she got the call confirming she got the job, and she has been working at the same branch continuously for two years.

In addition to her love of the products, she was taken with the brand's socially and environmentally conscious image. As a sociology major, she said that she understands issues of global inequality and cares deeply about environmental issues. This brand advertises that it does not use harmful chemicals and that all ingredients are ethically sourced. She felt that the image and vision of the brand represents who she is and the issues she cares about. To Heather, working at Fresh shows who she is as a person, her social and political views, her aesthetic, and her worldview. She loves that the company donates some of the proceeds from some of the products she uses to charities in a give-back program, making her feel good about her consumption.

Two years into her work at Fresh, Heather averages twenty to twenty-five hours per week, mostly afternoons and weekends. Her typical shifts are five to eight hours long, during which she assists customers, does product demonstrations, works the cash register, and trains other employees. These days, her location is understaffed and not many employees know how to open the store, so she has been working the opening shift. The tiny store is usually packed with customers who have detailed questions about the products, ask for samples and product demonstrations, and are sometimes upset about the prices and the lack of coupons and discounts. She does not mind working in such close quarters with her coworkers during these long, hectic shifts, as she feels emotionally close to them. "They are my best friends," she said, referring to her coworkers, and "my boss is awesome—we are friends." She said that the people who work as Fresh are like her: she sees them as similar in their worldviews, personalities, and social and political attitudes. "We get to play our own music. I get to show my passion and excitement for the products I like." During the interview, she did seem to be genuinely excited about the products. "I use everything," she said, referring to the brand's face masks, shampoo, conditioners, facial cleansers, scrubs, shower creams, and moisturizers.

She also told me that the customers "are really cool—well, mostly. Sometimes, they are very difficult. Mostly we are very nice, but we are on the expensive side, and people get upset about the prices. We have a way of explaining [that] every ingredient is natural; like, they are not putting chemicals in their shampoo, everything is locally sourced, and money goes back to the growers, so there is a reason. Usually after explaining, they understand, but sometimes they don't. They are upset we don't have sales or coupons."

Heather is one of many female service and retail workers who staff the endless counters of our increasingly service-oriented economy. Retail and service-sector jobs are essential to the contemporary American economy, especially given the decline of manufacturing jobs in the recent recession (Korczynski and Macdonald 2008; Macdonald and Sirianni 1996; Williams and Connell 2010). During the 2008 economic crisis, construction experienced a 23.3 percent decrease in employment, while manufacturing and trade experienced a 16 percent decline. Similarly, transportation and utilities also experienced a 7.6 percent decline, and administrative and waste services experienced an 18 percent jobs loss (Blank 2010; Gatta 2014). Today, more than 10 percent of the total labor force in advanced economies is composed of retail workers (Bozkurt and Grugulis 2011). Ödül Bozkurt and Irena Grugulis, in their edited volume *Retail Work*, observe that "retail work is in many ways the new generic form of mass employment in the post-industrial socio-economic landscape. If the factory and the assembly line came to represent the quintessential workplace under industrialism . . . [the workplace] of the post-industrial era may be Wal-Mart rather than Google" (2011, 2). With the growing importance of retail in today's economy, we have witnessed a growing interest in the sector. Scholars have studied the fast-food industry (Leidner 1993; Ritzer 2000), call centers and customer service (Callaghan and Thompson 2002; Taylor and Bain 2002), and working conditions in these sectors (Ehrenreich 2001). Typically, these service and retail jobs are characterized as unskilled, low-pay, inflexible jobs with automated and scripted work experiences (Frenkel 2003; Kalleberg 2011; Kalleberg, Reskin, and Hudson 2000; Misra and Walters 2016; Mouw and Kalleberg 2010; V. Smith 2012). Because these jobs have typically been what Arne Kalleberg (2011) characterizes as "bad jobs," they were also seen as easy to get. Chris Tilly and Françoise Carré (2011, 298) characterize the job interview process as a mirror test (hold a mirror up to see if it fogs up) or a pulse test (does the candidate have a pulse?).

While the recession of the late 2000s has mostly affected manufacturing jobs, retail and service-sector jobs have also experienced a decline due to the recession, as well as an increase in the pace of automation. Because these sectors employ predominantly male employees, the recent recession was dubbed as a "mancession" (D. Thompson 2009). But despite the media depiction of the recession as a man's recession, women have experienced some obstacles, as well. Especially during the recovery period, women in retail sectors have experienced job losses (Gatta 2014). The retail and service jobs that used to be readily available are no longer there, and competition for the remaining positions has increased, allowing employers to subject potential employees to treatment like the four-month wait Heather experienced. In addition, retail and service-sector jobs have become more difficult to get because of aesthetic-labor requirements.

Rise of Aesthetic Labor

Heather told me that Fresh workers all have a certain "look." According to her, "It's hard to describe, [but they all look] young, fresh, and clean." The store has a distinctive look, as well as an easily recognizable scent. "We are not forced to use the products," she said, but employees are encouraged to do so. That said, Heather said that employees do not need to be forced, because the workers are recruited from existing, devoted customers. "We all care about the products a great deal, and it shows." Her excitement for the products she sells seems genuine, and she said the customers pick up on that: "They know we are not just working on commission—we really love the products." She was already a big fan of the facial masks and the natural moisturizer, as well as some of the hair products. She simply continued to use them after she started working at the store.

The employee discount helps with her continued use of the products, as do the free samples. In addition to the products she regularly uses, she tries out new products as they are introduced at the store. For example, she did not use their shampoos before working there, but once she was introduced to them, she began to use them, along with a myriad of new skin products. Unsurprisingly, this means that she spends a substantial amount of money on the products she sells. She told me that last week, she spent more than one hundred dollars on products from her own store. For holiday and birthday gifts, she buys gifts exclusively from this store. "Sometimes I feel like all the money I earn goes back to the company," she said.

At a regular shift, she is expected wear all black and an apron with the company logo. She has a choice in what she wears, but it has to look high quality and put together. Most importantly, her skin has to look fresh, young, and clean, and it must be clear. Because of this requirement, not only does she use the products, but her skin-care regimen is central to keeping the job.

Like many of the other retail and service-sector workers I interviewed, she told me that how she looks on the job is very important. Employees in these sectors have to look good, be nice, and smell nice. Heather explained, "We don't have a uniform, [but we wear] mostly all black and white. We have an apron, but we have to wear all black. My wardrobe has become all black and white." For Heather, her work appearance requirements dominate her social life. "We are told to look like we use the product and not like we need to use products, and we all take it to heart. . . . We all have, like, really nice skin. I don't buy perfume anymore: I am supposed to smell like the product." She is especially careful about smells: even when she and her friends go to the food court to get lunch, they work to cover up any lingering food smells when they return to the store, even in the absence of explicit requirements that they do so.

In addition to looking and smelling a certain way, Fresh employees also have to be "nice." It is important that the workers be friends with each other, Heather said: she does not hang out with her classmates from college, but some of her coworkers at Fresh are her best friends. That "nice" environment is very important: in her perception, the company is all about being nice and ethically responsible and creating a happy, peaceful world, so that niceness and calmness should be conveyed during the shift.

Heather embodies the new aesthetic-labor requirements of retail and service jobs in the United States. Today, many retail and service jobs are much more diverse than the mirror-test jobs previously described, involving boutique retailers, high-end establishments, and specialized services in addition to the fast-food jobs that were the focus of much of the early work in the field. Bozkurt and Grugulis explain:

> Despite the popular cultural shorthand used to depict all retail workers as automatons who cannot wait to get out of these jobs if only the opportunities were there, retail work is widely diverse. The labour market spans a range from attractive, middle-class dominated "style" labour markets . . . to the poorly paid shift work offered by mass retailers. (2011, 5)

High-end boutiques and specialized services, despite the low pay and poor working conditions, opt for workers who will most positively represent their brand as the customer-oriented face of the corporation. "Looking good and sounding right," as Dennis Nickson and Chris Warhurst (2001) put it, has become a prerequisite for many retail and service-sector jobs. Companies like the one Heather works for are not selling a product or service but a brand. Anybody can learn to serve coffee or sell sweaters, but these companies are not just selling the products or the services; they are selling the service experience, and employees are essential in creating that branded service and selling a certain environment. For that, they not only have to look good and sound right but also have to embody the look of the brand. This puts new demands on the potential employees. As Nickson and colleagues argue, this is

> leading to the development of what is termed "aesthetic labour," involving the manner in which employees are expected to embody the product in industries such as service and hospitality. . . . This labour refers to the hiring of people with corporeal capacities and attributes

that favorably appeal to the customers' senses and which are organizationally mobilized, developed and commodified through training, management and regulation to produce an embodied style of service. As a part of this process of embodiment, employees are expected to . . . demonstrate soft-skills associated with personality and attitude to "look good" and "sound right." (2011, 69)

This is in diametric opposition to the idea of automated, interchangeable workers in identical uniforms reading from a script (Leidner 1993; Ritzer 2000). Nickson, Warhurst, and Dutton (2004) refer to this as a style-labor market: even when franchises are identical and using scripts, they make it seem like each store is unique, individualized, and custom made. Many high-end boutiques, restaurants, and retailers are adopting a similar strategy: even the city of Glasgow is branding itself as a fun city with style labor to attract more tourists (Nickson, Warhurst, and Dutton 2004).

Young people have an advantage with the rising aesthetic-labor requirements. Certain young workers have become sought-after vehicles to create the ultimate product experience. Who better to represent a brand than vibrant, youthful employees—especially ones who are enthusiastic about the brand and the products? Young people have always been part of the labor supply for the service sector, but with the rise of the style-labor market, they have become the faces of the corporation. Nickson and colleagues argue that "students are deemed to be particularly attractive to retail employers due to their flexibility, cheapness and highly developed soft-skills" (2011, 69; see also Canny 2002; Nickson, Warhurst, and Dutton 2004).

In creating a brand experience, it is not enough for young workers to be young and energetic; they also need to project a desired image (Besen-Cassino 2014; Gatta 2011; Pettinger 2004; Williams and Connell 2010). In a crowded retail and hospitality market, such style requirements help brands differentiate themselves (Nickson Warhurst, and Dutton 2004, 10). It is not enough for Heather to be knowledgeable about the products. She has to use them and signal to the customers that she uses them: she has to embody the brand at the same time she is selling it.

It is not just about looking good and sounding right, or just looking attractive, but employees need to look fashionable and fit the look of the company. This requires the employees to invest in their looks: buy new clothes, shoes, makeup, and accessories. Lynn Pettinger, for example, in her ethnographic study of high-end London boutiques, finds that "fashion orientation is one facet of brand strategy and the ability to present a fashionable appearance is one of the skills needed by sales assistants in many stores" (2004, 468). Wearing the clothes and accessories sold in the store not only creates a fashionable image for the company but also helps potential customers aspire to the lifestyle the brand wants to project.

Attractiveness and use of the products are important, but so is self-presentation. An employee working at Hot Topic will inevitably have a different look than an employee of Ann Taylor or Abercrombie and Fitch. David Wright argues that "physical attractiveness, particular style of dress, and types of physical comportment all contribute to the production of the retail space as meaningful and aesthetically pleasing to the customer" (2005, 305).

Borrowing from Pierre Bourdieu, the bodies of these young workers become the vehicles of retail success. Employee bodies are shaped and molded to project and maintain the image of the corporation. This goes beyond projecting a fashionable image: by using the products being sold, young workers create a bond with the customers more easily. As Sophia, a political science major who works at a high-end clothing store targeting younger women, recalls, her manager's hiring of a teenage girl who spent much of her time and money at the retail store was not an impulse decision but a calculated one. The girl looked like her customers, and it would be easy for the customers to ask her questions and talk about the products with her.

David Wright's ethnography of bookstores in the United Kingdom emphasizes the knowledge and interest in the product sold in retail. He argues that employees of a bookstore are not just there to sell books, but they are supposed to enjoy books and reading. He interviews a manager who tells him that "people come into book selling because they like books, and in my experience of interviewing several hundred people, the 'click' point in an interview is when you find out that someone is genuinely passionate about reading or books on any level. . . . It might be that they read, it may be that they write or review or anything else, but they'll have an engagement and that's the people worth having. If they don't have that, they're not worth having in a bookshop" (2005, 305–306). Similarly, Prue Huddleston, in her interviews with employees at sporting-goods stores, finds that the managers want workers who look "like they do the sports themselves, for example, we've got people who are interested in skateboarding, cycling, climbing, that sort of thing, it's a lifestyle thing, and of course, those are the sort of youngsters we get coming here looking for jobs" (2011, 115).

To create and sustain the right look, many retail and service jobs require, or at least strongly encourage, the workers to buy and use the company's products. Huddleston shows that in fashion outlets, even part-time employees are expected to purchase the products sold and wear them on the shop floor. Similarly, Mary Gatta (2011), in her qualitative study of boutique retail stores in New Jersey, shows that employees are expected not just to buy the uniform but also to keep purchasing the products sold at the store constantly, to keep up with the look requirements. The idea behind this expectation is that young workers are not simply selling the products but also acting as mediators between the customer and the product (Gatta 2011). Their bodies become the brand: the look, the lifestyle, and the environment being marketed are embodied by these young workers.

Gender and Emotion Work in the Service and Retail Sectors

Historically, the feminization of the service sector is a relatively recent phenomenon. With the rapid shift into a service economy, many studies of labor have continued to focus on manufacturing, which has employed predominantly male workers (Otis 2011). Service work, on the other hand, has been feminized and characterized as an extension of house chores and home-care responsibilities and therefore excluded from promotion into managerial positions (Kanter [1977] 1993). Typical studies of labor see a clear demarcation between service and manufacturing jobs, even though such dichotomies undermine the similarities of both sectors and mostly deemphasize the physical requirements of service-sector jobs (Kang 2010).

"It is mostly women," Heather said, describing the workers on her shift. "There are very few guys—but we are all ambassadors." Her shift consists mostly of young women who use and love the products. There are a few men who work with her, and sometimes male customers gravitate toward them, as do the older women. Even though there are very few men working at the store, they get more interest and attention and do more sales, and they are thought to be more special.

Emotion Work: Dealing with Difficult Customers

While traditional studies of labor have characterized work in the service sector as unskilled labor, sociologists have begun pointing out the social and interactive skills involved in service jobs. In *The Managed Heart*, Arlie Russell Hochschild (1983) points to the importance of what she refers to as emotion work, in which service-sector workers are expected to alter their own emotions to convey a certain affect. It is a "kind of labor that calls for a coordination of mind and feeling, and it sometimes draws on a source of self that we honor as deep and integral to our individuality" (Hochschild 1983, 7). Regardless of their own experiences, emotions, and states of mind during the shift, service-sector workers are expected to change their own emotions in order to elicit the emotions the company wants in the customers. In addition to altering one's emotions, Hochschild finds, in her detailed study of flight attendants, that changing one's emotions often involves an ability to read other people's emotions and use appropriate physical expressions of the necessary emotions. This is a complicated set of skills required by the emotion-labor component of service-sector jobs. According to Hochschild, "Behind the most effective display, there is a feeling that fits it, and that feeling can be managed" (1983, 34). Therefore, the mental state of the workers is controlled and managed throughout a shift to elicit the desired demeanor. Therefore, in addition to being expected to perform certain behaviors and gestures, workers are expected to feel a certain way. The control of feelings and emotions, not just their display, is central.

For Heather, her job requirements are not just to smile and be happy, young, and upbeat, as the previous research has shown. Her company's brand, Fresh, is all about calm and peace. Heather asked me to imagine taking a nice relaxing bubble bath after a long day. The employees are expected to convey that level of "peace, calm, and nice," she said. Most retail workers I spoke with pointed to challenging customers shouting at them, being aggressive, and being frustrated, but Heather was an exception. Yes, she definitely remembers having to deal with challenging customers, the ones who were upset about the prices or who wanted special discounts or special treatment. However, one thing that sets her store apart is the nice, calm, peaceful environment. "Even when the customers are angry, they see how nice we are, so they decide to act nice, too." Part of her emotion labor, then, is not just smiling but being "nice" "calm" and "peaceful." Almost all existing accounts of emotion work point to smiling and being happy and upbeat, mostly to convey a certain look, sound, or attitude to fit the image of the brand. However, in this case, the emotion work is used as a tool to manage customer service and assuage angry customers. The lived experience of staying calm and peaceful all the time, and coordinating with others to maintain a calm, peaceful environment, is often challenging. Heather told me she finds it very challenging to stay calm and peaceful under some circumstances, such as when someone is shouting at her. She told me that in her store, it is the female employees who are asked to handle those cases, as they are naturally calmer and more peaceful.

Michael, a twenty-year-old who has been working in a clothing store for some time, said he does not mind working with people so much, but he adds that at times he might get too angry and not know how to handle challenging customers, so at his job there is a young woman who is "good at dealing with difficult customers." "She does yoga," Michael said, indicating that she is calmer and better suited for dealing with angry customers. Zoe, on the other hand, a twenty-two-year-old female student, has been working at a retail store for a year. Even though she likes her coworkers and her "cool boss," she was told to do the opening shift at very early hours. Her boss told her that some of her coworkers were not very nice and pleasant in the morning, but Zoe would be ideal for this shift because she would be more upbeat and cheerful in the morning. As a result, she has been waking up early and often skipping her morning run because she has to do the opening shift, which she describes as her least favorite part of the job.

April, a twenty-year-old college student, has been working at a clothing store, where her friends also work, since high school. Her specialty, she tells me, is "dealing with difficult customers," a task she also calls the worst part of her job. She takes pride in the fact that she is the best at dealing with challenging customers, who come in at least once per shift, leading the other workers and management to come find her when a customer is becoming problematic. Many of the women I spoke to said they were asked to handle difficult or rude customers. Typically, supervisors tell young female employees that they are very good with people and that their good social skills are essential to the job. While these skills may be valuable, April and others report having been moved from cash registers, where they handled money and performed managerial tasks, so that they could deal with rude customers.

Shifting between Aesthetics

Today, many retail workers work part time, are given limited hours, and are unlikely to qualify for health-care or other benefits, with many retail and service-sector workers reporting that they work at multiple service and retail jobs to piece together adequate hours (see Bureau of Labor Statistics 2016). For example, according to the Bureau of Labor Statistics *Occupational Outlook Handbook* (2015), one in three retail workers work part time. Many participants in my study worked for multiple retail and service jobs to piece together enough hours to support themselves, or at least to be able to pay for some of their expenses. Such arrangements are complicated by aesthetic-labor and emotion-work requirements.

Kiara, an African American full-time college student who works two jobs because she needs the hours, pointed to the problem of shifting emotions and aesthetics every day. For the past year, she has been working twenty-five to thirty hours a week at Sport Central, a sporting-goods store. "I am so ready to leave it," she said of the job, which she found through a track-and-field teammate at her large state university. She described the interview process: "I interviewed with the apparel manager and then the head manager. You take the survey; then if you don't pass, they send you home. Then you meet the managers one on one. It was different. I am used to different interviews— like, what are your downfalls? Your strengths? Where-do-you-see-yourself- like questions. It was none of those questions. It was like, 'If there is this issue, what would you do? If a customer is upset, what would you do?'"

She got the job, she thinks, because of her athletic background: because she does track and field at her university, she fits in with the other workers, who are current or former athletes. "It is rare to see a nonathlete working there," she said, and "even [the nonathletes who work there] look pretty athletic. They work out or something." During her shifts, she needs to project that athleticism. "You can wear anything athletic, but [it] has to be athletic, and no tank tops—[a top] has to have sleeves. Hair has to be a natural color, or [you have to] ask for permission to have your hair colored. Shoes cannot be Uggs [comfortable boots]—we have them [at the store] but cannot wear them; [we have to wear] athletic shoes." Even though she gets a 25 percent discount, she said she still cannot afford to shop there. She knows some friends who try to keep up with the new sneakers, new yoga pants, and new brands all the time, and they end up in serious debt. She is expected to look athletic, so she constantly looks for bargain leisure and athletic wear at places like discount retailers. The employees are expected look "sporty," which is not something a person can accomplish just by putting on athletic wear. However, she feels that she has the expected muscle tone and looks like she is an athlete because of her track-and-field schedule at school. Employees are also supposed to be knowledgeable about sporting goods. She tells me that she needs to know which shoe is good for running, what people need for yoga, and where people can find spin shoes. She told me:

> You have to be in a certain mind-set. The customers are the worst—I work at a rich town, so their money speaks for them. I want to leave. I have to mentally prepare myself [for working the cash register]. I had, like, shoe boxes thrown at me. People throw shoeboxes. We don't take expired coupons, competitor coupons. They compare us to [two sporting-goods competitors]. [We would like to tell them,] "Then go there," but if you say that, there will be a bigger argument. The customers are not friendly; [friendliness] is rare. You have to be upbeat and friendly [and] greet every customer, [but] then we get complaints because we greet too much.
>
> Some [customers] directly go to the managers and complain that we didn't directly help them after greeting them. It's not our job to shop for [them], [but] they expect us to put [their purchases] in a cart and walk around the store with them. They want to tell us what their child is doing—like hockey or soccer—and they expect us to shop for them. It is very tug-of-war.

She told me that she sits in her car in the parking lot before her shift begins, just after ending her shift as a receptionist at a pediatric orthopedic practice, and tries to mentally prepare herself to deal with these types of customers.

What she finds especially challenging is shifting in and out of the roles and images of her different jobs quickly. "I don't get enough hours in either place, so I have to work both, but when they clash, it is so hard. . . . Like, Saturdays, they clash: I work the receptionist eight to five, then sporting goods five to ten, [but] they are twenty minutes apart. [If the] four o'clock parent [at the medical office] pays ahead, I leave early so I can make it, and I have to look and sound different. By the time I see the customers, I am so tired. Just scream at me."

The athletic look of Sport Central is a stark contrast to the look expected of a receptionist at a practice working with children with scoliosis. She has been working at that office since her aunt recommended her about a year ago. She gets ten to fifteen hours a week, depending on the schedule, but her hours are never enough. She likes that she gets to work with children. Since she is a receptionist, she has to look polished and grown up for the adults, yet she also needs to look nice, caring, and friendly toward the children. She explained the look required of her: "Business attire twenty-four-seven. Sometimes I wear a suit jacket and a blouse [with] black pants, no colors. It is very strict. Hair can't be bright colors, no blue. No open-toed shoes, no sandals." Since she is the first person the patients and their parents see and interact with, she needs to look serious and professional, but, at the same time, she needs to avoid scaring away the kids. "You are the first person they see, so you have to be upbeat. Like, 'Hi, how is your day?' I don't always feel up to it, especially when I am coming from school. I am like, 'Okay, here we go.' I have a mental talk: 'Kiara, three to four hours—you can do it.'"

The customers she deals with are just as aggressive and angry, but it is different. "They can get upset when the insurance does not pay. Sometimes the insurance company pays what it does, and the rest is like sixteen hundred dollars, and they are upset and vocal about it. Now I have to deal with them. There are some regulars [who] will just scream at you—you need to mentally prepare yourself. You just take it." Sometimes the manager tells her she is so good at dealing with hostile customers that she should deal with these "regulars."

Young Women of Retail and Service: Doing Gender

While women have become almost synonymous with retail and service-sector jobs, the other large source of workers for retail and service jobs is young workers, particularly students (Gatta 2009; Nickson et al. 2011). While female workers are seen as cheap, flexible labor with the required soft skills (Scott 1994), young workers have emerged as equally attractive options for retail and service positions. Students are particularly of interest to retail and service employers because of their willingness to work for low wages, their flexibility, and their willingness to work nonstandard shifts, especially nights and weekends, as well as not needing full-time hours (Canny 2002; Nickson et al. 2011; Nickson, Warhurst, and Dutton 2004). In addition, student workers have youthful energy and are capable of fulfilling the soft skills and aesthetic requirements of retail and service jobs. While extensive research has focused on women in retail and students in retail, the intersection of these groups has received scant attention. Typical studies have treated these two groups as distinctly separate pools of workers. However, their intersection—young female students—deserves the most attention and academic inquiry.

As these young women fill service and retail jobs, they are not simply performing a job, but they are "doing gender" (West and Zimmerman 1987). Candace West and Don Zimmerman (1987), borrowing from Erving Goffman's framing theory, offer a theory of gender as a series of actions and displays based on appropriate gender expectations, and they introduce the concept of "doing gender." According to West and Zimmerman (1987) gender identity is not passive; as active agents, we do gender in our everyday lives, and through everyday practice, individuals constitute, reconstitute, reaffirm, and reinforce gender identities and expectations (Ely and Meyerson 2000; Martin 2003; Mendez and Wolf 2001; Quinn 2002; Rantalaiho et al. 1997). These gendered identities are reaffirmed, and appropriate behaviors for men and women are internalized through practice in all major arenas of our lives, such as school, work, family, and relationships. Almost like riding a bicycle, to a point, gendering becomes automatic (Martin 2003). As young women go to work to sell soap or fold sweaters, not only are they socialized into the rules of the workplace, such as being on time or multitasking, but they internalize *gendered* rules of the workplace. Feminist scholars have long argued that seemingly neutral institutions and bureaucracies are heavily gendered (Calas and Smircich 1997; Cockburn 1988; Collinson and Hearn 1994; Martin 2001; Ridgeway 2001). Patricia Yancey Martin (2001), for example, shows that everyday interactions and everyday work experiences are central in workers' reinforcement and retention of gendered assumptions in the workplace (see also Cassirer and Reskin 2000; Collinson and Hearn 1996; Ely and Meyerson 2000; Kerfoot and Knights 1996; Martin 1990, 1994; McGuire 2002; Reskin and McBrier 2000; Whitehead 1998). Every day when young women and men go to work, they not only learn the gendered rules of the workplace but also perpetuate and strengthen gendered stereotypes and assumptions (Quinn 2002; Ridgeway 2001).

Borrowing from the postmodern feminist philosopher Judith Butler (1993), doing gender is a performance by actors, almost like a play, in our everyday lives, whether at school or at work. As Patricia Yancey Martin argues,

"Performing gender reconstructs gender practices in a way that stabilizes gender as an institution but that also provides material for future gendering practices/practicing of gender" (2003, 353; see also Campbell 2000). Using these concepts of gender performance, doing gender, and gender practice, R. W. Connell focuses on performing masculinities as "a configuration of practice within a system of gender relations" (1995, 84), rather than doing gender. Today, many gender scholars have applied this concept of practicing and doing femininities and masculinities in work and organizations (Bird 1996; Britton 1999; Dellinger and Williams 2002; Quinn 2002; Wharton, Rotolo, and Bird 2000). Through everyday work experiences, young women in retail and service jobs not only do gender at work but are also socialized into the gendered values of the workplace.

Women as Embodiment of the Brand and Debt

Jules, a twenty-year-old college student majoring in sociology with a minor in criminal justice, remembers her work experience at Seymour and Smith, where she worked when she was a high school student. "During my senior year in high school, I decided to find my first job. Many of my friends were working at the mall close to my home. So I decided to find a job in retail. I applied for a job at Seymour and Smith because I knew people who worked there, and I really liked their clothing. Working at Seymour and Smith gave one status back in the day. It was cool and the hottest place. If you told someone you worked at Seymour and Smith, they held you to a different standard. Since this was my first job, I had nothing on my résumé. The hiring process for this job was fairly easy. I showed up to a group interview and answered meaningless questions. I still remember being asked, 'What is your favorite animal?' There were no questions like 'How would you contribute to our company?' 'Do you see yourself working here in five years?' I had no experience. All I had was personality and appearance; that's what I brought to the table."

Jules was tall and slender, with an athletic build and long brown hair, which was always blow-dried. She looked like the embodiment of Seymour and Smith. As a high school student, she was ecstatic to work there, as the status of the company conferred status to her—a major affirmation of self-esteem. She told me among her high school friends, getting a job at Seymour and Smith was an important event because "it was like being chosen. Not everyone can get a job at Seymour and Smith. You have to be very thin, athletic, and attractive." It was an affirmation of beauty, and she remembers how she felt because she was excited to be chosen, as though she had been granted membership into an exclusive club.

Debt and Investment

Jules does not look back fondly on her experience working at Seymour and Smith, because her aesthetic requirements to fit into this exclusive club did not stop once she got the job. For her, it was a constant struggle to keep up with the look requirements. The employees were encouraged to purchase new items every week. It was not just the management, she told me; the employees had created a culture of constantly buying new products. Whether it was a new color of polo or new sandals, she got into the habit of purchasing something, sometimes many things, each week. Every employee on her shift acted similarly, excited about the brand and the new products, and during the time she worked at Seymour and Smith, she got sucked into a cycle of consumption. She felt that she had to purchase the new products and keep up to maintain the look of the company and keep her job. By the time she left Seymour and Smith, she had accumulated a level of credit card debt that rivals her student loans.

Jules's experience in the retail sector is not an exception. Of the women I interviewed, all of them reported having spent money at the store where they work. Nina, a sophomore in college, reported having spent $1,000 in the previous two months on clothes at the retail store where she works. Many retail workers feel that they are replaceable if they do not keep up with the look requirements. Sally, a first-generation Lebanese student majoring in sociology, is interested in fashion and merchandising. She remembers working at Tower Limited when a young woman who shopped regularly at that particular branch was hired on the spot when she came in to spend over $1,000. It was not uncommon for stores to hire existing customers, as those customers were already knowledgeable about the products and would easily display the clothes or accessories the store was selling. Therefore, for many of the female workers, consumption of the product is a signal of their commitment to the workplace and knowledge about the product. By using the products, they show commitment to the brand and ensure they keep their jobs.

While the $1,000 purchase was among the highest of the participants I interviewed, and many did not spend nearly as much, they almost universally invested substantial amounts of money to keep up the look of the company. Kendra, for example, is a nineteen-year-old who has been working at different retail and service-sector jobs from a young age; at the time of our interview, she was working at a high-end clothing store. When she was being interviewed for the job, she spent around $600 buying clothes and accessories and preparing her looks to fit the image of the company. Because of that, she says her interview took only thirty minutes, because when the managers saw her, her commitment to and knowledge of the brand were evident from her looks, and she had the job. It did not stop there for her, as she has continued to purchase new merchandise constantly, driven by worries that she will not look the part and her commitment to the brand will be questioned. In the past month, she has spent $300, which is typical for her. Even though she makes $9.15 an hour, most of her earnings go to supporting her clothing budget. Everything she earns goes back to the store, she jokes, but it does not end there: she has been using, and even maxing out, her credit card to keep up with the new merchandise. Abby, an eighteen-year-old white retail worker, said she loves the clothing store where she has been working for a year. Unfortunately, she only gets eight hours per week at $10.50 an hour. She loves the clothes that the store sells and regularly feels pressured to buy them. In the past month, she spent around $150 to buy new clothes, and she said that she has to spend about $120 a month on clothes to keep up with the look requirements of the store, a sentiment echoed by other workers I spoke with.

While the men in my sample reported similar aesthetic-labor requirements, there are major gender differences. First, while women reported both being hired and witnessing the hiring of devoted consumers, the men in the sample did not report experiencing this. While many of the women, like Sally, reported that stores hire from existing customers, the men in my sample did not report that they were hired because of their past shopping habits. It seems that young women consumers tend to be targeted more by the corporations and may be more likely to be hired as they are shopping.

Second, the male retail workers report spending money for the initial job interview but far less to keep up with the aesthetic requirements of the job. For example, John, a nineteen-year-old, white male student, has been working at a retail clothing chain for some time. He typically works twenty hours per week at $11 an hour, usually nights and weekends, to accommodate his school schedule. He remembers having to spend $100 before his interview to buy clothes and get a haircut to make sure he looked professional, but once he got the job, he did not continue this spending. He did not report feeling the pressure to consume that the young women do. When I asked him if he remembers purchasing anything from the clothing store, he told me that he had not bought anything from the store where he works in a few months.

A final component of "looking good" in the workplace, in addition to buying the products and accessories, is weight management. Young women, especially those who worked in clothing stores, mentioned dieting and exercising to fit into the clothes they sell. Sally, who started working as a teenager, said that as soon as she started working at Tower Limited, she began to dislike her curves and wanted to fit into smaller clothing sizes. She would skip meals, drink meal-replacement shakes, and often try fad diets. Her coworkers on her shifts would know her clothing size, so she wanted to be able to fit into smaller clothes and look like the models. Similarly, Theresa, a twenty-one-year old who works at a high-end clothing store, remembers a workplace culture in which she and her coworkers would compare their diets, go on diets together, and set fitness goals. Her mother would tell her she needed to lose to weight but to do so by eating her vegetables and exercising; nevertheless, she remembers some very unhealthy diets. Not only did she buy the clothes, but she constantly felt like she did not look right in the clothes.

Off-the-Clock and Last-Minute Help

In addition to shopping requirements, young women who work in retail are more likely to be asked to help off the clock and train others. Sally has worked at Tower Limited continuously for years, in addition to being an avid consumer of the company's products. She loves their clothing and accessories. Because of her knowledge about the products, she has often been asked to stay after her shift to train others. Lina, similarly, is a full-time college student and an aspiring musician: she plays the guitar and sings in a band. She works part time at a coffee shop, where she is employed as a barista, in addition to bartending some nights at a local bar. She tells me that the coffee shop where she works is not one of the large chains but an independent shop that sells higher-end, more socially and environmentally conscious coffee. Often at the end of her shift, she ends up staying to help train new staff, teaching them about the coffee machine.

In addition to the off-the-clock help these workers provide to the friends they work with, many young women have complained about last-minute requests to work. Shannon, a nineteen-year-old, has been working at an office for a year. When the office gets busy, especially over the weekends, Shannon usually gets a call asking her to come in at the last minute. This last-minute scheduling assumes that she can change her schedule for school, other potential jobs, school assignments, or extracurricular activities, but her supervisor does not call the other employees.

"You're in It for the Discounts"

Overall, young women pointed to inequalities in investment in aesthetic labor, accumulation of debt, job assignments involving challenging customers, higher unpaid hours, and last-minute scheduling. But what about pay? What happens when they ask for a raise? Despite being at work almost every day and never missing a shift, Mary, when she asked for a raise, was told she was not really committed to her job. This is especially surprising because during the time I observed her work habits (described in more detail in

Besen-Cassino 2014), she was always at the Caffeine Bean. She would come to the Caffeine Bean even when she was not scheduled, just to hang out with friends, talk about the workplace and the products, and help train her coworkers. Despite all of this, a manager told her that she was not committed to the store but that she was just working there because of how much she enjoyed the product. She did, in fact, enjoy the gourmet coffee beans they sold, and she paid attention to the places of origin and knew a great deal about the flavor profiles. However, her commitment to the job was questioned because she liked the product, leading to the perception that she was only working there in order to get an employee discount. This is a major paradox: on one hand, she was expected to enjoy the product, but on the other hand, her commitment to the work was questioned because she enjoyed the product.

This is something many young women in retail positions I spoke to told me that they have heard over and over: "You're in it for the discounts." Aesthetic labor, embodying the look of the company and using the products of the corporation, is a central factor that helps workers get their jobs. However, for young women, the aesthetic requirement becomes problematic: management regularly warns young women that their use of the product or the consumption of the goods demonstrates a lack of commitment to the job as serious work. For example, when Kendra inquired about the possibility of a raise, she was told that she had a generous discount at the store, and she was there to buy the clothes and was not genuinely interested in the job. This makes it extra challenging for young women: after all, if managers perceive them as not really interested in the money or in gaining skills for future work, why should the store give them a raise or train them in skills that might advantage them, or the company, in the future?

Sofia, a twenty-year-old Hispanic college student, is studying education as well as working at a doctor's office as a secretary. She introduced me to her eighteen-year-old sister, who works at the frozen yogurt and smoothie shop Pink Strawberry. The younger sister does not care much about the product; what matters to her is the work environment. "It drives our mom crazy," Sofia said. "My sister has been working at Pink Strawberry for years. She only took the job because all her best friends work there, too. They always schedule shifts together so they can hang out." Sofia told me that her sister's manager always says that she and her friends are there for fun and not for the job. But, Sofia says, her sister does a much better job because of the fun she has on the job. She works hard and never misses shifts, despite the fact that she is there to hang out with her friends.

Many scholars point to the recruitment of retail and service-sector jobs from existing employees' friends, or like-minded workers with similar interests, just to create a happy, pleasant, relaxed shopping environment or project a cool brand image (Besen-Cassino 2014). Heather's employer, for example, recruits friends who get along just to create a calmer, peaceful, spa-like environment to sell cosmetics and spa products. Some coffee chains recruit from more socially desirable groups of friends to project a happy, cool environment that attracts customers. Many young women I spoke to pointed to working with friends: they either became friends with their coworkers because the employers recruited people with similar interests and hobbies, or they sought out jobs where their friends already worked (Besen-Cassino 2014).

Whitney, a twenty-year-old white student, has been working as a server at a restaurant chain for years. She averages twenty hours per week and makes around one hundred dollars per five-hour shift, including tips. She said, "My coworkers are my best friends." Even though she gets good tips and her customers are happy, she told me, "My boss has recently gone crazy," questioning her work quality and claiming that she comes to work just to see her friends. When she asked for a raise, she was told that she is there only to see her friends. Alia has been working in the service sector for over a year and makes minimum wage ($8.38 an hour). Usually, she works odd shifts on nights and weekends, but her hours are erratic and based on demand; in the week before I interviewed her, she did not get any hours. One of the reasons she was hired was that she was friends with the other workers. She said she picked that particular place to work because of its "friendly atmosphere, with wonderful employees." The fact that she would help create a cool, hip, friendly environment for the customers was the selling point and one of the reasons why she was hired, so it was a surprise to Alia to find out that her interactions and the sociability that got her hired was also a reason given for not paying her more.

Talia, too, got her current job at a retail store selling clothes because it was an opportunity to see her friends and socialize. In her suburban life, she felt disconnected from her friends and found it challenging to socialize and meet new people, which is why, she said, she took the job at a famous retail chain selling fashionable clothes to young people. Her friends worked at that particular store, but Talia said that since the store employs people with similar interests and similar social and aesthetic views, she made friends with a lot more people her age when she started working there. She described her coworkers as "funny and nice" and said she is good friends with them, but her commitment to the job is questioned because of this. Other retail and service-sector workers said this phenomenon puts workers at a disadvantage. Hank, a twenty-one-year-old student, has been working in the service sector for years. He typically works eight hours a week for $8.50 an hour. He said that his job, typically at the cash register, is boring and repetitive, and the only thing that makes the time pass are the other people and the social aspect of the job. "This job helps me socialize," Hank said. The social atmosphere makes the workers happier and may attract more customers, but the female workers are penalized for propagating it.

The conflicting requirements are particularly challenging for the young female retail and service-sector workers. On one hand, during the recruitment process, employers recruit from existing customers and friends of workers (Besen-Cassino 2013, 2014). Many corporations actively recruit retail and service-sector workers who "look good and sound right" in order to create a high-end brand experience for the customers (Williams and Connell 2010). To attract these employees, companies use specific techniques, such as offering discounts and recruiting from existing customers who look like the brand, are able to afford the brand, and are knowledgeable about the product (Besen 2006; Besen-Cassino 2013; Williams and Connell 2010). While these techniques actively encourage workers to be avid consumers of the brand and be friends with their coworkers, the same techniques used to recruit also become causes of criticism; they are used to question the workers' commitments to their jobs.

Not My "Real" Job

The social aspects of the job often obscure the everyday reality of the job. There are numerous social benefits of part-time jobs (Besen-Cassino 2014), which have become more important as opportunities for young people to socialize in the suburbs have become increasingly limited. As such, workplaces provide space away from the supervision of adults for teenagers to socialize, see their friends, and meet new peers. These workplaces also are instrumental in providing teenagers with a social identity and help them express their social and political views (Besen-Cassino 2014). However, these social benefits often obscure the potential problems with a job. The social benefits of retail and service-sector jobs have important ramifications for young workers, often making young workers less likely to complain about the everyday problems of jobs. For example, April had been working long hours—she had been at work every day of the week I spoke with her, including the weekend, as the store has been especially busy. Because of the increased hours on her feet, she has been coming home to bleeding feet. She has been physically exhausted. She cannot do homework and does not even want to hang out with friends; she just wants to sleep or rest in front of the television. However, she never complained, because, for her, the job was about seeing her friends and hanging out. When I asked her to describe her job, she emphasized how much she likes her coworkers. It is not really a job, she told me: she goes there to hang out with her friends.

The work carries emotional tolls, as well. The retail workers I spoke with almost universally agreed that dealing with rude customers was the worst part of the job, and the young women were frequently asked to do this. But even when they are said to be good at dealing with such customers, being shouted at takes its toll, and many of the workers I spoke with reported feeling upset after their shifts were over. The problems are not limited to physical exhaustion and rude customers. Joanna has been working at a restaurant chain as a server for a while. "It is a toxic environment for women," she said, referring to the back of the house (the kitchen and the staff). As a women's studies major, she told me that she knows the studies and the literature on sexual harassment, but despite the endless sexual jokes and comments that bother her, she has not reported or complained to the management about them. "It's not my real job," she said. It is just something she is doing to until she finishes college.

The social benefits do not really take away the reality of the job: the low pay, physical demands, rude customers, and demanding employers, as well as sexual harassment. Everyday problems on the job arise in these retail and service jobs for many teenagers, but many of them said that it is not the same as it would be in a "real" workplace. From sexual harassment to bullying to working conditions, many problems arose for young women I interviewed. However, many echoed the same sentiment, saying, "It's not my *real* job." The fact that these jobs were for part-time employment during school years often resulted in underreporting of work-related problems. However, even though the lived experience or personal definitions of the job differ, these jobs are still real jobs, and these definitions result in the normalization of problems in the workplace.

Overall, young women are at the heart of retail and service-sector jobs, being recruited for low-paying jobs with high aesthetic-labor requirements and strong emotion-work components. Individual narratives of young women point to being recruited for traditionally feminine traits, such as being pleasant, nice, and friendly, as well as for their social skills. Their narratives also emphasize their role as consumers of the products they are selling: they are hired because they are avid consumers, so potential customers can relate to them easily, and they can put forward a desirable face of the product. However, even though their social skills and their consumption are highly encouraged by the corporations they work for, when it comes to higher pay, their product commitment and the friendly atmosphere they create in the workplace are used as counterarguments against them: they are perceived as not committed to the job but, rather, there just for the discounts or to see friends.

In addition, the everyday lived experiences of the jobs are not the same for the young men and women of retail. Based on the in-depth interviews, I identified two major differences. First, young women were more likely to be placed in positions to deal with difficult customers and more likely to mentor and help their male counterparts. Because they are told that they are good with people, or better at handling problematic customers, they are placed in positions where they get yelled at, have shoe boxes thrown at them, and are harassed more often than their male counterparts. Even at the same stores or at seemingly similar positions, young men and women in the retail and service sectors simply do not experience the same job. This has important repercussions. Even though some of the young women take pride in hearing that they are naturally good with people, this puts them in more challenging situations, creating inequality in the workplace. Furthermore, when young women are told that they are good with people, this skill is presented as being in opposition to being good at other skills, like money or managerial duties such as scheduling shifts.

Second, young men and women retail and service workers experience differential levels of aesthetic-labor requirements. While young men reported having to buy the products and look good and sound right, most of the men I spoke to purchased products before getting the job, and then stopping. The young women, on the other hand, feel that they are expected to keep up with the aesthetic requirements of retail and service-sector jobs. This involves keeping up with the consumption requirements and spending large sums of money to buy the products. Many young women reported having to shop extensively and accumulating substantial amounts of debt in order to keep the jobs they have.

Finally, aesthetic-labor requirements are not limited to buying products but also refer to the way young women look—particularly, their weight. Young women working in the retail and service sectors reported feeling overweight and reported dieting, exercising, and skipping meals in order to fit the look requirements of the corporations they work for.

Policy Implications

Young people's part-time work is ubiquitous in the United States. Youth start working in retail and service-sector jobs as early as fourteen, and while they themselves might enjoy the social benefits of discounts, cool brands, and meeting new people, these social benefits do not obscure the serious problems these early work experiences bring. These workplaces are important for many young people: they are where they spend vast amounts of their free time and where they interact with their friends. Parents, educators, and administrators might see these early work experiences as just something kids do, but early work experiences are not just socially significant; they are also important in shaping job expectations. These early jobs, where young people spend long hours for many years on end, are the first experiences of the workplace.

Many young people's job expectations, gendered assumptions, and views of the workplace are formed in these early years.

In recent years, there have been many campaigns, programs, and initiatives to help young women equalize the pay gap. These programs often target schools, parents, or peer groups at school to change young women's leadership roles, self-esteem, and body issues. For example, many programs at school encourage young women to rise to leadership roles, encourage young women to get jobs in science, technology, engineering, or mathematics (STEM) fields, or work with numbers and money. Similarly, many programs target schools and parents to help young women achieve better self-esteem and healthier body images. There are also many initiatives that encourage women to negotiate and ask for more money. However, these initiatives generally target schools and parents and leave the workplace outside of the realm of change. No matter what young people are told at school or by their parents about gender in the workplace, they are learning about gender at work by working, and unless we change the workplace, these initiatives are doomed to fail.

This chapter looks at the immediate effects of such gendered messages. In Chapter 4, I explore inequalities with an intersectional perspective and explore the roles of race and class.

4

Race, Class, and Gender Inequality

An Intersectional Approach

Kiara explains:

> [Before the start of my shift,] I am like, "Ugh, okay, here we go." In my car, I have a mental talk, like, "It's just three hours, four hours; you can do it." There are a few days when I don't feel up to it. Luckily, at the physical therapy place, they hired another receptionist, and we switch sometimes. I go to the back. We changed our billing, so there is a lot more to be done. That isn't much easier either, though. There's a lot of children, . . . there are lots of phone calls, calling insurance companies and clients. A lot of people forget that insurance companies pay what they want to pay, and they don't always [pay everything], and the clients are stuck with the bill. A lot of the times, the rest is like sixteen hundred dollars—like, a huge amount. They are very vocal about it. There's a few that . . . , you know, they are going to shout at you. Like, you mentally prepare yourself, like you know it—get ready to be shouted at. You know the regulars, once you see them.

Kiara has been juggling her two jobs for some time now. As an African American woman, her experience in the service and retail sectors have been markedly different than her white peers. She expects people to shout at her because of decisions made by an insurance company, and her job at the sporting-goods store is not much better, she said. "I work in a very rich town," she explained. "The customers expect everything. They are [even] more demanding than the clients dealing with insurance companies, and more upset."

Typical accounts of service and retail jobs point to some advantages of women in the retail and service sectors (Bozkurt and Grugulis 2011; Skillsmart 2007). According to the Bureau of Labor Statistics (2016), more than half of the service- and retail-sector workforce consists of women. Past accounts pointed to social, interpersonal, and communication skills of women to explain why women might dominate the service sector or emphasize women's role in nurturing and helping others. These same accounts would assume it was easier for women to find work in these sectors. In recent years, studies have also pointed to the relative ease of young people in getting these retail and service-sector jobs (Besen-Cassino 2014; Gatta 2011).

Because companies want young and energetic people to represent them, being the face of the brand has emerged as an important consideration in service and retail jobs (Grugulis and Bozkurt 2011; Gatta 2011), and young people have emerged as a natural pool of applicants for these jobs. Young women have become especially desirable in retail and service-sector jobs, especially high-end clothing stores, designer boutiques, and artisanal shops, as they possess the right look and the appropriate set of soft skills (Gatta 2011). Lynne Pettinger's (2004) ethnographic study of London retail stores emphasizes the desirability of fashionable young women in high-end clothing boutiques. Young, attractive women become the face of these stores and project the desired image the corporation wishes to put forward to its customers. "Fashion orientation is one face of brand strategy and the ability to present a fashionable appearance is one of the skills needed by sales assistants in many stores" (Pettinger 2004, 468). Physical attractiveness, youth, and attractiveness are important, as is self-presentation. David Wright's work shows that "physical attractiveness, particular style of dress, and types of physical comportment all contribute to the production of the retail space as meaningful and aesthetically pleasing to the customer" (2005, 305). After all, retail companies sell not simply the goods and services displayed but also a certain brand experience: the workers are not simply selling the products but rather mediating the relationship between the customer and the product, creating an interactive relationship between the products and the workers (Gatta 2011; see also Pettinger 2006).

Young workers, especially young women, have become central to the brand strategies of these companies, but these experiences can vary widely for white and African American workers and for workers from lower socioeconomic backgrounds. The emotional and aesthetic requirements asked of an African American worker, like Kiara, are very different from those asked of the young white women in my sample. Even for young, attractive people, race still matters, and does so in unexpected ways.

When I spoke with Shawn, a junior at a state university, I heard many old biases echoed. He told me that young women have it easy when it comes to finding jobs. Shawn has been working as the Easter Bunny at the nearby mall. Born and raised in Newark, New Jersey, he is the first in his family to go to college. He is double majoring in sociology and political science; he is also an African American man, over six feet tall, with a large build. "I dress as the Easter Bunny," he said. "They [the parents] would never let their kids sit on my lap if they knew what I really looked like." He told me that aesthetic-labor requirements have made it difficult for him to find jobs. He applied to many retail and service jobs but was turned down. "I didn't have the right look. I never have the right look," he told me. "When I wait at the ATM, the line in front of me clears very quickly: they [the other customers] think I am going to rob the bank."

He said that many high-end boutiques in town or retail establishments at the nearby mall toss his application aside when they see his Newark address. Locally, Newark is seen as crime-ridden—somewhere people would go only if they were called in for jury duty. To avoid putting a Newark address on his applications, he uses his campus address. "College girls," he said, "have an easier time getting jobs."

African American female students might have an easier time getting jobs than do their male counterparts, if they fit the aesthetic of the store to which they apply. Kiara remembers that when she first got her job at Sport Central, her experience running track in college and high school helped her immensely. She said that even though she could not afford the sporting goods sold at the store, she had an easy time getting the job because she fit the athletic aesthetic they were going for. As Prue Huddleston observes, quoting the manager of a sporting-goods store, the store looks for employees who look "like they do the sport themselves, for example, we've got people who are interested in skateboarding, cycling, climbing, that sort of thing, it's a lifestyle thing, and of course those are the sort of youngsters we get coming here looking for jobs" (2011, 115). Kiara's case was similar: she had another athlete friend working for another department, and she got the job at Sport Central easily. Her athletic look, muscles, and sporty attire are what got her the job. Of course, this same aesthetic made it more difficult for her to get a job elsewhere, especially in the apparel industry. She got rejected from many clothing stores because she did not have the right look. Getting a job may have been easier for her relative to her African American male peers, but it was not nearly as easy as it is for white classmates.

The actual experience of working at the store is not easy, and it may be made harder by race. Kiara told me that the sporting-goods store requires "a whole different level of mental preparation, especially if you're working the cash register." As detailed in Chapter 3, in addition to the mental switching she does before she comes into the store, she has to prepare herself for tasks that she knows will be unpleasant, such as dealing with difficult customers. Kiara felt the expectations of customer service from her were different from workplace expectations of her peers: there was extra pressure, and not all women her age were treated the same way. Lisa, a white college student from an affluent suburb, for example, works at a yoga chain, and she said she has not experienced that type of customer behavior. She said her customers respond to her calm, quiet demeanor and overall zen attitude.

Race and Class in the Youth Labor Force

Race and ethnicity play a large role in access to jobs for adolescents at any age. Starting as early as fourteen and fifteen, white adolescents are more likely to have jobs (Herman 2000). According to the "Report on the Youth Labor Force," white adolescents are more likely to be employed than are African American and Hispanic youth in both employee-type jobs and freelance jobs when they are fourteen and fifteen (Herman 2000).

As we have seen in the previous chapters, the 2008 recession adversely affected employment rates for young people, as they are in competition for jobs with a larger pool of applicants, including the elderly, immigrants, and those who lost jobs in the manufacturing industry. In addition, fewer employers were hiring during the recession, resulting in a smaller pool of available jobs. Before the recession, 64 percent of white youth ages fourteen and fifteen were employed while still in school, though the labor-force participation rates of African American and Hispanic youth ages fourteen and fifteen were only 43 and 41 percent, respectively. The racial inequality is also not just limited to employee-type jobs: African American and Hispanic teenagers had lower employment rates in freelance jobs, as well. Of white fourteen- to fifteen-year-olds, 48 percent were employed in freelance jobs, while freelance labor-force participation for African American and Hispanic teenagers in the same age group remained at only 33 and 30 percent, respectively (Herman 2000).

While all racial and ethnic groups experienced an increase in their labor-force participation as they got older, the racial and ethnic differences remained among older teenagers. According to the Bureau of Labor Statistics (2016), as of 2016, the employment rate for white youth between ages sixteen and twenty-four is 62.7 percent. It is 53.8 percent for African American youth and 56.2 percent for Hispanic youth. For African American youth, not only are the employment rates much lower, but they have also experienced a rapid 2.6 percentage point decline in employment rates since 2007. Similar racial and ethnic inequalities exist in unemployment rates. The unemployment rate is 11.5 percent for white youth between sixteen and twenty-four, while it remains at a staggering 20.6 percent for African American youth.

The labor-force participation rates and unemployment rates both before and after the recession show that African American and Hispanic teenagers have a marked disadvantage in the workforce, as they are less likely to find jobs—both employee-type and freelance. The Economic Policy Institute's report "The Kids Aren't Alright: Labor Market Analysis of Young Workers" points to racial inequality in finding jobs for young people, especially after the economic recession (Edwards and Hertel-Fernandez 2010). The authors show that while the economic recession has adversely affected young people (sixteen- to twenty-four-year-olds), these adverse effects are not experienced equally by every group: "The disparities between the unemployment rates of white, black, and Hispanic young workers are also stark. Black 16–24 year-old workers had the highest rate, starting 2010 at 32.5%, followed by Hispanics (24.2%), and then whites (15.2%)."

The report further breaks unemployment down by age and focuses solely on sixteen to nineteen-year-old student workers, showing that this group experienced record high unemployment rates; in particular, African American youth in this age bracket had unemployment as high as 49.8 percent. This inequality is just exacerbated with age and with the recent recession. Prior research suggests that African American teenagers are less likely to be hired in general (Ahn et al. 2010). Thomas Ahn and colleagues find that African American teenagers experience the biggest inequality in hiring and that white teenagers are 72 percent more likely to be hired.

Employment status and inequality in hiring is heavily dependent on neighborhood factors. Existing studies point to the importance of geographic location in young people's employment success. John Bound and Richard Freeman (1992) show that one of the causes of racial inequality in employment is the scarcity of jobs in areas where African American teenagers live. Jobs available to teenagers tend to be concentrated in predominantly white and more affluent locations, making it challenging for African American teenagers to get to these jobs. Such concerns are especially important to younger teenagers, for whom transportation can be a major limiting factor. Even after potentially getting their driver's licenses, many may not have a car or reliable access to one. As public transportation is often limited to less affluent areas, getting to and from jobs adds substantial time and cost to teenagers' job searches and work experience. Rosella Gardecki (2001) finds that residence constraints, nonownership of a car, long commutes, and high commuting costs often result in lower employment rates and limited job searches for minority youth. These differences are not just confined to the early teen years: Gardecki finds that they persist even for workers between the ages of sixteen and twenty-four.

The jobs that are available in the neighborhoods where these youth reside may be unavailable to them for other reasons: for instance, they often include heavy industry, which minors may be prevented from entering. In fact, Katherine M. O'Regan and John M. Quigley's (1996a, 1996b) analysis shows that minority youth in white and higher-income areas are more likely to be employed because more jobs are available to them.

Neighborhood characteristics do not just affect job availability, but they heavily influence young people's networks. High unemployment among youth in a given area results in reduced networking opportunities; young people in the neighborhood are not able to relay job-opening information to friends and acquaintances (Weinberg, Reagan, and Yankow 2000). Word of mouth and informal networks are central methods for finding jobs, and if a teenager's immediate friends, family, and acquaintances are not employed, then his or her chances of hearing about jobs are much lower. Kiara, among many other young workers I spoke with, found her job through a friend: when fewer students in an area know someone with a job, they are unable to find jobs for their friends, and so on, creating a cascade effect. This sort of effect has been described by Bruce A. Weinberg, Patricia B. Reagan, and Jeffrey J. Yankow (2000), who find that large numbers of youth being unemployed in the same geographic area results in demoralization and the normalization of unemployment. The same effects have been found even within families: Albert Rees and Wayne Gray (1982) show that although parents' work status and characteristics have no effect on youth's employment, those of older siblings do: when older children are unable to find employment, their siblings, all else being equal, become less likely to do so, as well.

Neighborhood effects can also result in differential rates of criminal behavior. Many researchers point to the complex relationship between work and crime and suggest that working is an important factor in staying out of criminal activity (Blumstein and Wallman 2006; Bushway and Reuter 2001; Freeman 1983; Levitt 2001, 2004). Later studies attribute these differences in criminal activity and work to selection effects: it is not that young people with jobs are less likely to engage in criminal behaviors but that youth engaged in criminal behaviors are less likely to have jobs, perhaps because employers are reluctant to hire young people with criminal records.

In addition to differential employment rates and job availability, race affects the wages earned by young people. Overall, African American youth have much lower wages than their white counterparts (Herman 2000), but part of this is due to the fact that they might not be working at the same places. While it may seem as though the retail and service-sector jobs where young people work are all about the same, there is great variance among these jobs. Minority youth are concentrated in fast-food jobs, and white, affluent youth tend to get higher-paying jobs with better working conditions in more upscale stores. Even within a workplace, minority youth are given tasks with less visibility and harder working conditions: working in the stock rooms, for instance, as opposed to at the cash register. It has also been shown that aesthetic-labor requirements push many African American young people out of more desirable retail and service-sector jobs with better pay and working conditions, as they do not have the right look or are not consuming the products and goods sold at higher-end establishments (Besen-Cassino 2014).

Gardecki (2001) finds that even though white and African American teenagers have similar rates of looking for jobs, African American teenagers are much less likely to hold jobs. These early unemployment experiences are important not just because of any immediate impact but because they influence future employment and wages (Gardecki 2001; Ruhm 1997).

The lower rates of employment, and lower wages or worse conditions for those that find jobs, seem to have long-term effects for these young people. Doris Entwisle, Karl Alexander and Linda Steffel Olson (2000), in their study of Baltimore teenagers, find that nonwhite students are at a significantly higher risk of dropping out of school as a result of their work experiences. Overall, the existing literature points to the existence of racial inequalities in the workforce for adolescents. In addition to inequalities in hiring, pay, and job placement, researchers also point to the differential effects of working and potential negative outcomes for African American teenagers.

Socioeconomic Status

Highly correlated with race is the socioeconomic status of the youths. Our traditional images of working youth are Dickensian chimney sweeps or children in unventilated sweatshops in developing countries. In the past, researchers linked youth work with economic need, which would imply that young people from lower socioeconomic backgrounds should be more likely to work.

However, recent studies point to a more complex picture. According to the most recent Bureau of Labor Statistics "Report on the Youth Labor Force" (Herman 2000), adolescents from higher socioeconomic backgrounds are more likely to work than those from lower socioeconomic backgrounds. Adolescents that come from families with annual incomes of less than $25,000 are least likely to work: 21 percent of fourteen-year-old adolescents from the lowest-income group work, as opposed to 25 and 27 percent of adolescents working from higher-income groups. The same socioeconomic inequality persists as adolescent grow older. Among fifteen-year-olds, 32 percent in the lowest household-income group held a job, compared to 40 and 42 percent in higher-income groups. Data from the Current Population Survey also show lower employment rates for fif-teen- to seventeen-year-olds from lower-income backgrounds (Herman 2000). The "Report on the Youth Labor Force" also shows that youth from single-parent families are less likely to work than youth from two-parent households, despite the fact that youth from single-parent families generally have lower household incomes (Herman 2000). Of fourteen-year-olds from two-parent households, 61 percent worked, compared to 54 percent of fourteen-year-olds from households led by single women. Herman (2000) shows that not only are youth from lower-socioeconomic-status backgrounds less likely to work but when they do work, they work fewer hours.

It is not clear why adolescents from lower socioeconomic backgrounds are less likely to work, but Herman (2000) speculates this might be because young people from lower-income backgrounds might have less adult presence in the household. The absence of adults would mean more household chores for young people, leaving limited time for paid work. Having fewer adults, or having adults working multiple shifts, also means fewer adults able to drive young people to paid jobs. Herman (2000) also argues that lower-income areas have higher unemployment rates with limited job availability and fewer businesses, and, therefore, young people from these lower-income areas have a harder time finding jobs. Other research points to systematic bias against adolescents from lower-income backgrounds, as higher-end retail and service-sector jobs prefer hiring higher-income adolescents who embody the look of the brand (Besen-Cassino 2014).

Socioeconomic background and racial inequality are not two different forms of discrimination in the workforce; they are linked, and both may be hidden by income levels. Research finds that many African American and Hispanic youth are less likely to be employed, which may be linked to the lower average household-income levels among these groups. Mary Corcoran and her research group (1992) show that among teenagers, the number of welfare recipients in families and in communities decreases the likelihood that young people will be able to find a job. Many studies also point to the interaction effect of race and class: African American youth from lower so-cioeconomic backgrounds, like Shawn, who was able to get a job only when it required him to wear a full-body costume, have a much harder time getting jobs, and the ones who really need the jobs often get shut out of the system, have longer job searches, or end up in fast-food jobs.

Emotion Work

As discussed earlier, an important component of many service-sector and re-tail jobs today is emotion work. In Arlie Russell Hochschild's (1983) study of flight attendants, she argues that women in the service sector do not just em-body interactive components, but they also embody middle-class-ness. Most flight attendants in her study are not only women but also from middle-class backgrounds, and in their work, they need to not only perform emotion labor but also embody middle-class standards of appearance and attributes. Their middle-class-ness and middle-class interactive social skills are attributes they are assumed to have acquired at home and be able to translate into the work-place (Leidner 1993; Hochschild 1983; Otis 2011; Pierce 1995).

In addition to the class component, such expectations of self-presentation and emotion-labor displays are not devoid of a racial component. Emotion labor, in addition to being gendered and classed, is also raced. Adia Harvey Wingfield (2009), for example, shows that the same emotions have different social meanings dependent on the gender and race of the employee. For exam-ple, the social meaning of anger, and expressions of it, is different for African American men than it is for others. While African American men's expressions of anger and frustration are perceived as threatening and induce fear, white women's expressions of anger in the workplace are trivialized and not seen as real threats. Similarly, women's anger and frustrations in the workplace are interpreted as menstruation-related and not really tied to work conditions. Be-cause women's anger and frustration are seen as extensions of biology, they are more likely to be dismissed as irrational. Bodily self-presentations and expres-sions of emotions also rely heavily on gender stereotypes. Men and women are socialized to learn and internalize appropriate behaviors and expressions, and they come to be seen as natural (Butler 1993; West and Zimmerman 1987).

Aesthetic-labor and emotion-labor requirements often involve double standards based on racial and ethnic background. According to Eileen Otis, "aesthetic labor highlights work involved in class distinction and focuses on the body as a vehicle of symbols that generates profits" (Otis 2016), and these aesthetic expectations and body rules are different for different situations (Otis 2011; see also Gottfried 2003; Mears 2014; Warhurst and Nickson 2007; C. Williams 2006; Williams and Connell 2010) and these rules re-quire individual-level adjustments from workers (Gruys 2012; Kang 2010; C. Williams 2006). Yet extensive research shows how these individual-level adjustments are highly correlated with race. While the expectations have double standards, the responses to the unequal expectations are varied. In plus-sized clothing stores, Gruys (2012) finds that African American work-ers adjusted their responses to customers' bodies based on the race of the customers: with white customers, they tended to emphasize the slimming effect of the clothing, while with African American and Latina customers, they tended to emphasize the shapeliness and desirability of bodies. Christine Williams, in her study of toy stores, found that African American workers expressed irritability toward some white customers to avoid racial stereotypes associated with servility and because they felt white, privileged customers would "walk all over them" (2006, 119). Being too pleasant did not have the same meaning for all workers, and African American workers used aesthetic labor as a tool of resistance.

Kiara said her aesthetic is accepted at the sporting-goods store but not necessarily everywhere: she remembers the challenging time she had finding jobs. Her athletic build and muscles do not really fit the "look" of clothing stores she applied to: to them, she simply was not feminine enough. Another African American woman I spoke with, Janelle, was told that her hair was a problem, that she had to control it, and that it did not look polished and professional. "Polished and professional hair" was described as straightened and nontextured: her natural hair was not considered appropriate for the brand. Of course, there are other ways in which aesthetic labor can prevent young people from getting jobs: when Janice, an African American college student applied to one popular clothing chain, she was told she would not really fit into the clothes (which are not manufactured in her size) and was told she would not be a good fit because of her weight.

Double Standards of Emotion Labor

In addition to aesthetic requirements, emotion work is a central component of retail and service-sector jobs, as discussed in Chapter 3. Not only are women working in the retail and service-sectors expected to serve, but they are expected to serve with a smile. In Chapter 3, young women working in the retail sector pointed to the complex requirements of emotion work that go beyond serving with a smile, demanding that they control and embody a wide range of emotions. For example, the spa-like, high-end cosmetics store where Heather works expects their female employees to look calm and display an aura of serenity. The calm voice and attitude of the workers were supposed to emphasize the spa-like quality of the brand. With their own skin regimens and scents, and their calm, pleasant demeanors and soft voices, the girls of Fresh aim to create a spa-like environment. The emotion work is also useful as a tool of customer service, as the calm voice and demeanor of the employers can placate irate customers.

However, niceness and a pleasant demeanor are not met with the same response for all racial groups. When Heather and her coworkers, who are all white, display a calm, nice, and peaceful demeanor, the customers respond to that by matching the demeanor of the workers. Heather said Fresh uses the demeanor of its employees consciously, as a tool to calm angry customers. When angry and upset customers are met with happy, calm, and pleasant employers, according to Heather, the majority of the time, the customers match the demeanor of the employers. However, some African American workers experience the opposite. Kiara said that when she is extremely nice, the customers shout at her even more. Several times, when angry customers complained about expired coupons, she was met with extra-angry customers. In fact, she told me that she has been told that she was not genuinely nice but was just pretending to be. Despite the fact that she tries very hard to serve with a smile and mentally prepares herself before every shift to be nice and pleasant, her niceness is not met with the same reaction from the customers. While the niceness of the white girls is seen as genuine, the niceness of an African American girl is viewed as a ploy and met with anger.

The expression of emotions in the workplace is an important topic that has received vast academic and popular attention. The control of emotions in the workplace is important not just because of the ubiquity of emotion work in retail and service-sector jobs but also to control and regulate interpersonal relationships in the workplace (Hochschild 1983; Lively 2000). The norms and rules that govern which emotions are appropriate to display often appear to be neutral, but extensive research has pointed out unequal expectations about who can display which emotions and which emotions are available to which groups (Wingfield 2009). Therefore, just as institutions can appear to be neutral and still perpetuate gender inequality, the range of emotions available to employees are gendered and serve to perpetuate gender inequality (Acker 1990). These researchers point out that some emotions are acceptable for men and not for women, and the social meanings of the same emotions differ based on the gender of the employees. For example, Kieran Snyder (2014) points to the double standards of emotions for men and women in the workplace. Based on 248 reviews from 180 people—105 men and 75 women—from twenty-eight different companies of varying sizes and specializations, he finds important differences based on gender. Assertiveness, being outspoken, and expressions of anger are normalized and even praised for men, while women's similar expressions are considered abrasive, often resulting in negative evaluations in the workplace.

Similarly, Jennifer Pierce (1995) finds that the expressions of deference and care are different for men and women paralegals. Women paralegals are expected to show more deference and do more emotion work, while their male counterparts are discouraged from such work. Similar studies also confirm that among professors who are assertive, women receive lower evaluations than men (e.g., Boring, Ottobani, and Stark 2016). While assertiveness is considered a traditionally male trait and is celebrated when men display it, the same trait is judged differently for women. In addition to the gender inequality in emotional displays in the workplace, the range of emotions that are available to workers differs greatly based on race. These emotional displays and the expectations of emotional displays are selectively applied to different racial and ethnic groups.

Some new studies point out similar racial inequalities in the workplace (see Harlow 2003; Kang 2003; Wingfield 2012, 2015). Kiran Mirchandani (2003) argues that emotion-work studies assume white heterosexual male workers as the norm in the workplace: workplaces assume the white male heterosexual body as the norm, and anything that deviates from the norm is considered an anomaly. An example of this is the assumption that men's bathroom breaks are the norm, and compared to the men in the office, who typically do not have to wait in line, women take longer bathroom breaks and are punished in the workplace because of it. Adia Harvey Wingfield (2015), in her qualitative study of African American professionals, finds that emotional norms and expectations are highly racialized in the workplace. Wingfield found that displaying anger and irritation was not as readily available to them:

> Black professionals, however, suggest that the feeling rules that guide the expressions of anger do not apply to them. This is not to suggest that they are free to show anger in any way; in contrast, respondents suggest that a different set of rules apply to them altogether wherein they are not permitted to show anger under any circumstances. They cite numerous examples of white workers who have openly expressed feelings of frustration or annoyance in ways that they believe are simply unavailable to them as black employees. Respondents argue that as black professionals, they would be punished for displaying anger in the same ways their white colleagues do. (Wingfield 2015, 204)

Similarly, despite having shoe boxes thrown at her and being shouted at periodically, Kiara had a very difficult time expressing anger and frustration. She would sit in her car to mentally prepare herself, or take breaks, but she rarely expressed her frustration in the workplace. She told me that arguing with the customers "would make it worse." When customers shout at her, she just takes it. When she complained about the customers to her supervisor or coworkers, she was met with little sympathy.

While Wingfield's research suggests that anger and frustration are off limits to African American professionals in the workplace, they are also expected to be pleasant. However, in the case of Kiara, attempts to be nice and pleasant were met with suspicion from the customers, and she was accused of not being genuine. One time, Kiara remembers, a customer complained about her to her supervisor, because the customer felt she had been greeted by store employees too many times. Another time, when she smiled and was trying to help, Kiara was accused of not being sincere. Her coworkers have not had this problem, but she has consistently been singled out for failing to show sincere emotion. My discussions with Kiara and many other young African American women further these ideas, showing how African American women employees in service-sector jobs may find themselves at an impasse. They are not allowed to express frustration, but when they are pleasant and nice, their niceness is not seen as genuine.

The experience of Kiara and my other interviewees is far from unique. Scholars have argued that emotion-labor requirements prioritize the white body. Miliann Kang's (2003) study of Korean and African American nail salons shows that the intersections of race and gender shape emotion work. Borrowing from Hochschild, Kang builds her qualitative analysis of nail salons on the concept of body labor. This seemingly commercialized labor is not simply an economic transaction. According to Kang, a manicure is also a display of deference and power: "The manicure is not simply an economic transaction. It is also a symbolic exchange that involves the buying and selling of deference" (2010, 134). Therefore, for white women in upscale nail salons, the manicure is a symbolic exercise by which they can display privilege and exercise entitlement.

Overall, race and class play significant roles in employee-type jobs. My qualitative interviews reveal the ways in which African American women have a harder time finding jobs in the service and retail sectors compared to their white counterparts. Aesthetic requirements—looking good and sounding right, to project the image of the brand—can leave nonwhite and lower-income adolescents out. In the service and retail sectors, an intersectional approach helps to reveal the multiple levels of inequality and how gender inequality can be exacerbated for young people in some racial and income groups. Not only are African American women expected to be nice, pleasant, and calm, but their niceness, pleasantness, and calmness are not met with the same response as the same traits displayed by their white counterparts. Their frustration is not considered acceptable, and their niceness is not seen as genuine. Either way, emotion labor and aesthetic labor present an enormous challenge for young African American women.

No Complaints: Not My Real Job

Earlier, I discussed how many young women failed to report sexual harassment in their workplaces because they did not see their positions as their "real" jobs. Even Johanna, who takes classes in women's and gender studies, or Emily, who talked about her mother working in human resources, who were both keenly aware that workplace behavior was inappropriate, failed to report what they had experienced. Such experiences are especially important because of the extent to which they conflict with the messages these girls receive in school and even from their parents. When they are receiving one set of messages about pay discrimination and harassment from some sources and another from their actual jobs, which are they going to believe? As these dynamics exist for gender-based issues, it seems likely that they would also exist for race-based issues.

Legally, there have been numerous lawsuits involving racial inequality among young workers, especially in retail settings. *Gonzalez v. Abercrombie and Fitch* argued that the company discriminated on the basis of race and gender when hiring. The corporation's "natural classical American style," according to the plaintiffs, excluded nonwhite applications. They claimed the look of the company was "virtually all white" and "the attractive look the employer was seeking was not just pretty, but pretty and white" (Corbett 2007, 155). The plaintiffs also argued that in addition to racial discrimination in hiring, young employees of color were excluded from front-of-the-house tasks like greeting customers and working cash registers and were instead placed in positions where they were not visible to customers. This particular case was settled in 2005 for approximately $50 million, and Abercrombie and Fitch agreed to implement programs to increase diversity.

As exemplified by this case, aesthetic-labor requirements have become problematic in hiring and have made it easier for corporations to discriminate on the basis of race with little accountability. There have been numerous lawsuits in which courts have sided with corporations on discrimination on the basis of aesthetics: after all, it is illegal to discriminate on the basis of race but perfectly acceptable to discriminate on the basis of how well an individual embodies the desired look of a brand. Lawsuits like *Gonzalez* show how the American retail and service sectors have become increasingly look-oriented, and these look-oriented hiring practices can lead to discrimination on the basis of race and socioeconomic status.

African American Babysitters

While racial and class inequalities are prevalent for adolescent girls in the service and retail sectors, little has been written about inequalities in free-lance jobs. My interviews show that while young African American women have trouble finding retail and service-sector jobs, they may have an easier time with freelance jobs, such as babysitting jobs, which they tend to find through large informal networks—neighbors, family, friends, and friends of friends.

For example, LaShonda, a young African American woman residing in Newark, New Jersey, remembers how challenging it was for her to find the jobs she wanted in fashion retail. In addition to being flatly turned down from many places, she remembers the lengthy waits that employers used to weed out the less affluent workers who need the jobs. Heather, who eventually got her desired job at Fresh, told me that she waited months after her application before getting an interview call. As Heather did not really need a job, and would not have taken a job at a different store, the wait did not matter to her. But for a young person from a lower socioeconomic background—for someone who really needed a job—the long wait would have been a deal breaker. Such tactics allow companies to ensure that they are not hiring anyone who really needs a job, without engaging in any sort of actionable discrimination. LaShonda needed a job, and the long waits ensured that she would not get one in the sort of high-end retail establishments she was interested in. Of course, LaShonda could easily find a fast-food job, but she did not want to come home smelling like french fries. Their neighbors needed a babysitter, so she started babysitting. Today, she still works as a babysitter. She told me that "people have children and babies in every community, so as long as people keep having babies, I have a job."

Even though the African American babysitters I spoke to described finding babysitting jobs easily, there is still discrimination in hiring in this field. Kara, a twenty-year-old African American college student trying to balance two majors, told me, "Of course there is discrimination" in the babysitting market. Kara has been working as a babysitter for four years, during which she has cared for four children, including a baby, for three different families. "I feel like I have to prove myself if I am looking for a job outside of Newark," she said. Outside her immediate community in Newark, where she got her job easily because her mother knew the families, it is complicated. "Mothers tend to approach white college girls; they don't approach me," she said, echoing the experiences of white babysitters, who told me about how mothers would approach them and ask if they would be interested in babysitting.

Kara's friend and classmate, Lulu, had a similar experience. Lulu, a white, full-time college student, was working at the front desk at a child-oriented gym and did not have any experience babysitting. "The mother came to me," she remembers. "I didn't even think about babysitting." There were no interviews, and she got the job on the spot: "I couldn't believe it." The mother told her she had an honest face and looked like she was good with children, despite the fact that the mother had not actually observed her working with children.

One of the problems with freelance jobs, as discussed in Chapter 2, is that girls stay in lower-paying freelance jobs while boys move into employee-type jobs, which contributes to the gender wage gap. Freelance jobs pay lower than employee-type jobs, and they lack rigid work-leisure boundaries, potentially creating endless work for young women. Roxanne, an African American full-time student at a large state university, where she would like to study business administration, turned twenty this year and has been working as a babysitter for eight years. When she started, at age twelve, there were not many options for her, so babysitting seemed ideal. She started working as a babysitter for the two children of acquaintances. It was supposed to be just an occasional babysitting job, and when she was able, she started to look for retail and service-sector jobs, but her choices were limited. There were very few chains or franchises in her working-class, predominantly African American town, so with no driver's license or access to a car, options in retail and service-sector job were limited. With no other options, she started working for another family, introduced to her by the first family. By the time she got to college, she was still living close by and had her driver's license and a car, but she was turned down from the clothing chains where she wanted to work.

"Eight years feels like a lot: too much," Roxanne said. At some point, she wanted to get out, but now she works almost full time for a third family, taking care of their three school-age children, arranging their care and driving them around after school, and sometimes before. Occasionally, she still babysits for the first two families, looking after the children if the parents are going out on a Friday night or have a work emergency. Even though she said she loves hanging out with the kids, she did not expect that she would be babysitting this many years. Though she sometimes gets annoyed during her long shifts—especially when the "kids give her attitude"—she knows she does not have many options.

Young African American women I interviewed pointed to the ease with which they found jobs, as well as the problems they had marketing themselves as higher-end babysitters or asking for more money. While finding local babysitting jobs may have been easy for them, some also noted what they saw as discrimination in the job market, including an inability to find work with higher-income white families. They also say that they had to justify their qualifications in a way that the white babysitters did not report and that they were given fewer perks on the job.

Hallie, an African American college student, started babysitting as a high school student, and when she started college, she started working almost full time for one family. Typically, she spends thirty-five hours per week looking after three children for $13 per hour. Even though she lives far away, she says the parents are inconsiderate, not thinking about how she gets home after late hours, especially with multiple bus connections. Now that she has a car, her gas costs $30 per week, but they have not offered to help with transportation costs. While some white young women have pointed to not being compensated for their transportation costs, oftentimes they lived much closer to the families they babysat for, and very few white participants in my sample traveled long distances. However, for the African American babysitters in my sample, the travel distances were much greater.

Katie remembers when the mother of the family she works for had a United Nations connection, and Katie asked her for help applying for an internship there. Katie, a twenty-one-year-old Latina majoring in sociology, with a family and child studies minor, at a large state university, was scheduled to graduate at the end of the spring semester. "The mother was genuinely surprised I applied for an internship," Katie said. "I have a life outside of Cheerios and Gymboree classes, you know!" She said that the family had no problem helping her find another babysitting job, but internships or real jobs were out of the question. "It's not that she didn't want to. She genuinely was surprised. She didn't even think!"

Overall, this chapter makes use of an intersectional approach in understanding gender and race differences within the youth labor force. The retail and service sectors are becoming increasingly middle class and white, both in America and internationally (Nickson et al. 2011). In the United Kingdom, service and retail sectors are dominated by middle-class and white students, who take away jobs from the long-term unemployed and older working-class workers (Nickson et al. 2011). In the context of the United Kingdom, Anne Witz, Chris Warhurst, and Dennis Nickson (2003) refer to embodied dispositions: aesthetic attributes, social and physical capacities, and soft skills required and preferred by employers in many interactive retail and service-sector jobs. However, these social skills are highly correlated with social class, race, and ethnicity, meaning that their application can lead to race- and class-based discriminatory outcomes, even without intent: Deborah Leslie (2002) finds that the soft skills required and preferred for retail and interactive service align with being white. Because these jobs' aesthetic requirements prioritize middle-class-ness and whiteness, African American and lower-socioeconomic-status young people have a challenging time on the market.

In retail and service-sector jobs, poorer and nonwhite young people have a harder time finding jobs. Some, especially African American women of lower socioeconomic status, are left out of the formal job force completely, despite the fact that they may need the jobs the most. The extra income from these jobs could help keep these students in school, contribute to their family income, and aid them with extra money. Even when they were able to find jobs, on average, African American adolescent girls took longer than their white counterparts to find jobs, which has both economic and social repercussions for these young women.

In addition, the rules of emotion and aesthetic labor were different for young African American and white women. While niceness, pleasantness, and calmness were appreciated and rewarded for white girls, for African American girls, the same emotions were not rewarded in the same way. For African American girls, these emotions were met with suspicion and were not considered genuine. In addition, African American adolescent girls were also asked to do more in service and to aid white shoppers more. Finally, while they themselves were not allowed to express frustration, the African American girls were more likely to be targets of frustration. Kiara and many others reported customers shouting at them and targeting them for their frustrations with the corporation.

Young African American women had an easier time finding babysitting jobs—a welcome change from the challenges they face getting jobs in the retail and interactive service positions. Though babysitting positions were easier to find, these jobs were also problematic. First, as many young people move to higher-paying retail and service-sector jobs, these girls start in freelance jobs with lower pay. Even within those jobs, the African American girls I spoke with often were paid less than their white counterparts. This is partly because babysitters often find jobs through their networks, and lower-income African American girls are more likely to get stuck in babysitting jobs for lower-income households and find themselves unable to move into jobs with higher-income households, especially white ones.

Previous chapters look at the immediate effects of such gendered messages; in Chapter 5, I explore the long-term effects. What happens to these young women when they grow up and get "real" jobs? How do these early work experiences affect young women's careers in the long run? What are the long-term repercussions of these early gendered messages?

5

Long-Term Effects

Jules worked for Seymour and Smith throughout her high school years. She told me that being chosen to work at Seymour and Smith meant that she was special and that she saw Seymour and Smith as an exclusive club of similar, like-minded people: a cool-kids club. For her, being hired by Seymour and Smith was an affirmation that she was attractive, cool, and fashionable. Today, though, she said, she views her years at Seymour and Smith as the biggest mistake of her life. Her good looks were enough to get her the job, but to keep the job, she felt that she had to keep shopping. Even though Seymour and Smith provided employee discounts, they were not enough to make the clothes there affordable for her. Soon, she had three different credit cards, and every week she would buy something new: a polo shirt in a new color, new flip-flops. Soon, she started to feel like she was struggling to keep up. She said she felt like her shopping was getting out of control, that it seemed like she was bringing home a new item of clothing after almost every shift.

It was not just the clothes at Seymour and Smith that she spent money on; she also invested in her looks. She would always get her hair professionally blown out and would get highlights: darker in the winter and gradually lighter over the summer to go with the beachy, surfer-style look of the store. She would also get regular manicures and pedicures and would occasionally go to the tanning salon. She felt she had to keep up with her friends; if she did not look the part, she thought, she would not be able to keep the job or fit into the environment anymore. She remembers feeling constantly inadequate: it was challenging for her self-esteem. The people she worked with were so perfect: their hair, teeth, clothes, and athletic bodies fit the look of the store but made her constantly feel bad. She started dieting because her coworkers on her shift were all very slender and athletic. During that time, she tried everything from low-carbohydrate diets to meal-replacement shakes or bars. Her coworkers constantly talked about dieting and compared notes, she said, inculcating her into a culture of dieting. They would start their diets together, bringing their water bottles with lemon slices to work and having salads together for lunch. She does not remember anyone telling her she was overweight, but while working there, she felt bad about her body and dieted constantly, and she joined a gym. Her coworkers not only were slender but exercised regularly. Some of them took exercise classes together, and some of them went running regularly, so she started to join in. As the new merchandise came in, Jules started to compare herself with the models and felt she did not hold up. She remembers that when the store got the summer merchandise delivered, there would be panic among the employees: "The short shorts and bikinis—we would really start dieting."

Jules stopped working at Seymour and Smith some time ago, but when she met me at a coffee shop on campus, she still carried her water bottle with lemon slices and her diet meal-replacement shakes, and she refused the coffee drinks and the wall of pastries, instead sipping on an herbal tea during our interview. From her days at Seymour and Smith, Jules not only carries a large amount of credit card debt; she also internalized many values of the workplace, including the company look and weight. Leaving the interview, I wondered about the long-term effects of teenage work: the messages that young people receive from their workplace are often at odds with those that society may want to instill, but these adverse messages may well be durable. Adolescents work at these part-time jobs during important, formative years. In the past, it was argued that these early jobs built character and taught responsibility, work ethic, and the value of money. While they may do some of that, they may be teaching other values, as well.

The previous chapters explore the effects of gender on earning for teenage workers. Chapter 1 finds that while twelve- and thirteen-year-old workers make the same amount of money, by the time they reach fourteen and fifteen, we see the emergence of the first gender wage gap, which widens with age. One of the reasons for this pay inequality is that girls at that age tend to concentrate in more freelance jobs, while boys are more likely to move into employee-type jobs in the retail and service sectors. Even within freelance jobs there is sex segregation: girls babysit, and boys do yard work and snow removal. But even after controlling for many potential confounds, at the same level and for the same job, the pay gap remains among teenage workers.

After establishing gender inequality in pay for early teenagers, the next two chapters focus on the lived experience of inequality in freelance jobs and employee-type jobs. In the fields I examine most closely, babysitters working freelance and retail and service-sector workers, I document the everyday mechanisms that create and reinforce gender inequality in the workplace. These chapters show how girls in babysitting jobs and retail and service-sector jobs end up being paid less, and they identify the everyday mechanisms that result in the widening of the wage gap with time. Throughout the chapters, I adopt an intersectional approach to gender inequality among teenage workers: while all teenage girls may experience the pay gap, pay inequality is exacerbated by race and class.

In addition, these early jobs may lead young women to hold certain values, which may be enormously gendered and may extend beyond their youth work experiences. In this chapter, I explore the long-term effects of these early work experiences on men and women. What happens to teenagers who worked part time when they grow up and enter into adult careers? Are these wage inequalities limited to the teenage years, or do these early work experiences have long-term effects? Are these effects gendered? More importantly, do early experiences of gender inequality translate into lower wages later?

Prior Work: Short- versus Long-Term Effects of Work

The effects of early work experiences have occupied researchers for decades, as they have tried to capture the magnitude and direction of the effects of early work experience on various spheres of young people's lives. While research projects have focused on the effects of working on teenagers, most of these studies focus on the immediate or short-term effects of working. One central and obvious area of this work has been on the effects of working on academic performance and schooling. Scholars have explored the effects of having a job on academic performance, measured through students' grade-point averages, scores on standardized tests, absenteeism, high school completion, college matriculation, and school engagement (Lee and Staff 2007; Marsh and Kleitman 2005; McNeal 1997; Mortimer 2005; Mortimer and Finch 1986; Staff, Messersmith, and Schulenberg 2009; Staff and Mortimer 2007; Warren and Lee 2003; Warren, LePore and Mare 2000), as well as attendance rates (Marsh 1991; Mortimer and Finch 1986; Shanahan, Mortimer, and Krüger 2002; Staff, Schulenberg, and Bachman 2010).

Other scholars have moved the debate away from immediate academic effects to the effects of work on other spheres, such as emotional and psychological development (Greenberger and Steinberg 1986; Marsh and Kleitmen 2005), interactions with family and friends (Finch et al. 1991; Greenberger and Steinberg 1986; Lewin-Epstein 1981; Mihalic and Elliot 1997; Paternoster et al. 2003). These scholars have argued that given the age of the workers, they might not be emotionally and psychologically ready to be involved in the world of work and that such involvement could interfere with young people's development, creating stress and taking time away from their relationships with friends and family and participation in extracurricular activities.

Scholars have also explored the effects of working on behaviors such as drug and alcohol use, delinquency, truancy, and school misconduct (Longest and Shanahan 2007; McMorris and Uggen 2000; Mihalic and Elliot 1997; Steinberg, Fegley and Dornbush 1993; Uggen and Wakefield 2007) and crime (Hansen and Jarvis 2000). Working part time can provide young people with both unsupervised time away from parents or other adults and their own spending money with which to purchase drugs or alcohol. Students who work are also introduced to older workers and, through these networks, could obtain illegal substances and become involved in criminal activity.

Findings from these studies on the immediate or short-term effects of working have been contradictory, without much agreement on the magnitude, or even the direction, of the effects. Herbert Marsh (1991), for example, found that hours worked in high school have significant negative academic outcomes, lowering grades and the number of hours spent on homework, as well as increasing rates of getting in trouble in and out of school. Later researchers supported these findings, arguing that working part time during high school leaves little time to complete homework assignments, prepare for examinations, get extra help from teachers, and complete other requirements for coming to class ready for learning. However, in some later studies, researches such as Michael Shanahan and Brian Flaherty (2001) found no direct link between paid work and the amount of time spent doing homework. Among ninth, tenth, and twelfth graders, part-time workers and nonworkers had no difference in time dedicated to school work. Among eleventh graders, workers spent more time on homework. Similarly, Jeylan Mortimer, Michael Shanahan, and Seongryeol Ryu (1993) document the effects of high school work on lowered grades, poor attitudes toward school, less time invested in homework and extracurricular activities, and a higher risk of delinquency. Other studies document the detrimental physiological effects of working on young people, noting that working students get less sleep and less exercise and are more likely to skip breakfast (Bachman and Schulenberg 1993; Safron, Schulenberg, and Bachman 2001).

However, other studies identify positive effects of working (D'Amico and Baker 1984), depending on whether the teenager is college bound and the type and intensity of the work. Youth who work more than twenty hours per week during the school year report having less time to do homework and report lower test scores (see also Lewin-Epstein 1981), but youth who work fewer than twenty hours per week do not seem any different from those who do not work at all (Carr, Wright, and Brody 1996; D'Amico 1984; Marsh 1991; Marsh and Kleitman 2005; Steinberg and Dornbusch 1991; Steinberg, Fegley, and Dornbusch 1993). Similarly, school absenteeism and dropout rates are higher for intensive workers (generally defined as working twenty hours or more per week), but not for those who work fewer hours (Schoenhals, Tienda, and Schneider 1998; Warren and Lee 2003).

Some involvement in paid work does not seem to restrict time for homework, school activities, and reading outside of class (Mihalic and Elliot 1997; Schoenhals, Tienda, and Schneider 1998; Shanahan and Flaherty 2001), but intensive work does seem to have detrimental effects. High-intensity workers also seem to have significantly higher absenteeism rates at school (Marsh and Kleitman 2005; Schoenhals, Tienda, and Schneider 1998), as working such long hours may lead to conflicts with a school schedule. In fact, recent studies point to students choosing work over school when they are in conflict, as they feel more connected and needed at work than at school (Besen-Cassino 2014). High-intensity workers are also less likely to be engaged in community and extracurricular activities at school, which are considered important because they promote learning and reinforce school-related values (McNeal 1997; Osgood 1999; Schoenhals, Tienda, and Schneider 1998). High-intensity work necessarily limits schedule flexibility for young people, making it more difficult to fit in such activities. This work would also be expected to limit the amount of time spent hanging out with friends and family (Lewin-Epstein 1981). Intensive workers are also shown to be more attracted to unstructured activities and unsupervised spaces, such as going to parties, riding in cars, or going to bars, as they are used to greater autonomy and less parental supervision (Longest and Shanahan 2007). Such autonomy and lack of supervision are also strongly linked to school misconduct and delinquency and crime (Bachman and Schulenberg 1993; McMorris and Uggen 2000), problem behaviors (Osgood 1999; Safron, Schulenberg, and Bachman 2001), and increased drug and alcohol use (Mortimer and Johnson 1998; Staff and Uggen 2003).

Despite the lack of consensus on the effects of work, almost all of the prior research has focused on the immediate effects of the work experience on teenagers. Some studies have explored short-term effects, such as whether working as a teenager helps workers find better jobs when they complete their education (D'Amico and Baker 1984; Marsh 1991; Meyer and Wise 1983; Mortimer and Finch 1986; Stephenson 1981; Stern and Nakata 1989), finding positive short-term (one to four years after graduating) effects on employment rates and wages. Of course, these results are conditional, with the positive effects pertaining only to those students who are not college bound but finding no effect for those who do attend college. Other studies have also explored whether working part time affects dropout rates, providing structure and funds to help keep teenagers in school for longer (D'Amico and Baker 1984; McNeal 1997). However, despite the positive effects of teenage work on short-term future employment for some, scholars suggest that these benefits are only short term and would be offset in the long term by the lack of school commitment and lower educational outcomes, though the results again seem to be conditional. Rhoda Carr, James Wright, and Charles Brody (1996) and Christopher Ruhm (1997) found that the intensity of work still mattered beyond immediate effects, with intensive work during high school decreasing college attendance and completion of four or more years of college. On the other hand, Jeylan Mortimer (2005) reports that teenagers who worked moderated hours in their high school years were more likely to receive bachelor's degrees by their mid-twenties.

Even these studies, though, look at relatively short-term effects of a few years out; long-term effects have proven more difficult to study, partially because of data restrictions. Carr, Wright, and Brody (1996), in one notable example, measure the long-term effects of working in high school on both educational attainment and work twelve years later, finding a negative effect of working on educational attainment. In the same study, though, students who had worked in high school had higher levels of labor-force participation, employment, and income. Thomas Mroz and Timothy Savage (2006) explore the long-term effects of youth unemployment. Using data from the National Longitudinal Survey of Youth (NLSY97), the authors find that being unemployed as a young person has lasting effects on future employment. In the short term, they find that experiencing involuntary unemployment as a young person results in underinvesting in human capital. These early underinvestments in human capital result in unemployment in the long term, as well as lower wages.

In addition, there are few studies that focus on the gendered effects of working. Constance Stevens and her coauthors (1992) explore the role of gender in work orientations among adolescent workers, comparing adolescent boys' and girls' aspirations and plans about achievement, family life, and work using data from 1,001 students. They find that adolescent boys who work develop more traditional family orientations, while employed girls expect less involvement in marriage and family life. They argue, "Paid work is traditionalizing for boys, promoting optimism about, and commitment to, numerous adult life domains; but for girls, formal work lessens interest in traditional female gender roles" (Stevens et al. 1992, 153). However, this research looks at the attitudes, aspirations, and orientations of young people, not the actual effects of working; the material effects of working, such as future wages, future promotions, and other related effects, remain outside the scope of their inquiry.

These studies have been limited by data availability and restrictions. Typical datasets do not collect data on very young adolescents, especially because of access issues and institutional ethics board restrictions. Therefore, younger workers who work in freelance jobs are typically left outside the realm of datasets of formal employment. Furthermore, especially because of high costs, time investment, and logistic complications of longitudinal studies, few longitudinal studies exist on this topic. For a comprehensive study on the long-term effects of teenage work, a longitudinal research design is central. Datasets would need to start collecting data on individuals as young as twelve to capture very early work experiences, with regular follow-up interviews into adulthood. The costs, as well as the logistical hurdles needed to carry out such research, are enormous, and, thus, high-quality data is mostly limited to the NLSY97.

The aim of this chapter is to explore the long-term effects of teenage work and capture the differential effects based on gender inequality. Such a focus fills the gap in the literature by addressing both the long-term effects of work and the potentially gendered effects. I hypothesize that working part-time as a teenager has differential effects for boys and girls. While the existing literature is generally positive about the effects of work on work-related outcomes, such as future wages and finding jobs, such research has not explored how these outcomes may differ based on the gender of the worker. Just as students not attending college receive greater benefits from work than those who do, I hypothesize that boys experience long-term benefits of work more than girls do in the long run. In addition, I hypothesize that the effects of early work are not confined to educational attainment and future work outcomes but include values and attitudes learned on the job. While working, both boys and girls are socialized into work values, such as aesthetic-labor requirements, how boys and girls should look, and other work-related assumptions. If the acculturation that young workers receive from their early workplaces extends into adulthood, working, especially in certain industries, could have enormous detrimental effects on women.

For the reasons discussed in Chapter 1, the NLSY97 is an ideal dataset for this sort of analysis. It follows cohorts of young people from their early teenage years through their twenties on an annual basis, allowing for the capture of the effects of various types of youth employment for years afterward. In addition, it has a large sample size, allowing us to estimate effects on various subgroups. Using NLSY97 data, we can track the effect of early employment (age seventeen or before) on the earnings of women at ages twenty-seven to twenty-nine. What are the long-term effects of early work experiences for young people? More importantly, what role does gender play? Do these early work experiences have different effects for men and women? I estimated an ordinary least squares (OLS) regression model predicting income. The distribution of income is presented in the methodological notes. Of the overall sample, 52 percent of respondents are white; 26 percent are black, 49 percent are female, and 51 percent are male. In the OLS regression model, I predict overall income. In this model, I include education (coded 0–7; mean 2.3) as a control.

In light of my qualitative findings in Chapter 3 on retail and service-sector jobs, I also include a series of variables on weight. In Chapter 3, I show how my qualitative interviews with retail and service-sector women, especially ones who work in clothing stores, point to the effects of working on their bodies. Many of them pointed to feeling overweight, dieting, and exercising during their time working at clothing stores. While these qualitative findings pointed to short-term immediate effects of working, I wondered if such early experiences had lasting effects on women. Therefore, I included weight-related questions in my model to see if early work experiences result in future weight-related issues. To test that, I included a variable on respondents' actual reported weights, as well as a variable that measures respondents' own assessment of their weight. Regardless of their actual weight, this variable measures respondents' own evaluations of their weight—that is, whether they feel overweight or see themselves as overweight.

In addition, I included a series of work-related variables. First, I included a variable to control for the type of industry. In addition, I included a variable that measures how much young people work: 94.8 percent worked at least one week (94.6 percent for girls and 95 percent for boys). The detailed distributions and descriptive statistics for these independent variables are presented in detail in the methodological notes, as well as in the detailed results of the OLS regression.

Positive Effects of Part-Time Work: Only for Boys

What do these regression results tell us? Among boys who worked as teens, more work equaled more earnings once they became adults. With all other conditions remaining the same, boys who did not work at all as teens earned about $36,000 per year at age twenty-nine, going up to about $44,000 per year for those who maxed out their work (211 weeks—just about every week from sixteen to nineteen; see Tables A.6 and A.7 in the Appendix).

While men enjoy the monetary benefits of early work experiences, these benefits are not experienced by women. Women get the same benefit from

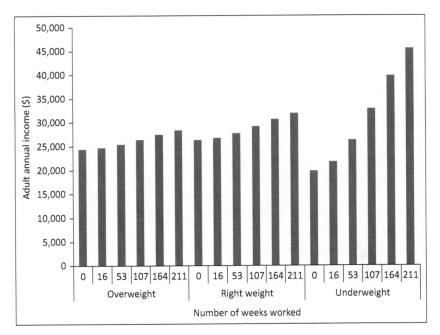

Figure 5.1 Effect of teen work time and weight on adult income

working—but only if they are (self-described as) underweight, controlling for adult weight. For girls who are any heavier than that, there is only a slight, but insignificant, positive effect of teen work experience on adult earnings. Basically, we can conclude that boys benefit from working as teenagers, but not all girls do. To put it in context, the study measures weight categories as follows: "underweight" girls average 105 pounds; "right weight," 117 pounds; "overweight," 143 pounds; and "very overweight," 166 pounds. Only underweight girls enjoy comparable long-term benefits. Therefore, we can conclude that working during the teenage years has different long-term effects for men and women: it benefits men's earnings in the long run but not women's (Figure 5.1).

The Longer Girls Work in Customer Service Jobs, the Less They Earn as Adults

In the previous model, I look at the overall work experience and its gendered long-term effects. With this model, I wanted to capture the differential effects of different sectors. I estimated another OLS regression model. The dependent variable is earning as an adult. Education, SAT scores, marital status, weight, race, and first industry worked in were included as control variables. Key variables of interest are weeks worked as a teen (also discussed in the first model) and whether they worked in the joint restaurant/apparel category. The details of these variables are discussed in the methodological notes.

The results point to differential effects of working for some industries, particularly apparel and restaurants. The results show that the more a girl works in apparel or restaurants as a teen, the farther she falls behind girls who worked in other industries, as well as boys. Girls who work in apparel or restaurants make slightly *less* as an adult as the number of hours they work increases, and they fall farther behind the girls who worked elsewhere.

In addition to the net negative effect of working in apparel and restaurants, how much they work is also important. The more hours they work, the more negative the results are in the long term. The whole effect is moderated by time spent in the job, as that undercuts a selection-effect argument: girls who work in apparel might be different from girls who do not, but how are girls who work in the industry for a long time different from those who work for just a year?

On the basis of the analyses presented here, early work experience has important long-term consequences for young women, at least through their late twenties. First, working in apparel or the related restaurant sector as an adolescent results in reduced overall wages when women reach adulthood and start working in "real jobs" (Figure 5.2). Even though these workers do not

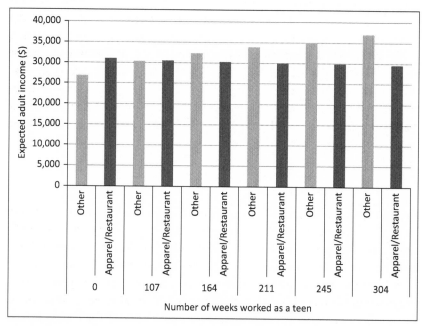

Figure 5.2 Long-term effects of working by industry

generally continue to work in the apparel sector, the more time they spent in the apparel sector, the lower their earnings are, relative to women who worked in other sectors when they were young. Given what my interviews revealed about the norms of these workplaces, it is unsurprising that the young women would internalize some of these values, and that these values would affect their future work experiences.

Such long-term effects are surprising because the early jobs students take generally appear unrelated to their future careers. Few young people—college bound or not—continue to work in the same sector or in similar positions as adults, so why would working in apparel as a teenager reduce wages for a thirty-year-old working as a financial planner? Because the content of the jobs and the required skill sets are vastly different, we would expect little connection or long-term effects. However, working part time does not just teach work-related skills; it also trains young people in "doing gender." The aesthetic-labor requirements of many retail and service-sector jobs—in the apparel industry in particular—mean that young women are expected to "look good and sound right." These analyses show that such early work experiences have lasting effects.

Interestingly, working seems to have greater detrimental effects on some young women than it does on others. Young women who consider themselves to be very skinny at the time they take their first job actually seem to benefit about as much as young men from their work experience. Explanations for this can be found in the interviews described in previous chapters: if young women are valued in these positions because of their ability to represent a brand effectively, women who consider themselves to be of a normal weight may well be marginalized and undervalued in such positions, a marginalization that seems to undercut their income for years afterwards. This is especially interesting given that the regression model controls for women's actual weight as adults, so the effects cannot simply be chalked up to heavier women having lower levels of income.

Body Image and Apparel Jobs

In addition to the effects on earnings, work in certain industries as a young adult has an enormous effect on women's body images. Mary Douglas (1966) finds that the body is a blank surface on which cultural expectations, biases, and hierarchies are inscribed. So, by understanding the body, we can shed light on those cultural values and expectations. Similarly, Schepher-Hughes and Lock (1987) look at the body as a "natural symbol" with which to understand cultural expectations and values. Today, in the United States, body image and gender have attracted vast academic and popular attention.

According to one study, 82 percent of white Americans girls have dieted, even though 62 percent of them are at a healthy weight (Storz and Greene 1983). Research from the National Eating Disorders Association finds that 40 to 60 percent of children ages six to twelve worry about how much they weigh; 70 percent wish they weighed less (Roberts 2012).

Past research also points to differences in body images and weight based on race. African American girls show healthier body images and tend to be happier with their body size, weight, and body shapes, even when they are heavier (Akan and Grilo 1995; Lovejoy 2001; Parker et al. 1995; Rucker and Cash 1992). Compared to their white counterparts, African American girls in that age group also have lower rates of eating disorders such as anorexia and bulimia (Abrams, Allen, and Grey 1993; Akan and Grilo 1995; Rand and Kuldau 1990), despite having higher rates of obesity and compulsive overeating (Kumanyika, Wilson, and Guilford-Davenport 1993; White 1991). In sum, despite being heavier on average, African American girls have higher body satisfaction and self-esteem and feel better about their bodies than all other racial and ethnic groups.

In studies of body image, many researchers have made use of silhouettes of continuums of body types, asking participants to rate which ones are underweight, average, and overweight. In these studies, white girls tend to rate silhouettes as fatter than they actually are, showing a bias toward thinness. They also tend to consider themselves as heavier than they actually are, showing bias in evaluations of weight (Desmond et al. 1989; Rand and Kuldau 1990; Story et al. 1995). They also tend to have much higher rates of not just eating disorders (Kumanyika, Wilson, and Guilford-Davenport 1993; Rand and Kuldau 1990; Story et al. 1995) but also other problematic eating behavior, such as binge eating, use of laxatives, purging, fasting, and fear of fat (Abrams, Allen, and Gray 1993; Akan and Grilo 1995; Rand and Kuldau 1990).

Despite these differences, the culture of thinness and problems with body image seem to be problematic because they target young women and prescribe oppressive—and often unattainable—standards of what is and is not appropriate. Feminist theorists, especially in the social-control school, argue that these images of how to look, how much to weigh, and how women's bodies should look are mechanisms of social control. Through dieting and excessive exercise (Bordo 1993; Kilbourne 1994; Rothblum 1994), these idealized versions of what women's bodies should look like result in control and oppression of actual women's bodies. Naomi Wolf (2002) argues that the attempt to create an idealized body for women and the cult of thinness are society's attempts to restrict and control women's gains in both the political and economic arenas in the previous decades. In this view, these images in the media, the cosmetics industry, and advertising are the cause of eating disorders and the cult of thinness (Bordo 1993; Kilbourne 1994; Rothblum 1994). By promoting weights substantially lower than women's actual weights, our culture traps women within a cycle of self-hate, dieting, restricting food, and denial of self. Such a cycle distracts women from economic and political struggle.

Jean Kilbourne, in her *Killing Us Softly* documentary (2010) looks at the role of media and advertising in promoting ultrathin, often Photoshopped, and otherwise physically impossible images of women's bodies, often with the intent to sell beauty and fashion products and promote the cosmetic surgery. These industries target women and, through advertising, promote unrealistic beauty ideals with the promise that women can attain this beauty if they buy the right cosmetics or clothes. Overall, as Susan Bordo (1993) argues, these practices result in women contributing to their own oppression and feeding into what Michel Foucault (1979) would call a system of auto-control.

However, not all feminist scholars agree on this. Some argue that body-image issues, dieting, and eating disorders are the results of shifting gender roles and changing expectations of women (Root, Fallon, and Friedrich 1986). Women are expected to be loving, nurturing, pleasant, assertive, and achievement oriented all at the same time, and the conflict between these expectations is reflected in body-image issues and eating disorders. According to Susan Bordo (1993), this relatively new ideal of thinness is the embodiment of that very conflict. By becoming extra slender, women can achieve traditionally feminine roles: they can be submissive, fragile, small, and not take up much space. At the same time, dieting and limiting food is quintessentially a masculine endeavor of mastery and self-discipline. Through dieting, women also eliminate traditionally feminine features, such as larger hips and breasts, which, historically, have been associated with motherhood and caregiving, as a rebellion against potentially restrictive roles of motherhood and marriage.

Other studies on body image and weight issues focus on mother-daughter relationships, the changing role of gender (Orbach 1986; Perlick and Silverstein 1994; Theriot 1988), and the role of college education (Silverstein et al. 1993). Brett Silverstein and colleagues (1988) find that rates of eating disorders are higher among girls who aspire to go to college. Other studies have found that adolescent girls whose mothers experienced academic or professional disappointment are more likely to experience eating disorders and body-image issues (e.g., Horend and Perdue 1990). Research has also identified the role of eating issues and body-image issues in dealing with trauma and traumatic life experiences (B. Thompson 1992).

What many of these studies leave out, though, is the role of the lived experiences of young women with these body-image issues. Throughout the literature, the traditional culprits are media, the cosmetics industry, and the fashion industry (Kilbourne 1994) for creating and sustaining unrealistic images for women's bodies, but while these unrealistic images play a role, so, too, do the social roles that young women take on. Some of this can be seen in the work on family effects, where daughters are seen as taking on certain roles to compensate for the failings of a mother, but the effects of work on women's body images has largely been ignored. My interviews point to the unrealistic body images and expectations that are present in the workplaces of young women, and it would be unrealistic to assume that these are not internalized to some extent. The interviews show how these images and expectations affect a large group of women. While it may be the case that women involved in modeling or high-level athletics may have problematic relationships with food, the overall impact of such relationships are limited by the relatively small number of women implicated. On the other hand, hundreds of thousands of young women are employed in retail apparel or in restaurants, meaning that even small influences of such work on body images have potentially enormous effects.

The Apparel Industry Disabuses Girls of the Notion That They Are Skinny

Using the same NLSY97 data, it is possible to trace the effects of a woman's first job on their body image a few years later, when they are of college age. This time, we look at the change in how girls perceive their weight from before their first job to after their first job. Most girls tend to think they are heavier before than after, but girls in the apparel industry are much more likely to stop saying that they are underweight. Basically, there a lot of girls who think they are too skinny, but girls who work in the apparel industry are much more likely to stop thinking that. This is made worse by the fact that we are controlling for how much they actually weigh: for any given weight, girls who work in apparel are more likely to think they are fat.

The dependent variable is whether girls moved up a class in their perceived weight between the ages of fifteen and twenty (37 percent did). Table A.8 in the Appendix shows the overall breakdown for girls: negative values mean moving down (from "overweight" to "right weight," or from "right weight" to "underweight," for instance). Interestingly, working in restaurants made girls a little less likely to think that they were heavier. This could be because they are surrounded by food and people who consume food. Further research is needed to explore why the restaurant industry is different.

Based on the results, 82 percent of fifteen-year-olds who said they were "very underweight" thought they were heavier when they were twenty, but that increased to 96 percent for girls who worked in apparel (Figure 5.3). Of the girls who thought they were underweight at fifteen, 63 percent rated themselves as heavier at twenty—but that's 76 percent of girls who worked in apparel. Because of ceiling effects, girls who initially rated themselves as overweight were less likely to say that they were heavier later, controlling for how much they actually weigh.

Much of the research on body-image issues notes that teenagers are especially vulnerable to messages about their bodies and has therefore criticized magazines and media sources marketed to teenage girls that show and idealize unrealistic or impossible body images. This focus on the media, however, may well obscure the enormous effects of early workplace experiences on how young women see themselves. The earlier analyses show that young women who work in service-oriented industries tend to have lower incomes as adults, but these analyses show that working can lead young women to have worse body images, as well. Young women, like Janice, who works for a trendy clothing chain, who compare themselves to catalog models, in an environment where the arrival of summer styles causes panic among the staff as they engage in binge diets in order to fit the brand image, cannot help but internalize these values, and thus they feel worse about themselves and their bodies.

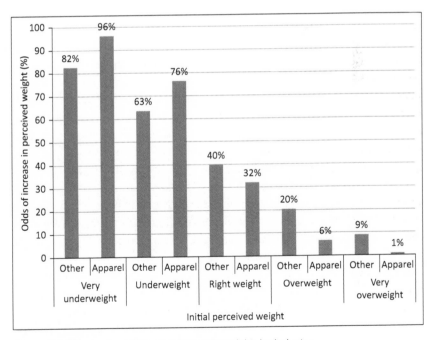

Figure 5.3 Effects of working on feeling overweight, by industry

In understanding workplace inequality, most research and policy typically focuses on home and school. While home and school are certainly important areas for young people's socialization and their learning of gender roles, they are not the only places where young people are socialized. Today, almost every student works at some point throughout his or her school years. Many work over twenty hours per week, some as many as forty hours per week (Herman 2000), and this work is a socially and culturally important part of young people's lives. Work provides not only a common space for young people to socialize and meet new friends but also a common vocabulary with which they can relate to their peers and build up independent identities (Besen-Cassino 2014).

One of the criticisms of research on at the effects of employment is that there might be self-selection effects with young people who work, especially ones who engage in intensive work. Some scholars argue that working does not necessarily have such effects on school performance and school and community engagement but, rather, that teenagers who choose to work, especially in intensive jobs, have either less interest or less ability in academic studies, or they have fewer community and school ties, and therefore look for work to create ties (Bachman et al. 2003). Ideally, such concerns could be resolved by randomly assigning young people to various jobs, but as that is ethically and logistically impossible, researchers have tried to address the issue by looking at how many weeks a given respondent worked as a teenager, rather than how many hours were worked in each of those weeks. It may make sense to say that young women who choose to work forty hours a week differ from those who work fifteen hours a week, but that does not explain why a young woman who works—for any number of hours—throughout their teen years is different from one who works for only a few months. The fact that the effects pertain to the length of exposure to the workplace, rather than to the mean number of hours worked, tends to undercut a selection bias explanation and promote a socialization one.

While early job-related skills might not directly translate into future jobs, biases in the workforce and gendered expectations seem to be learned at an early age and are reinforced in the everyday lived experience of work. To borrow from Candace West and Don Zimmerman (1987), young workers "do gender," even as they are pouring coffees or folding sweaters.

The Negotiation Trap

One of the most prominent ways in which activists have sought to reduce the wage gap is by increasing the rates at which women negotiate salaries with their employers. Research shows that women's starting salaries in the job market are lower than those of their male counterparts, and this inequality in starting salaries contributes to the gender wage gap (Bowles, Babcock, and McGinn 2005; Small, Gelfand, Babcock, and Gettman 2007). One reason for lower starting salaries is lower salary expectations for women: since men traditionally make more, they expect higher starting salaries (Hogue, DuBois, and Fox-Cardamone 2010). Parallel with the expectations of the workers, there is a gender bias among employers, who expect to pay more for male employees (Belliveau 2005; Solnick 2001; Williams, Paluk and Spencer-Rodgers 2010). Hannah Bowles and Linda Babcock (2013) refer to these expectations as a self-fulfilling prophecy in which both employers and employees reinforce existing stereotypes and inequality in the context of salary negotiations, especially in the absence of transparent salary information and pay standards (see also Bowles, Babcock, and McGinn 2005).

Some studies have put the responsibility on women to negotiate for higher wages and potentially reduce the wage gap (Kaman and Hartel 1994; Stevens, Bavetta, and Gist 1993), an approach was has been generally supported by the literature. Some studies have suggested that negotiation leads to higher salaries (Malhotra and Bazerman 2007; Pinkley and Northcraft 2000; Stevens, Bavetta, and Gist 1993). On the other hand, other studies have been more skeptical of the power of negotiation, pointing to potential problems for women. Similar to the results found in the babysitter experiment described in Chapter 2, Hannah Bowles, Linda Babcock, and Lei Lai (2007) show that female managers who negotiated were perceived as less nice and more demanding, resulting in coworkers not wanting to work with them. Simply put, while negotiation may help women reduce the wage gap, the social meaning of negotiating for men and women is quite different. Women's negotiation violates gender stereotypes (Ridgeway and Bourg 2004) and is therefore socially costly for women. In particular, negotiation over salary disrupts the gendered assumption that women are caring, nurturing, and more other-oriented and, at the same time, is in line with men's gender roles of breadwinning, being a go-getter, and assertiveness, all traditionally masculine traits (Amanatullah and Morris 2010; Bowles, Babcock, and Lai 2007; Latu et al. 2011; Moss-Racusin, Phelan, and Rudman 2010; Rudman and Glick 1999). Research also shows that adult women are generally apprehensive toward negotiating (Amanatullah and Morris 2010; Bowles, Babcock, and Lai 2007), perhaps because they see the potential social cost attendant with it. To overcome this gender expectation gap, some research has suggested that women use psychological tools to better negotiate (Ridgeway and Bourg 2004). Because negotiating and asking for more money is perceived as a traditionally masculine trait that violates feminine roles, some suggest, women can minimize this potential problem by invoking traditionally feminine attributes, such as caring and displaying concern for others (Amanatullah and Morris 2010; Bowles, Babcock, and Lai 2007; Wade 2001) during their negotiations.

However, the experiment presented in Chapter 4 offers insight into the potential downfalls of such an approach: for babysitters, being nice and caring actually hurts their chances of getting a pay raise. While lack of concern and lack of care do not fit traditionally feminine traits and are treated harshly during negotiations, young babysitters who show concern do not have an advantage. Caring and showing concern for the child *while* asking for more money is met with extra anger from the employers, as it is viewed as manipulative. Therefore, at a young age, babysitters have firsthand experience of what happens when they ask for more money. Of course, not showing emotional connection is not a good option, either: babysitters face being stereotyped whether they show care or treat their jobs with emotional distance. While emotional distance makes them look cool, aloof, and not nice, being emotionally involved traps them in another gendered stereotype. Either way, babysitters are faced with employers who refuse to give them higher pay, but for different reasons.

Research suggests that this experience of the babysitters is mirrored by women and employers throughout the economy. Other research demonstrates long-term effects of negotiating for women that go beyond being turned down for a salary increase. Even if women are more successful in negotiating in the short term, asking for a higher salary has long-term negative consequences for them (Higgins and Kram 2001). Among my participants, some babysitters asked for a raise and were successful—though they were a minority. For example, Francesca asked for a raise when the newborn she was babysitting got older and more mobile and also got a younger sibling. She said she felt her job description changed drastically. Now, she was babysitting two children and was actively running after the children. In fact, the parents wanted her to speak Italian, as well. She decided to ask for a small raise from the ten dollars an hour they agreed to initially. The parents agreed to give her a raise, but after she asked, she said, the parents' attitudes changed. They lowered her hours, and Francesca felt that they were more formal and less friendly. They used to ask her about how school was going, which classes she was taking, and how she did on her finals, but they do not anymore. During the holiday season, before she asked for a raise, they always got her a gift card to a coffee shop or a restaurant, but this year they did not do so, and Francesca believes it is because she asked for a raise.

As a result, women seem to internalize learned helplessness: by the time they enter the adult labor force, they have already asked for raises, been turned down, and experienced the negative effects of negotiation firsthand. During their education, teachers, parents, and administrators put enormous emphasis into teaching girls about success in the workplace and the importance of negotiating for higher salaries, and they provide classes and workshops. However, during the same years, these students experience the world of work firsthand, including experiences with negotiation and asking for a raise, and their firsthand experience differs vastly from the theoretical knowledge provided in schools. In the same way that young women internalize gendered messages about workplace roles from their early work experiences, they also internalize messages about the consequences of asking for more money and the likely results if they do. These messages are yet another way in which early work feeds the gender pay gap that young women experience for years afterward.

Overall, this chapter demonstrates several long-term effects of the early jobs taken by young women. Rather than being just something teenagers do, these jobs—folding sweaters, serving coffee, working cash registers—have important long-term consequences. They not only hold the origins of the gender wage gap but create the internal states in women that reinforce the gender wage gap. While many early jobs appear unrelated to women's (and men's) future careers, they have significant effects on women's future earnings and their body images. This chapter shows that working as a teenager has generally negative effects for women, while the effects are positive for men. Furthermore, working as a teenager in the apparel and service sectors—especially in retail and service jobs with the most intense aesthetic-labor requirements of "looking good and sounding right"—results in women having negative body images and feeling overweight, many years after.

This chapter shows how, during the teenage labor years, both men and women learn to do gender (West and Zimmerman 1987), as well as learn to labor (using Willis's [1977] formulation): they discover the rules of the workplace and socialize into the world of work. These rules are highly gendered, and women are socialized into gendered, oppressive rules, including unequal pay, from young ages. In the Conclusion, the analysis turns to the effects of the recent economic recession and the policy implications of the findings presented in the chapters.

Conclusion

Work, Recession, and Future Direction

n June 2015, the Pew Research Center released a research report on the decline of youth employment as a result of the recession that began in 2008 (DeSilver 2015). Part-time youth employment during the school year and summer months, which had peaked in the 1980s, has lagged behind other areas in the economy, and has yet to fully recover. Among sixteen- to nineteen-year-olds, the Great American Summer Job declined first with the recession of the early 1990s and then more substantially with the more recent recession. Using all of the available data—which goes back to 1948—the researchers conclude that teen employment historically increased with economic boom times and decreased during economic recessions, but it remained within a 46 percent to 58 percent range (2015). However, starting with the recession of 1990–1991 and through the 2001 and 2008 crises, teen employment has never fully recovered, especially in the area of summer employment, as competition for low-paying entry-level jobs has increased. Karen Sternheimer (2016) refers to this phenomenon as the "privilege of a summer job."

These findings are troubling, because they mean that fewer young people are able to reap the benefits of working as an adolescent, which was once an almost universal experience and an important part of our culture. The idea that adolescent employment might be a privilege is emblematic of the existing research, which is based on a uniform understanding of both adolescents and part-time jobs. If nothing else, though, the interviews and analyses presented in this book show that the jobs held by young people are not created equally, and even the same job can lead to very different experiences, depending on the race and gender of the young person holding it. While these early jobs may benefit young men, the effects are generally negative for young women in both the short and the long term. Beliefs about the positive effects of young people's work are based on the view that white men are the default category, and it is when we move outside of that category that things get complicated.

The same Pew report also points to the emerging inequalities in the postrecession economy. While the jobs are becoming increasingly scarce, not all adolescents are experiencing joblessness at the same rates. Both the Bureau of Labor Statistics (2015) and Pew (DeSilver 2015) find that race and socioeconomic status are important factors in young people's job searches. White adolescents from higher socioeconomic backgrounds have an easier time finding and keeping jobs, while nonwhite youth, especially from lower socioeconomic groups, have a harder time. According to the Pew Report, after the recession of 2007–2009,

> white teens are much more likely to work over the summer than teens of other races and ethnicities. Last year, for example, the summer employment rate for 16- to 19-year-old whites was 34.0%, versus 19.3% for blacks, 23.0% for Asians and 25.0% for Hispanics (who can be of any race). About 1.3 million more teens were employed in July 2014 than in April, a rough gauge of summer jobholding; 1.1 million, or 84.2%, were white. (DeSilver 2015)

Karen Sternheimer's (2016) work also supports this finding, as she observes that having a part-time job is becoming a privilege. More affluent teenagers are easily finding jobs, yet their less affluent counterparts are having a more difficult time, taking longer to find jobs or being shut out of the workforce altogether (Besen-Cassino 2014).

But despite a more competitive job market with fewer available jobs and higher aesthetic-labor and emotion-labor demands, the social importance of jobs for young people persists, with many adolescents wanting to work part time (Besen-Cassino 2014). It is this social aspect of jobs that so many studies in the past have overlooked. While past studies of youth typically have focused on school, extracurricular activities, and families as prime agents of socialization, teenagers at work spend long hours away from parental supervision and adult scrutiny. During that time, they keenly observe the messages and norms provided by the workplace and, according to the results presented here, internalize them, leading to significant long-term consequences. For example, typical studies have focused on schools, families, and peer groups in predicting which majors or areas of specialization male and female students will choose, showing how experiences in these arenas can reinforce gender biases. However, work is just as important a facet of young people's lives, making it necessary to understand the role of early work experiences in internalizing societal gender biases.

Similarly, studies of gender inequality and of the pay gap in particular have looked at the adult pay gap after the completion of formal education and entry into the adult labor force. However, by the time students complete their formal education to enter the adult labor force, they have already spent years in the workforce and have already internalized social biases and gender inequality. Therefore, in order to better understand the gender pay gap, it is vital to examine the role of early work experiences.

Findings: An Overview

The findings presented in this book show the complexity of the work experiences of young student workers. Using a mixed-method approach—both quantitative analysis using NLSY97 data and qualitative data, such as in-depth interviews and personal narratives—I show that the gender wage gap starts well before adult employment. First, by looking at very early work experiences, I identify the emergence of the pay gap among very young workers. When young people are twelve and thirteen, male and female workers make the same amount of money. But by the time they reach fourteen and fifteen and begin moving to employee-type jobs from freelance jobs, we see the emergence of the gender wage gap, which widens with age. Among fourteen- to fifteen-year-olds, I find that the wage gap is partially explained by boys' movement to employee-type jobs, while girls stay in freelance jobs, such as babysitting. But even within freelance jobs and employee-type jobs, pay inequality based on gender remains, even after controlling for all relevant individual-level factors.

Such a finding sheds light on a persistent problem in our economy. Typical inquiries of the gender wage gap focus on later years in the workforce, but these results show that by that time, the gender wage gap has already emerged as a social problem, and the mechanisms through which it is transmitted are embedded in social and economic structures. This analysis of the gender wage gap among the youngest workers is also important because it allows us to do away with many of the individual-level explanations that are typically offered for the adult wage gap. Like a social laboratory, looking at the youngest workers allows us to control for factors including the unequal distribution of house chores, child care, differences in years of education, and differences in skills and practice, which are simply not applicable for this age group. Even when none of these factors is driving it, the gender wage gap exists, so by the time adolescents start their "real jobs," they already have internalized values and expectations to bring with them. While the pay gap at these ages might not appear to be substantial in real dollars, it is substantial as a percentage of their earnings, and it undercuts the idea that youth work is some kind of gender utopia.

I also tested the dominant theories of the pay gap that might apply to these young workers, looking at the relative importance of individual factors, occupational characteristics, and differences in values. I find that male and female students do not value different things at work, with both saying they value the social aspects of the job, such as the opportunity to meet new people and socialize with friends. Importantly, both male and female students are equally likely to value money, so even if differential values were a source of the adult gender wage gap, they cannot be driving the gap among young people.

Using qualitative interviews, I focused on two types of employment common to young women: babysitters and workers in the retail and service sectors. Given that one of the main contributors to the gender wage gap is the movement of boys into employee-type jobs, it is important to understand why young women stay in freelance jobs, like babysitting. From the perspective of the young women, there is enormous pressure to stay put, as they are "too valuable" and "too important" to the survival of families and the children's well-being. But despite being told they are essential for the family and the children, they are not offered higher pay. Most of the young women interviewed reported a substantial change in their job description since they started their jobs, going from one child to multiple children and from occasional date-night babysitting to everyday child care, but such changes in their job description had little to no affect on their pay. In addition, many of the babysitters spent unpaid hours talking to parents, making playdates and arrangements, and coming up with games in their own time. In addition, they are often expected to complete other tasks, such as cooking, cleaning, picking up dry cleaning, and running other errands for the family. In this sense, they are being asked to work as what amounts to a replacement mother, carrying out the tasks that would have been done by a wife in the era of single-earner households. The gendering of such tasks is made evident from interviews with male babysitters, who reported much more professional experiences, with none of these additional tasks even countenanced. They had more rigid hours and shifts, were rarely asked to take on other house chores, and were not asked to care. Rather, their connection to the children was based on tasks or skills, such as being able to play sports with the children.

Most of the babysitters I interviewed found their jobs through informal networks, what Mark Granovetter refers to as "the strength of weak ties" (1973, 1360). While these informal networks are useful for finding jobs, they also stop babysitters from asking for more money. Because the babysitters are connected to their employers, asking for more money or negotiating over salary is rather more difficult than it would be in less emotionally fraught, more traditional employer-employee relationships.

In addition, babysitting jobs had central care components, in which babysitters were expected to be emotionally engaged with both the children and the family. Because this emotional investment is defined in opposition to money, asking for more money is construed as a sign that the babysitter does not really care about the children. Therefore, while many young women were working under challenging conditions with extra tasks, they did not feel as though they could complain or ask to be compensated for the additional time required for them to demonstrate their care. The general narrative put forward in the literature is that they are being underpaid because they do not negotiate or ask for additional money, but would they have gotten the raise if they asked for it? The perception of the babysitters I interviewed was that they would not, making a socially and emotionally awkward attempt pointless. To test whether this was the perception of the babysitters or if this was reality, I designed an experiment, the results of which confirmed the perceptions of the babysitters. When they did not show care and personal connection, the female babysitters were denied a raise and were disliked by the employers, and they seemed to be disliked because such women do not fit the stereotype of caring and nurturing women. When they did show care and emotional connections, they were better liked by the employers, but when they asked for a raise, they were described as manipulative and still did not get the money. Such mechanisms were not at play for male babysitters: they did not seem to be evaluated on the basis of care and emotional connection, but unless they appeared to use a connection to ask for a raise, they were given one. These results demonstrate that the roots of the wage inequality go much deeper than a simple failure to negotiate.

Chapter 3 explores gender inequality in retail and service-sector jobs. In this chapter, I show that the aesthetic-labor requirements of many retail and service-sector jobs disproportionately affect young women. Young women are sought after to be the face of corporations and to represent brands, and while this can make the job hunt easier, it also means that young women are more likely to be pressured to conform to aesthetic-labor requirements: to look good and sound right. To achieve the right look, these young women are pushed towards using the products that they are selling. This encourages a cycle of consumption, leaving young women in substantial credit card debt. Despite being asked to consume the products as part of the job, when they asked for a raise, young women I interviewed were told that they do not really care about the job and that they are only working for the discounts. They can get these jobs because they like the products, keep the job by buying the products, and still have their consumption of the products held against them by management when it comes to getting more money. Similarly, many young women in retail and service-sector jobs are encouraged to be nice and friendly to create a pleasant shopping environment for customers and are hired through their social connections with existing workers. However, when they ask for a raise, they are denied because, they are told, they do not really care about money and are simply at work to spend time with their friends.

Finally, young women are more likely to be in customer-service positions because they are "better with people" and have superior "people skills." This often results in young women being tasked with dealing with challenging customers, in what workers in these sectors universally describe as the worst part of the job. When young women are told they are good with people, they do not see it as a compliment but rather as an indication that they are not good with numbers or have poor managerial skills. Such tasks may also lead them to miss out on training for tasks that might help them in other jobs later in life.

Chapter 4 offers an intersectional perspective to understanding gender inequality in the youth labor force. While gender matters a great deal, not all young women have the same experience in the workforce. In the adolescent workforce, as the jobs become scarcer, race and socioeconomic status become increasingly important factors in hiring. While young women are seen as having an advantage in the job market, women of color have a harder time finding jobs: their job searches take longer, and oftentimes they end up taking lower-paying, less desirable jobs. In addition, their lived experience of part-time jobs is much different. Young women of color experience more customer harassment and are expected to show greater deference. Yet even when they provide service with a smile and show the expected deference, it is not met with the same praise as it is for their white counterparts. The sincerity of their emotion work is called into question in a way that it is not for whites, a charge which will hurt them in the short and long term.

Chapters 1–4 focus on gender inequality, identifying its causes and unraveling the mechanisms in the youth labor force. Chapter 5 takes these immediate effects and moves the discussion from the short-term, immediate effects to long-term repercussions. While part-time jobs held by young people may appear trivial, young people's experiences in the workforce have important, long-term repercussions. The benefits of these early work experiences are not uniformly experienced: working as a teen benefits men when they are older but does not have the same benefits for women. Even a decade later, and while working in unrelated sectors, inequalities learned and internalized in the youth labor force affect people's jobs. Working in the apparel industry is especially destructive for women: working in these sectors as young adolescents lowers women's self-esteem and results in women having more negative body images when they are older, presumably because of the aesthetic- and style-labor requirements of that sector. The workers in the apparel sector need to look good and sound right, and they are expected to wear and model the merchandise they are selling. Despite the fact that most of the women in the dataset do not work in the apparel industry anymore, the gendered expectations of apparel work continue to plague the women, with these early effects resulting in lower wages.

Policy Implications and What We Can Do

In studying young people, school, activities, parents, and peers have been the central actors, and studies have focused on home, schools, and peer groups in understanding young people's worlds. In the United States, work is such as central component of young people's lives, with young people spending a substantial portion of their day at their part-time jobs (Besen-Cassino 2014). Work also provides a sense of identity, offering a common vocabulary and a central space to socialize with friends. Today, young people have limited social space, especially in suburban settings, to gather and hang out freely without adult scrutiny. Today, movie theaters and shops ban teenagers or limit their movements. Even shopping malls, where teenagers used to freely roam, hang out, and congregate, are restricting their movement. Some malls have implemented parental escort policies for youth below the age of eighteen or twenty-one. The Atlantic Terminal mall in Brooklyn, New York, is even more restrictive: it bans groups of four or more unsupervised youth under the age of twenty-one (Schaefer 2010). For young people, the mere act of being in a public space is viewed as a suspicious activity, associated with drug use or crime. Working, for teenagers, means claiming some social space for themselves in which to socialize and build an identity.

However, while working as an adolescent can have social benefits, these benefits conceal the many potential problems they create. As a society, our vocabulary for talking about part-time adolescent jobs is a uniform one, lumping all adolescents and all part-time jobs together. However, not all adolescent jobs are of the same quality, and not every adolescent enjoys the benefits of working. It is important to adopt a critical view, acknowledging the inequalities and differential outcomes in the workforce. Despite some ebbs and flows in youth employment rates, rising with economic booms and declining with recessions, youth labor has continued to be an important part of our economy as well as an important marker of American culture. Starting as children at lemonade stands and becoming to babysitters, landscapers, retail workers, baristas, and restaurant servers, young people continue to be an important part of our economy, and work continues to be an important portion of their lives.

Many of the policies proposed to cut down on gender inequality target schools and parents. For example, there are many programs that target adolescent girls to encourage them to choose science, technology, engineering, and mathematics (STEM) fields of study in higher education. By moving more women into these male-dominated fields, it is thought that we can combat gender inequality in the job market. Similarly, there are many campaigns to encourage adolescent girls to take on management positions. Lean In, for example, targeted young women and encouraged them to take their place at the table and be more management oriented. There have been campaigns to ban the word "bossy," as it targets girls and discourages them from being in management positions. However, all of these efforts target the workers and seem to ignore the workplace. Women do not start working after finishing their education: work is an important part of young people's lives but is markedly absent from policy initiatives. Often at the same time that teenage girls are given positive, encouraging messages on gender equality at school and at home, they are learning very different lessons in a real workplace. They are told that that they are good with people and, therefore, not good with money or management; that money is in opposition to really caring about their work; and that their appearance needs to comparable to the models in a catalog and it is a failing on their part if it is not. The analyses of long-term effects show that when the messages from school and parents conflict with the lessons actually learned in the workplace, the workplace is winning out.

It is also important to acknowledge the problems of the workplace. As we send the younger generation to the workplace, most are not just learning job-related skills or work experience. An unintended consequence of part-time work, borrowing from Robert K. Merton (1996), is learning and internalizing the potential problems of the workplace. These problems of the workplace—such as sexual harassment, sexism, and racism—often go underreported. As work is an important part of young people's lives, it is important to educate young workers about their rights and responsibilities in the workplace. While our education and parenting often equip young people to deal with problems like bullying and harassment at school, workplace issues are often left out of the discussion.

Finally, it is important to focus on improving work conditions and hiring standards, creating transparent hiring practices for all jobs. These standards are especially important for young people, as they are socialized into the rules of the workplace from an early age.

Future Direction: Methodological Issues

As a result of the importance of work—both socially and economically—to young people, workplaces now constitute an important research site for sociologists. We have explored many aspects of young people's lives, including peer groups, family life, school life, and extracurricular activities, but work requires similar attention for us to fully understand the social development of youth. After all, work is where many of them spend large portions of their free time, and many define their identities and social and political views through work and brands (see also Besen-Cassino 2014).

In understanding important social problems such as the gender wage gap, early work practices are a potentially vital area of inquiry. The early years of employment function as a natural laboratory, controlling for some of the typical explanations for gender inequality at work. Because of temporal primacy, studying early work experiences has important social consequences, and, methodologically, it helps to pinpoint the emergence of the gender wage gap and identify the short- and long-term consequences of such work-based socialization. Such research not only helps us see the emergence and progression of this social problem but also helps clearly debunk common myths about the wage gap.

As many students work part time, it is also important to acknowledge the role of work in socializing young people and establishing their beliefs about work, gender, race, and inequalities. While many of our policies target schools, educators, parents, and guidance counselors in shaping young people's expectations about the job market and the types of jobs they should be taking, these policies need to incorporate discussions of management and workplace culture in the jobs taken by young people.

There is extensive research on the gender biases of teachers and administrators. For instance, young men are more likely to be reported for discipline issues, but young men are also likely to be praised by peers for acting out in class (Ferguson 2013). However, when female students break the rules of the classroom, they do not receive similar recognition and accolades from their peers, but they are also less likely to be reported to the administration. While avoiding discipline appears to be a positive thing, in reality, women's anger, frustration, and assertion are not taken seriously. Peers, teachers, and administrators evaluate the same acts differently, creating double standards of appropriate and acceptable behavior for men and women. Similarly, research has looked at the way girls and boys are socialized in school and home into gendered jobs, with teachers being less likely to encourage and mentor female students or push them towards STEM fields. Guidance counselors have also been problematized for the ways in which they channel students into different fields based on gender, race, and socioeconomic background (Auwarter and Aruguete 2008; Owens, Smothers, and Love 2003). Counselors' own assumptions and biases about what men and women should be doing affect how they counsel young men and women into gendered jobs and fields.

Researchers understand that early experiences with gender play a tremendous role in shaping lives, but without including actual workplaces, the scope of the work and the efficacy of policy resulting from it will necessarily be limited. Researchers and policy makers should focus on the role of workplaces and employers in shaping the gendered expectations of young people. While policies designed to encourage STEM education and women in management target young women in schools, they intervene probably too little, too late, because by then, young women are already learning how to do gender from their workplaces. The jobs these young people take are not simply offering the opportunity to make a few dollars to help with their consumption habits or school: they are classrooms themselves, and if we do not like the lessons that they are teaching, we need to do something about it. Many academic and nonacademic sources point to the positive effects of working in early years. Work potentially helps young people with their consumption habits, helps them pay for their cars and insurance, and, in some cases, helps them pay for their school expenses and help their families. Many parents and educators believe working teaches discipline and positive work habits, such as work ethic, discipline, money and time management, scheduling, multitasking, and professional self-presentation. Workplaces may do all of these things, but they also serve to socialize young people into the existing inequalities in the job force.

One of the findings of the book is that aesthetic-labor requirements encourage young people to consume the products they are asked to sell. In order to get and keep their jobs, workers were pushed to keep up with look requirements, and even employee discounts were not enough to make such consumption affordable. While I have examined the role of these jobs on future earnings, the next step is to uncover the effects of these early jobs on debt. While these early jobs result in short-term credit card debt, are there long-term effects of accumulated debt? Are young workers internalizing these consumption habits in a way that creates a culture of debt and consumption?

Young women experience many problems in their workplaces: racial discrimination, gender discrimination, sexual harassment, and being pressured to work off the clock. However, many of these problems are underreported, because young workers refer to part-time jobs as temporary. "Not my *real* job" becomes an excuse for young people to underreport, or simply laugh off, these important issues. They know that something is wrong in their workplaces, but they do not do anything about it, and so the problems continue.

A few years ago, I interviewed Lily, a university student majoring in biology while working at a coffee chain. Though her work as a barista has no bearing on her major or her future career, she worked every shift, often dealing with long lines or rude customers, carrying large trash bags to a dumpster outside, and being on her feet all day long, all while training the new workers coming through. By any objective measure, this was not a good job, but she never complained about the everyday difficulties This was not her real job, so she did not feel entitled to complain. But whether it is a career or not, a job is a real one to the person paying the employee, and it teaches employees real lessons about how to behave and what to expect from a workplace. While this book uncovers individual qualitative reports of labor issues, work complaints, and reports of harassment, the systematic study of them remains outside the scope of this book. It is vital for future research to focus on these undocumented and underreported issues and shed light on these social problems. Given the prevalence of work for young people, they need to be educated about work and their rights in the workplace in order to be empowered, even when it is not their "real" job.

Appendix

Methodological Notes

Introduction

My method for all the original data collection was approved by the Institutional Review Board (IRB) of Montclair State University. The in-depth interviews were conducted with students between ages eighteen and twenty-four. Following IRB guidelines, no participants younger than eighteen were interviewed; however, the participants were asked about their previous work history, including work they performed throughout their teenage years.

To recruit participants for the in-depth interviews, I employed snowball sampling. With the approval of the Montclair State University IRB, I offered five- to ten-dollar gift cards as incentives to participate; these amounts were small enough that they would not be viewed as efforts to coerce participants. The participants were also instructed prior to the start of the interviews that they could opt out at any time and that they would still receive the gift card. However, no participant opted out of the interviews.

Previous research has pointed to the challenges of collecting data from retail workers, and gift cards or similar incentives are often used in original data collection in qualitative studies to incentivize participation. Christine Williams and Catherine Connell (2010), for example, discuss the challenges of recruiting retail workers for interviews and have used gift cards as incentives. In my data collection, I did not experience similar challenges. While I interviewed retail workers, unlike in Williams and Connell's study, I focused on much younger workers. Younger retail workers were more willing to participate in the interviews.

Chapter 1

The National Longitudinal Survey of Youth 1997 (NLSY97) is one of a series of surveys of the labor market conducted by the Bureau of Labor Statistics of the U.S.

Department of Labor over a span of more than four decades. NLSY97 consists of a representative sample of the noninstitutionalized U.S. population born between 1980 and 1984, including 8,984 youth respondents who were between the ages of twelve and sixteen as of December 31, 1996. (An oversample of black and Hispanic individuals required the use of sample weighting.) Interviews for NLSY97 were conducted in five waves. The first interviews (Round 1) for the survey took place in 1997, when both the eligible youth and one of that individual's parents participated in hour-long personal interviews. In addition, during the screening process, an extensive two-part questionnaire was administered to gather demographic information on members of each youth's household and on his or her immediate family members living elsewhere. Youth were reinterviewed annually, and data from Rounds 1–5 of NLSY97 were released in May 2003. The aim of NLSY97 was to document the transition of youth from school to work and into adulthood through collection of extensive information about the behavior of youth in the labor market and their educational experiences over time. Employment data included details on methods employed for job searches and on the demographic background of the youth.

The data employed in Chapter 1 are from the first round of interviews for NLSY97. For my analysis, I used the full range of ages from NLSY97 (twelve through sixteen years) and NLSY97 data on the methods the youth employed for obtaining a job. In the survey, the employed youth were presented with a series of questions concerning their choice of method for finding a job. The questions were selected based on the results of a pretest and were in line with the standard phrasing of questions employed by the U.S. Census Bureau's Current Population Survey.

The descriptive characteristics of the variables used in my analysis are presented in Table A.1.

A simple linear regression is insufficient to sort out these effects, because of the expectation of a great deal of heteroskedasticity in the model. As the youth in the study

TABLE A.1 DESCRIPTIVE STATISTICS OF SELECTED VARIABLES

Variable	Min.	Max.	Overall Mean	Overall SD	Female Mean	Female SD	Male Mean	Male SD
Hours worked (weekly)	0	90	16.34	11.54	16.43	10.59	16.26	12.29
Grades	1	13	5.74	1.76	6.05	1.67	5.41	1.79
Freelance	0	1	0.36	0.48	0.39	0.49	0.32	0.47
Employee type	0	1	0.25	0.43	0.22	0.42	0.28	0.45
Age	12	18	14.31	1.48	14.32	1.48	14.29	1.47
Household income (monthly)	0	1,627	283.26	270.15	280.04	266.84	286.33	273.27
White	0	1	0.52	0.50	0.51	0.50	0.52	0.50
Logged income (yearly)	0	11	5.57	1.55	5.49	1.53	5.65	1.57

Source: NLSY97
Note: SD = standard deviation.

get older, there are simply more work opportunities available to them, leading to the expectation that the variance around the dependent variable should increase substantially with age. Also, as is almost always the case with income measures, the measurement becomes less precise as the dollar values grow larger. That is, in reporting income, an individual making several thousand dollars a year is likely to err by a few hundred dollars, while an individual who makes several hundred dollars is likely to make errors on a much smaller scale. A battery of heteroskedasticity tests on the model bears out this expectation. The results of the Breusch-Pagan test identify the presence of heteroskedasticity in the model. Of course, there are several ways in which this heteroskedasticity could be accounted for. The most common way of doing so is simply to make use of White-Huber estimation procedures to generate robust standard errors, inflated to account for the problems inherent in estimating a heteroskedastic dependent variable. However, the purposes of the book are better served by using a maximum-likelihood procedure to directly model the heteroskedasticity. Using such an approach not only allows us to achieve consistent parameter estimates while avoiding artificially inflated standard errors but also means that it is possible to test hypotheses regarding the nature of the variance. As noted, for reasons inherent in the data, it is expected that the variance will increase with both the age of the respondent and the amount of money that they make. However, our theoretical argument also holds that as youth age, their work patterns necessarily converge on those that they will hold as adults, moving more and more into employee-type jobs with standardized rates of pay and the gender wage gap that has been repeatedly shown to exist in adult employment. Thus, the variance that should increase with both age and income should decrease as a function of the interaction of the two. As youth become older and earn more, we would expect that the variance of the dependent variable should decrease as they converge to adult work habits.

The results of the model are presented in Table A.2.

To study the values and motivations of young people, I used the World Values Survey (WVS). This dataset has been used widely, especially among economists, political scientists, and sociologists, for examining differential beliefs about social institutions, government, and values, such as postmaterialism, individualism, and the role of women. It provides the ideal dataset for measuring the relative affects of economic and social factors in decisions to enter the labor market, because it offers a wide array of work-related variables, including economic and social factors for working among a large, nationally representative sample.

The WVS also defines work in much the same way that this book does: paid labor done outside the home, not including unpaid work, domestic labor, or agricultural labor. Most importantly, the dataset was constructed based on ethnographic, in-depth, face-to-face interviews with the respondents, which were conducted by social scientists and based on questions devised by survey methodologists according to the results of several waves of pilot studies.

To account for any potential confounding factors, however, the model described in the following section was run separately for college and high school students, and the resulting coefficients were then compared with F-tests against the null hypothesis that the coefficients are equivalent (and, thus, that the effects of the reasons for working do not vary across the groups). The analyses failed to reject the null hypothesis of no difference between college and high school students for all coefficients. However, students and nonstudents in the same age bracket behave quite differently in terms of their

TABLE A.2 MAXIMUM LIKELIHOOD REGRESSION OF LOGGED INCOME, WITH MODELED HETEROSKEDASTICITY

	Coefficient	Standard error	Z	P > Z	Dollar value
Gender*	−.134	.042	−3.14	.002	$93.05
Age*	.426	.018	24.19	.000	$295.67/year
Hours worked weekly*	.170	.002	7.60	.000	$117.99/weekly hour
Freelance*	−.353	.057	−6.15	.000	$245.01
Family SES*	.002	.001	2.10	.036	$104.11/multiple of poverty line
White/Asian*	.092	.047	1.97	.049	$63.85
Constant	−.691	.272	−2.54	.011	
Sigma					
Age	.027	.011	2.64	.014	
Income	.002	.000	7.92	.000	
Age × Income	−.001	.000	−7.42	.000	
Constant	.551	.159	3.47	.001	

Source: NLSY97
Note: Wald chi-squared = 908.68; p > chi-squared = .00; N = 2,564. SES = socioeconomic status.
*Significant at $p < .05$.

decisions to enter the labor market. Within the age bracket of interest, student status is highly correlated with socioeconomic status. Almost all sixteen- to nineteen-year-old nonstudents are economically deprived, although not all economically deprived youth leave school early. This creates a confounding factor in analyses of labor-market-entry decisions, because student status and socioeconomic status are often highly correlated, muting the independent effects of one or both of the factors. Unfortunately, the measurement of variables such as socioeconomic status is typically not precise enough in surveys to capture the relative degree of deprivation. Although such measurements are useful in accounting for more pronounced effects, they fail to capture more nuanced ones. However, adopting the student-nonstudent indicator provides a more fine-tuned measure of economic deprivation and low socioeconomic status. Although many teenagers are economically deprived, coming from lower socioeconomic backgrounds, only those who are extremely deprived do not go to school.

To better capture the differential reasons for working, the sample was separated into student and nonstudent subsamples for comparison. Within these groups, I could control for the effect of socioeconomic status, which allowed me to examine how socioeconomic status affects students and nonstudents differentially. In the WVS, youth—and all other respondents—were asked, "Did you work for money or benefits at least for one hour last week?" The answer is dichotomous; it was coded as 1 if the respondent worked for money or benefits for at least an hour in the reference week or 0 otherwise. There are several reasons for the choice of a dichotomous dependent variable rather than modeling the number of hours worked. Prior research has shown that the number of hours worked does not have significant effects on many aspects of employment (Entwisle, Alexander, and Olson 2000). This makes sense: it is unlikely that the factors that lead a teenager to take a job for ten hours a week differ considerably from those that lead a teenager to work twenty hours a week. Also, the number of hours worked in a week by teenagers is often highly inconsistent, varying by as many as ten hours from week to week. This not only renders measures of central tendency ineffective but also raises questions about the use of threshold effects. If we believe that taking a job of twenty hours per week is different from taking a job of fifteen hours per week, what should be done with a student who works more than twenty hours one week but fewer the next? Furthermore, the only findings that seem to show a difference based on the number of hours worked appear to indicate a threshold effect such that academic performance is hurt only after individuals work more than thirty hours per week.

In addition to questions about work status, respondents to the WVS were asked which factors they thought were the most important when choosing a job. They were then given fifteen cards, each representing a factor that they were told some people believe to be important in a job, and asked to choose which of the factors they personally thought were important. Respondents could choose as many or as few of the cards as they felt were applicable. It is important to note that *all* respondents were asked these questions, regardless of their work status. Moreover, the question was asked regarding respondents' beliefs about work in general and not in reference to any particular job. This is especially important because of the high turnover rates endemic to many youth-oriented jobs. The job factors listed were:

Good pay
Not too much pressure
Good job security
Good chances for promotion
A job respected by people in general
Good hours
An opportunity to use initiative
A useful job for society
Good holidays
A job in which you feel you can achieve something
A responsible job
A job that is interesting
A job that meets one's abilities
Meeting people
Pleasant people to work with

Each of the categories was treated as a separate variable, coded as 1 if the subject chose the reason and 0 otherwise. The majority of the independent variables in the model were constructed, as discussed earlier, from the respondents' beliefs about the importance of different aspects of jobs, both social and economic. The aspects of a job respondents were able to choose from include both economic factors (such as good pay, chances of promotion, and job security) and social factors (such as meeting people and having pleasant people to work with). The inclusion of such factors allowed me to compare the social and economic aspects of a job that respondents report as important in their decision to work.

In comparing the labor-market-entry decisions of student and nonstudent youth, in addition to the potential social and economic reasons for working, some control variables were included. First, a socioeconomic status measure was included. The WVS measures socioeconomic status based on the parents' type of occupation. The question presented to the respondents (not asked verbally by the interviewer but filled out on the written portion of the survey) asked them to classify their socioeconomic background in one of four categories: upper/upper middle class, middle class/nonmanual labor, manual skilled labor/nonmanual skilled labor, and unskilled manual labor. This breakdown was based on the definitions provided in the WVS and is in line with the common practice in academic studies on youth employment (Greenberger and Steinberg 1986). The exact specification in my model is discussed in detail at the end of this section. Another important distinction that must accounted for is whether youth live with their parents or not. The WVS provides a variable specifically to measure that. The respondents were asked, "Do you live with your parents?" The answers were coded 1 if the respondents reported living with their parents and 0 otherwise. Preliminary findings show no main effect of living with parents for U.S. students and nonstudents but significant effects for youth in other industrialized countries. The names of the variables were abbreviated for presentation of the model. Their definitions are as follows:

Y: The dependent variable, whether an individual works or not

Decision to work: Respondent's answer of "yes" or "no" to the question of whether he or she works or not

Good pay: Importance of good pay for both working and nonworking respondents in the decision to work in general

No pressure: Importance of having a no-pressure job for both working and nonworking respondents in the decision to work in general

Security: Importance of job security for both working and nonworking respondents in the decision to work in general

Promotions: Importance of possibility of promotions for both working and nonworking respondents in the decision to work in general

Respected: Importance of having a respected job for both working and nonworking respondents in the decision to work in general

Good hours: Importance of good hours for the respondent for both working and nonworking respondents in the decision to work in general

Initiative: Importance of having the opportunity to use initiative in the job for both working and nonworking respondents in the decision to work in general

Useful: Importance of usefulness of the job for both working and nonworking respondents in the decision to work in general

Good holidays: Importance of good holidays for both working and nonworking respondents in the decision to work in general

Achievement: Importance of the possibility of achievement for both working and nonworking respondents in the decision to work in general

Responsibility: Importance of having responsibilities at work for both working and nonworking respondents in the decision to work in general

Interesting: Importance of having an interesting job for both working and nonworking respondents in the decision to work in general

Meets abilities: Importance of having a job that meets the respondents' abilities for both working and nonworking respondents in the decision to work in general

Pleasant people: Importance of having pleasant people to work with for both working and nonworking respondents in the decision to work in general

Live with parents: A dummy variable that identifies respondents living with their parents; respondents living with their parents are coded as 1, and 0 otherwise

Because of the dichotomous nature of the dependent variable—an individual either works or does not—I employed logistic regression techniques to predict the likelihood of a respondent working, given the variables listed above as predictive variables. The model was run separately for student and nonstudent youth to demonstrate the uniqueness of the student population within the United States. Because the coefficients attached to logistic regression coefficients tell us very little about the effect of an independent variable other than its size and its significance, it was necessary to use Monte Carlo simulation to fully analyze the results. To this end, Gary King's CLARIFY plug-in for STATA was used (King, Tomz, and Wittenberg 2000). Monte Carlo simulations estimate unweighted, predicted probabilities at random one thousand draws. They offer expected values for each independent variable. To simulate the parameters, they use the point estimates of variance/covariance matrices of the estimates to randomly draw a multivariate normal distribution that enables determination of predicted probabilities. The numbers show the amount of change in the dependent variable for every change, from the lowest category to the highest category. In other words, the Monte Carlo values for each independent variable show how much the likelihood of working increases or decreases, moving from the lowest category of the independent variable to its highest value. Simply put, the Monte Carlo simulation allowed me to present numerically precise estimates of the effects of parameters of interest in a way that requires minimal statistical knowledge on the part of the reader. Certainly, the procedure was more complicated than some other approaches, such as odds ratios, but the interpretation and the visual representation of the results are much simpler with the aid of Monte Carlo simulations. As King, Michael Tomz, and Jason Wittenberg (2000) argue, with Monte Carlo simulations, the interpretation of the size and the magnitude of the effects is much simpler and easier to follow for readers, and the results are comparable across different models. Also, with Monte Carlo simulations, it is easier to visually observe the size and the magnitude of the changes (Table A.3).

Chapter 2

The experiment designed for Chapter 2 aims at capturing the parents and potential employers' perspectives. The experiment was pilot tested and took five minutes to complete. The participants were paid $1 at an ethical wage, higher than minimum wage. Because of the comparatively high benefit, the data collection was completed quickly.

These participants were collected by Amazon's MTurk. While MTurk offers a convenience sample, for the research design, it is not meant to be representative. This

TABLE A.3 LOGIT ESTIMATES OF VARIABLES INTERACTED WITH GENDER OF RESPONDENT

Variable	Coefficient	Standard error	Z	P > Z
Job respected by people	−1.275	0.801	−1.59	0.111
Achievement	0.576	1.200	0.48	0.631
Opportunity to use initiative	0.825	1.220	0.68	0.499
Good chances of promotion	−0.929	0.868	−1.07	0.285
Good holidays	−0.032	0.959	−0.03	0.973
Good hours	−0.781	0.868	−0.90	0.368
Job security	1.355	0.909	1.49	0.136
Job that makes use of abilities	1.670	1.187	1.41	0.159
Meeting new people	0.573	1.152	0.50	0.619
Not too much pressure	1.273	0.946	1.35	0.178
Pleasant people to work with	−1.290	1.223	−1.06	0.291
Responsibility	0.056	1.182	0.05	0.963
Useful to society	0.314	1.155	0.27	0.786
Socioeconomic status	−0.322	0.508	−0.63	0.526
Confidence in education	0.333	0.466	0.71	0.475

Source: World Values Survey

portion of the study is designed as an experiment, and the sample recruited by MTurk is comparable to any sample recruited on college campuses for typical experimental research. Typical experimental research designs often recruit college students using departmental subject pools. Such departmental or university subject pools are convenience-based samples. The subject pool used is similar to the typical subject pools used in experimental studies in the United States. I opted to use MTurk instead of a departmental subject pool because MTurk is similar to departmental subject pools in every way except that it allows the researchers to sample an older group, including parents. Such an option is not available with university subject pools, which typically consist of college students. For this research design, reaching parents and other adults is more desirable. The experimental design is presented in detail below.

The participants were exposed to two different babysitters, "Molly" and "Jake." There were two experimental conditions. First, I was trying to measure the effects of gender: Would the participants react differently to Molly and Jake? Does the gender of the babysitter affect how parents and potential employers feel about the babysitter?

The second experimental condition was caring about the students. One group of participants were told that the babysitter cares deeply about the child and the child has a deep connection to the babysitter. The babysitter also does emotion labor by bringing homemade snacks to the child. In the alternative, the babysitter is described as the same except for the emotional attachment to the child and bringing homemade snacks. Bringing homemade snacks and forming an attachment to the child are used as indicators of emotion labor. To account for the act of bringing something, so we are not measuring the effects of bringing goods to the child as a material benefit, the control group received snacks, but they were store-bought (not homemade) snacks.

Chapter 3

One quotation in this chapter, by Jules, who works at Seymour and Smith, was not obtained as a part of the data collected for this book. This interview was conducted as a part of a previous wave of data collection, but given the thematic affinity, I included the interview with the consent of the participant. I interviewed this participant numerous times after the initial interview.

The interviews included in Chapters 2 and 3 were conducted between January and September 2016, after IRB approval. Interview participants were recruited from a large, public university using fliers and snowball sampling. The in-depth, face-to-face interviews took from thirty minutes to two hours and, on average, lasted approximately one hour. Participants were offered gift cards to incentivize the interviews, and gift cards ranged from $5 to $10, depending on the length of the interview.

Interviews were semistructured; they were based on a list of questions as a guide, but the conversations were not limited to those questions. The guiding questions are as follows.

Do you currently work? By "work," I mean working outside the home for pay.
In the past week, how many hours did you work? What is your pay? How many hours do you normally work? What is your sector?
Have you ever worked as a babysitter? How many children did you care for? How long did you work as a babysitter? Did you have to drive the children anywhere? Did you have to plan activities? Did you do cooking or cleaning?
Have you ever worked in retail or service? Did you ever have to buy your uniform or purchase the clothes you were selling? Were you told to smile or change your accent?
What did you most enjoy about your job? What did you least enjoy about your job?

While majority of the interviews were one-on-one conversations, some of the participants, especially those who worked together at the same stores, wanted to be interviewed in pairs. I also reinterviewed some of the participants to request clarification or ask follow-up questions.

In addition, interviewees were asked to complete surveys, which included closed-ended questions about their demographic backgrounds (gender, age, race, income, marital status, and education). The surveys also allowed the participants to give background information on their past work experiences, including on topics such as work hours and shifts, night and weekend work, hourly wages, benefits, work expectations, management, and coworker relations. While participants of all in-depth interviews took the survey, not all survey participants were interviewed. The survey took fewer than ten minutes to complete, and participants who completed only the survey were not compensated.

Chapter 5

In this chapter, I look at the long-term effects on future income of working before seventeen. For the older sample, the exact age varies according to the wave of the study. Because data was not collected yearly on all participants, it is not possible to have exact start and end years for each. While it would have been more specific and much better to have exact ages, because of data collection limitations, that was not possible. Therefore, I define early work as work before seventeen and long-term effects as the effects evidenced by workers between twenty-seven and twenty-nine, since almost all are in that range. I estimated how working affects future earnings. I included education, income, number of hours worked as a teenager, and actual weight of the respondents as control variables. In addition to actual weight, I included respondents' own assessment of their own weight: whether they consider themselves overweight or underweight. The distribution of income is shown in Table A.4. The regression results are presented in Tables A.5–A.8.

TABLE A.4 DISTRIBUTION OF INCOME

Percentage	Income ($)
1	300
5	3,000
10	8,000
25	18,000
50	30,000
75	46,700
90	65,000
95	80,000
99	146,002

Source: NLSY97
Note: $N = 5,307$; mean = 35,413.97; standard deviation = 26,861.53.

TABLE A.5 OLS REGRESSION RESULTS PREDICTING INCOME

	Coefficient	Standard error	t	$p > t$
White	1,395.99	925.99	1.51	0.132
Black	−4,123.27	1,065.54	−3.87	0
Female	−13,781.10	7,742.72	−1.90	0.057
Education	6,593.93	258.00	25.56	0
Restaurant	−2,285.55	1,193.88	−1.91	0.056
Apparel	1,998.17	2,257.17	0.89	0.376
Construction	4,855.88	2,556.39	1.90	0.058
R's weight	−0.05	8.48	0.06	0.955
Weeks worked as a teen	7.93	33.32	0.24	0.812
Female × Weeks worked as a teen	113.66	55.79	2.04	0.042
R's perceived weight				
Underweight	1,999.38	5,592.17	0.36	0.721
Normal	2,619.59	5,122.96	0.51	0.609
Overweight	1,884.01	5,458.90	0.35	0.730
Very overweight	11,154.74	8,045.97	1.39	0.166
Female × Weeks worked × Perceived weight				
Underweight	−117.31	62.73	−1.87	0.062
Normal	−132.40	57.32	−2.31	0.021
Overweight	−126.94	9.17	−2.15	0.032
Very overweight	−29.60	77.46	−0.38	0.702
Constant	16,442.02	5,245.66	3.13	0.002

Source: NLSY97
Note: N = 4,668; $F(26, 4,641)$ = 41.47; $p > F$ = 0; R-squared = 0.1885; adjusted R-squared = 0.184; root-mean-square error = 24,137.

TABLE A.6 NET EFFECT FOR BOYS OF WORKING AS A TEENAGER ON FUTURE INCOME

Weeks worked	Expected adult income ($)	Standard error	Z	$P > Z$
0	36,267.84	990.7258	36.10	0
16	36,841.96	900.6701	40.91	0
53	38,169.60	712.3692	53.58	0
107	40,107.23	538.6021	74.47	0
164	42,152.51	592.8848	71.10	0
211	43,838.97	791.7547	55.37	0

Source: NLSY97
Note: These weeks correspond, respectively, to the 5th, 10th, 25th, 50th, 75th, and 90th percentiles of weeks worked as a teenager between the ages of sixteen and nineteen.

TABLE A.7 OLS REGRESSION RESULTS FOR EFFECTS OF THE INDUSTRY ON FUTURE INCOME

	Coefficient	Standard error	t	$p > t$
Weight as an adult	−26.8	8.923	−3.00	0.003
SAT math score	845.8	125.253	6.75	0
Ever married	769.7	866.142	0.89	0.374
Education	4917.7	442.022	11.13	0
White	−3911.1	1942.639	−2.01	0.044
White × Education	1650.4	538.303	2.83	0.005
Black	−1118.2	1228.608	−0.91	0.363
Grocery	−3993.8	2439.213	−1.64	0.102
Construction	−3200.8	8711.298	−0.37	0.713
Weeks worked as a teen	34.0	6.397	5.32	0
Working in service sector	4270.0	2698.761	1.58	0.114
Working in service × Number of weeks	−38.9	19.005	−2.04	0.041
Constant	17538.4	2245.214	7.81	0

Source: NLSY97
Note: N = 2,244; $F(12, 2,231)$ = 6,319; $p > F$ = 0; R-squared = 0.2537; adjusted R-squared = 0.2496; root-mean-square error = 19,429.

TABLE A.8 EFFECTS OF WORKING ON FEELING OVERWEIGHT

	Coefficient	Standard error	Z	$P > Z$
White	−0.1274	0.090236	−1.41	0.158
Black	0.0190	0.102724	0.19	0.853
Restaurants	−0.0246	0.120434	−2.05	0.041
R's weight	−0.0121	0.000658	−18.36	0
Perceived weight	−1.0692	0.053537	−19.97	0
Apparel	2.7642	1.184011	2.33	0.020
Apparel × Perceived weight	−1.0486	0.399827	−2.62	0.009
Constant	4.3394	0.205028	21.17	0

Source: NLSY97
Note: N = 4,372; likelihood ratio chi-squared(7) = 1,045.57; $p >$ chi-squared = 0; pseudo-chi-squared = 0.1812.

References

Abrams, K. K., L. R. Allen, and J. J. Gray. 1993. "Disordered Eating Attitudes and Behaviors, Psychological Adjustment, and Ethnic Identity: A Comparison of Black and White Female College Students." *International Journal of Eating Disorders* 14:49–57.

Abramson, Paul, and Ronald Inglehart. 1995. *Value Change in Global Perspective.* Ann Arbor: University of Michigan Press.

Acker, Joan. 1990. "Hierarchies, Jobs, Bodies: A Theory of Gendered Organizations." *Gender and Society* 4 (2): 139–158.

Ahn, Thomas, Peter Arcidiacono, Alvin Murphy, and Omari Swinton. 2010. "Explaining Cross-racial Differences in Teenage Labor Force Participation: Results from a Two-Sided Search Model." *Journal of Econometrics* 156:201–211.

Ajzen, Icek, and Martin Fishbein. 1977. "Attitude-Behavior Relations: A Theoretical Analysis and Review of Empirical Research." *Psychological Bulletin* 84 (5): 888–918.

Akan, G. E., and C. M. Grilo. 1995. "Sociocultural Influences on Eating Attitudes and Behaviors, Body Image, and Psychological Functioning: A Comparison of African-American, Asian-American, and Caucasian College Women." *International Journal of Eating Disorders* 18:181–187.

Aldrich, M., and R. Buchele. 1989. "Where to Look for Comparable Worth: The Implications of Efficiency Wages." In *Comparable Worth Analyses and Evidence*, edited by M. A. Hill and M. Killingsworth, 11–28. Ithaca, NY: ILR Press.

Alessio, John C., and Julie Andrzejewski. 2000. "Unveiling the Glass Ceiling: An Analysis of the Cohort Claim Effect." *American Sociological Review* 65:311–315.

Alexander, Karl L., Bruce K. Eckland, and Larry J. Griffin. 1975. "The Wisconsin Model of Socioeconomic Achievement: A Replication." *American Journal of Sociology* 81:324–342.

Allan, Janet D., Kelly Mayo, and Yvonne Michel. 1993. "Body Size Values of White and Black Women." *Research in Nursing and Health* 16:323–333.

Altonji, Joseph G., and Rebecca M. Blank. 1999. "Race and Gender in the Labor Market." In *Handbook of Labor Economics*, vol. 3C, edited by O. Ashenfelter and D. Card, 3143–3259. Amsterdam: Elsevier.

Amanatullah, Emily T., and Michael W. Morris. 2010. "Negotiating Gender Roles: Gender Differences in Assertive Negotiating Are Mediated by Women's Fear of Backlash and Attenuated when Negotiating on Behalf of Others." *Journal of Personality and Social Psychology* 98:256–267.

Anderson, Bridget. 2000. *Doing the Dirty Work? The Global Politics of Domestic Labour.* London: Zed Books.

Andreoni, James, and Lise Vesterlund. 2001. "Which Is the Fair Sex? Gender Differences in Altruism." *Quarterly Journal of Economics* 116 (1): 293–312.

Anthony, Susan B. 1868. "The Revolution." *Women's Suffrage Newspaper*, October 8.

Arons, Jessica. 2008. "Lifetime Losses: The Career Wage Gap." Available at https://cdn.americanprogress.org/wp-content/uploads/issues/2008/pdf/equal_pay.pdf.

Ashforth, Blake E., and Ronald H. Humphrey. 1993. "Emotional Labor in Service Roles: The Influence of Identity." *Academy of Management Review* 18 (1): 88–115.

Auwarter, Amy E., and Mara S. Aruguete. 2008. "Counselor Perceptions of Students Who Vary in Gender and Socioeconomic Status." *Social Psychology of Education* 11 (4): 389–395.

Babcock, Linda, and Sara Laschever. 2003. *Women Don't Ask: Negotiation and the Gender Divide.* Princeton, NJ: Princeton University Press.

Bachman, Jerald G., Deborah J. Safron, Susan Rogala Sy, and John E. Schulenberg. 2003. "Wishing to Work: New Perspectives on How Adolescents' Part-Time Work Intensity Is Linked with Educational Disengagement, Drug Use, and Other Problem Behaviours." *International Journal of Behavioral Development* 27:301–315.

Bachman, Jerald G., and John Schulenberg. 1993. "How Part-Time Work Intensity Relates to Drug Use, Problem Behavior, Time Use, and Satisfaction among High School Seniors: Are These Consequences or Merely Correlates?" *Developmental Psychology* 29:220–235.

Baughman, Reagan A., and Kristin E. Smith. 2011. "Labor Mobility of the Direct Care Workforce: Implications for the Provision of Long-Term Care." *Health Economics* 21 (12): 1402–1415.

Beck, E. M., Patrick M. Horan, and Charles M. Tolbert II. 1980. "Industrial Segmentation and Labor Market Discrimination." *Social Problems* 28 (2): 113–130.

Becker, Gary. 1964. *Human Capital.* New York: National Bureau of Economic Research.

Belkin, Lisa. 2003. "The Opt-Out Revolution." *New York Times*, October 26. Available at http://www.nytimes.com/2003/10/26/magazine/the-opt-out-revolution.html.

Belliveau, Maura A. 2005. "Blind Ambition? The Effects of Social Networks and Institutional Sex Composition on the Job Search Outcomes of Elite Coeducational and Women's College Graduates." *Organization Science* 16 (2): 134–141.

Berinsky, Adam J., Gregory A. Huber, and Gabriel S. Lenz. 2010. "Using Mechanical Turk as a Subject Recruitment Tool for Experimental Research." Available at http://qipsr.as.uky.edu/sites/default/files/Berinsky.Using%20Mechanical%20Turk%20as%20a%20Subject%20Recruitment%20Tool%20for%20Experimental%20Research.pdf.

Berinsky, Adam J., Michele F. Margolis, and Michael W. Sances. 2014. "Separating the Shirkers from the Workers? Making Sure Respondents Pay Attention on Self-Administered Surveys." *American Journal of Political Science* 58 (3): 739–753.

Berk, Richard A., and Sarah Fenstermaker Berk. 1979. *Labor and Leisure at Home: Content and Organization of the Household Day.* Newbury Park, CA: Sage.

Bertrand, Marianne, Claudia Goldin, and Lawrence F. Katz. 2010. "Dynamics of the Gender Gap for Young Professionals in the Financial and Corporate Sectors." *American Economic Journal: Applied Economics* 2 (3): 228–255.

Besen, Yasemin. 2006. "Exploitation or Fun? The Lived Experience of Teenage Employment in Suburban America." *Journal of Contemporary Ethnography* 35 (3): 319–340.

Besen-Cassino, Yasemin. 2013. "Cool Stores, Bad Jobs." *Contexts* 12 (4): 42–47.

———. 2014. *Consuming Work: Youth Labor in America.* Philadelphia: Temple University Press.

Bianchi, Suzanne M. 2011. "Family Change and Time Allocation in American Families." *The Annals of the American Academy of Political and Social Science* 638:21–44.

Bianchi, Suzanne M., Melissa A. Milkie, Liana C. Sayer, and John P. Robinson. 2000. "Is Anyone Doing the Housework? Trends in the Gender Division of Household Labor." *Social Forces* 79:191–228.

Bianchi, Suzanne M., Liana C. Sayer, Melissa A. Milkie, and John P. Robinson. 2012. "Housework: Who Did, Does or Will Do It, and How Much Does It Matter?" *Social Forces* 91 (1): 55–63.

Bielby, Denise D., and William T. Bielby. 1988. "She Works Hard for the Money." *American Journal of Sociology* 93:1031–1059.

Bielby, Denise D. V., and William T. Bielby. 1984. "Work Commitment, Sex-Role Attitudes, and Women's Employment." *American Sociological Review* 49 (2): 234–247.

Bielby, William T., and James N. Baron. 1986. "Men and Women at Work: Sex Segregation and Statistical Discrimination." *American Journal of Sociology* 91 (4): 759–799.

Bird, Sharon R. 1996. "Welcome to the Men's Club: Homosociality and the Maintenance of Hegemonic Masculinity." *Gender and Society* 10:120–132.

Bittman, Michael, Paula England, Liana Sayer, Nancy Folbre, and George Matheson. 2003. "When Does Gender Trump Money? Bargaining and Time in Household Work." *American Journal of Sociology* 109:186–214.

Blackburn, Robert, Jude Browne, Bradley Brooks, and Jennifer Jarman. 2002. "Explaining Gender Segregation." *British Journal of Sociology* 53:513–36.

Blair-Loy, Mary. 2005. *Competing Devotions: Career and Family among Women Executives.* Cambridge, MA: Harvard University Press.

Blank, Rebecca M. 2010. "The Impact of the Recession on Women." Presentation at the Congressional Breakfast Briefing, Washington, DC, January 21.

Blau, Francine D. 1977. *Equal Pay in the Office.* Lexington, MA: Lexington Books.

Blau, Francine D., Marienne A. Ferber, and Anne E. Winkler. 2006. *The Economics of Women, Men, and Work.* 5th ed. Upper Saddle River, NJ: Prentice Hall.

Blau, Francine D., and Lawrence M. Kahn. 2000. "Gender Differences in Pay." *Journal of Economic Perspectives* 14 (4): 75–99.

———. 2004. "The US Gender Pay Gap in the 1990s: Slowing Convergence." National Bureau of Economic Research Working Paper no. 10853. Available at http://www.nber.org/papers/w10853.pdf.

———. 2005. "Changes in the Labor Supply Behavior of Married Women: 1980–2000." National Bureau of Economic Research Working Paper no. 11230. Available at http://www.nber.org/papers/w11230.pdf.

———. 2006. "The Gender Pay Gap: Going, Going . . . but Not Gone." In *The Declining Significance of Gender*, edited by F. D. Blau, M. J. Brinton, and D. B. Grusky, 37–67. New York: Russell Sage Foundation.

Blinder, Alan S. 1973. "Wage Discrimination: Reduced Form and Structural Estimates." *Journal of Human Resources* 8 (4): 436–455.

Blum, Terry C., Dail L. Fields, and Jodi S. Goodman. 1994. "Organization-Level Determinants of Women in Management." *Academy of Management Journal* 37:241–268.

Blumstein, Alfred, and Joel Wallman. 2006. "The Crime Drop and Beyond." *Annual Review of Law and Social Science* 2:125–146.

Bobbitt-Zeher, Donna. 2007. "The Gender Income Gap and the Role of Education." *Sociology of Education* 80:1–22.

Bordo, Susan. 1993. *Unbearable Weight: Feminism, Western Culture, and the Body*. Berkeley: University of California Press.

Borghans, Lex, Bas ter Weel, and Bruce A. Weinberg. 2006. "People People: Social Capital and the Labor-Market Outcomes of Underrepresented Groups." National Bureau of Economic Research Working Paper no. 11985. Available at http://www.nber.org/papers/w11985.pdf.

Boring, Anne, Kellie Ottobani, and Philip B. Stark. 2016. "Student Evaluations of Teaching (Mostly) Do Not Measure Teaching Effectiveness." *Science Open Research*, January 7. Available at https://www.scienceopen.com/document?vid=818d8ec0-5908-47d8-86b4-5dc38f04b23e.

Bose, Christine, and Rachel Bridges-Whaley. 2011. "Sex Segregation in the United States Labor Force." In. *Feminist Frontiers*, 8th ed., edited by L. Rupp and Verta Taylor, 233–251. Boston: McGraw-Hill.

Boserup, Esther. 1970. *Women's Role in Economic Development*. London: Allen and Unwin.

Bound, John, Richard B. Freeman, and Jeff Grogger. 1992. "Arrests, Persistent Youth Joblessness, and Black/White Employment Differentials." *Review of Economics and Statistics* 74 (1): 100–106.

Bourdieu, Pierre. 1973. "Cultural Reproduction and Social Reproduction." In *Knowledge, Education, and Cultural Change*, edited by Richard Brown, 71–112. London: Tavistock.

———. (1980) 1990. *The Logic of Practice*. Stanford, CA: Stanford University Press.

Bourdieu, Pierre, and Jean-Claude Passeron. 1977. *Reproduction in Education, Society, and Culture*. Newbury Park, CA: Sage.

Bowles, Hannah Riley, and Linda Babcock. 2013. "How Can Women Escape the Compensation Negotiation Dilemma? Relational Accounts Are One Answer." *Psychology of Women Quarterly* 37 (1): 80–96.

Bowles, Hannah Riley, Linda Babcock, and Lei Lai. 2007. "Social Incentives for Gender Differences in the Propensity to Initiate Negotiations: Sometimes It Does Hurt to Ask." *Organizational Behavior and Human Decision Processes* 103:84–103.

Bowles, Hannah Riley, Linda Babcock, and Kathleen McGinn. 2005. "Constraints and Triggers: Situational Mechanics of Gender in Negotiation." *Journal of Personality and Social Psychology* 89:951–965.

Bowles, Samuel, Herb Gintis, and Melissa Osborne. 2001. "The Determinants of Earnings: A Behavioral Approach." *Journal of Economic Literature* 39 (4): 1137–1176.

Bozkurt, Ödül, and Irena Grugulis. 2011. "Why Retail Work Demands a Closer Look." In *Retail Work*, edited by Irena Grugulis and Ödül Bozkurt, 1–21. London: Palgrave Macmillan.

Brewster, Karin L., and Irene Padavic. 2000. "Change in Gender-Ideology, 1977–1996: The Contributions of Intracohort Change and Population Turnover." *Journal of Marriage and Family* 62:477–487.

Bridges, Judith S. 1989. "Sex Differences in Occupational Values." *Sex Roles* 20:205–211.

Bridges, Tristan, and C.J. Pascoe. 2014. "Hybrid Masculinities: New Directions in the Sociology of Men and Masculinities." *Sociology Compass* 8 (3): 246–258.

Britton, Dana. M. 1999. "Cat Fights and Gang Fights: Preference for Work in a Male-Dominated Organization." *Sociological Quarterly* 40 (3): 455–474.

———. 2000. "The Epistemology of the Gendered Organization." *Gender and Society* 14 (3): 418–434.

Brown, Charles, and Mary Corcoran. 1997. "Sex-Based Differences in School Content and the Male-Female Wage Gap." *Journal of Labor Economics* 15 (3): 431–465.

Browne, Irene, and Ivy Kennelly. 2006. "Stereotypes and Realities: Images of Black Women in the Labor Market." In *Race, Work, and Family in the Lives of African Americans*, edited by M. Durr and S. A. Hill, 185–208. Lanham, MD: Rowman and Littlefield.

Brumley, Krista M. 2014. "The Gendered Ideal Worker Narrative: Professional Women's and Men's Work Experiences in the New Economy at a Mexican Company." *Gender and Society* 28 (6): 799–823.

Budig, Michelle J. 2002. "Male Advantage and the Gender Composition of Jobs: Who Rides the Glass Escalator?" *Social Problems* 49 (2): 258–277.

Budig, Michelle J., and Paula England. 2001. "Wage Penalty for Motherhood." *American Sociological Review* 66:204–225.

Buhrmester, Michael, Tracy Kwang, and Samuel D. Gosling. 2011. "Amazon's Mechanical Turk a New Source of Inexpensive, yet High-Quality, Data." *Perspectives on Psychological Science* 6:3–5.

Bureau of Labor Statistics. 2011. "School's Out." Available at https://www.bls.gov/spotlight/2011/schools_out.

———. 2013. "Women's Earnings, 1979–2012." Available at https://www.bls.gov/opub/ted/2013/ted_20131104.htm.

———. 2014. "Women in the Labor Force: A Databook." Available at http://www.bls.gov/cps/wlf-databook-2013.pdf.

———. 2015. *Occupational Outlook Handbook*. Available at https://www.bls.gov/ooh.

———. 2016. "Employment and Unemployment among Youth Summary." Available at https://www.bls.gov/news.release/youth.nr0.htm.

Bushway, Shawn, and Peter Reuter. 2001. "Labor Markets and Crime." In *Crime: Public Policies for Crime Control*, edited by James Wilson and Joan Petersilia, 191–224. San Francisco: ICS Press.

Butler, Judith. 1993. *Bodies that Matter: On the Discursive Limits of Sex*. New York: Routledge.

Calas, Marta B., and Linda Smircich. 1997. "Predicando la Moral en Calzoncillos? Feminist Inquiries into Business Ethics." In *Women's Studies and Business Ethics:*

Toward a New Conversation, edited by Edward Freeman and Andrea Larson, 50–79. New York: Oxford University Press.

Calasanti, Toni M. 2001. "Retirement: *Golden Years* for Whom?" In *Gender Mosaics: Social Perspectives*, edited by Dana Vannoy, 300–310. Los Angeles: Roxbury.

Callaghan, George, and Paul Thompson. 2002. "'We Recruit Attitude': The Selection and Shaping of Routine Call Centre Labour." *Journal of Management Studies* 39 (2): 233–254.

Campbell, Hugh. 2000. "The Glass Phallus: Pub(lic) Masculinity and Drinking in Rural New Zealand." *Rural Sociology* 65 (4): 562–581.

Canny, Angela. 2002. "Flexible Labour? The Growth of Student Employment in the UK." *Journal of Education and Work* 15 (3): 277–301.

Caraway, Teri. 2007. *Assembling Women: The Feminization of Global Manufacturing*. Ithaca, NY: Cornell University Press.

Carey, Max, and Alan Eck. 1984. "How Workers Get Their Training." *Occupational Outlook Quarterly* 28 (4): 3–21.

Carr, Rhoda V., James D. Wright, and Charles J. Brody. 1996. "Effects of High School Work Experience a Decade Later: Evidence from the National Longitudinal Survey." *Sociology of Education* 69 (1): 66–81.

Carrell, Scott E., Marianne E. Page, and James West. 2010. "Sex and Science: How Professor Gender Perpetuates the Gender Wage Gap." *Quarterly Journal of Public Economics* 125 (3): 1101–1144.

Casselman, Ben. 2016. "Poor Kids Need Summer Jobs; Rich Kids Get Them." *FiveThirtyEight*, July 1. Available at https://fivethirtyeight.com/features/poor-kids -need-summer-jobs-rich-kids-get-them.

Cassirer, Naomi, and Barbara F. Reskin. 2000. "High Hopes: Organizational Position, Employment Experiences, and Women's and Men's Promotion Aspirations." *Work and Occupations* 27 (4): 438–463.

Castagnetti, Carolina, and Luisa Rosti. 2013. "Unfair Tournament: Gender Stereotyping and Wage Discrimination among Italian Graduates." *Gender and Society* 27 (5): 630–658.

Charles, Maria. 2003. "Deciphering Sex Segregation: Vertical and Horizontal Inequalities in Ten National Labor Markets." *Acta Sociologica* 46 (4): 267–287.

Charles, Maria, and Karen Bradley. 2009. "Indulging Our Gendered Selves? Sex Segregation by Field of Study in 44 Countries." *American Journal of Sociology* 114 (4): 925–976.

Cheng, Cliff. 1996. *Masculinities in Organizations*. Thousand Oaks, CA: Sage.

Chodorow, Nancy. 1978. *The Reproduction of Mothering*. Berkeley: University of California Press.

Chorn-Dunham, Charlotte, and Bernadette E. Dietz. 2003. "If I'm Not Allowed to Out My Family Members First: Challenges Experienced by Women Who Are Caregiving for Family Members with Dementia." *Journal of Women and Aging* 15 (1): 55–70.

Cockburn, Cynthia. 1988. *Machinery of Dominance: Women, Men, and Technical Know-How*. Boston: Northeastern University Press.

Cohen, Philip N., and Matt L. Huffman. 2003. "Occupational Segregation and the Devaluation of Women's Work across U.S. Labor Markets." *Social Forces* 81:881–908.

————. 2007. "Working for the Woman? Female Managers and the Gender Wage Gap." *American Sociological Review* 72:681–704.

Collinson, David L., and Margaret Collinson. 2004. "The Power of Time: Leadership, Management and Gender." In *Fighting for Time: Shifting the Boundaries of Work and Social Life*, edited by C. F. Epstein and A. L. Kalleberg, 219–246. New York: Russell Sage Foundation.

Collinson, David, and Jeff Hearn. 1994. "Naming Men as Men: Implications for Work, Organization, and Management." *Gender, Work and Organization* 1:2–22.

————. 1996. "Breaking the Silence: On Men, Masculinities, and Managements." In *Men as Managers, Managers as Men: Critical Perspectives on Men, Masculinities, and Managements*, edited by David L. Collinson and Jeff Hearn, 1–24. London: Sage.

Coltrane, Scott. 2010. "Gender Theory and Household Labor." *Sex Roles* 63:791–800.

Coltrane, Scott, and Michele Adams. 2001. "Men's Family Work: Child-Centered Fathering and the Sharing of Domestic Labor." In *Working Families: The Transformation of the American Home*, edited by R. Hertz and N. Marshall, 72–99. Berkeley: University of California Press.

Connell, R. W. 1987. *Gender and Power: Society, the Person, and Sexual Politics*. Stanford, CA: Stanford University Press.

————. 1995. *Masculinities*. Berkeley: University of California Press.

Corbett, William R. 2007. "The Ugly Truth about Appearance Discrimination and the Beauty of Our Employment Discrimination Law." *Duke Journal of Gender Law and Policy* 14:153–178.

Corcoran, Mary, and Greg J. Duncan. 1979. "Work History, Labor Force Attachments, and Earning Differences between the Races and Sexes." *Journal of Human Resources* 14 (1): 3–20.

Corcoran, Mary, Roger Gordon, Deborah Laren, and Gary Solon. 1992. "The Association between Men's Economic Status and Their Family and Community Origins." *Journal of Human Resources* 27 (4): 575–601.

Correll, Shelley J. 2001. "Gender and the Career Choice Process: The Role of Biased Self-Assessments." *American Journal of Sociology* 106:1691–1730.

————. 2004. "Constraints into Preferences: Gender, Status, and Emerging Career Aspirations." *American Sociological Review* 69:93–113.

Correll, Shelley J., Stephen Benard, and In Paik. 2007. "Getting a Job: Is There a Motherhood Penalty?" *American Journal of Sociology* 112 (5): 1297–1339.

Cotter, David A., Joan Hermsen, Seth Ovadia, and Reeve Vanneman. 2001. "The Glass Ceiling Effect." *Social Forces* 80 (2): 655–682.

Coverdill, James E. 1988. "The Dual Economy and Sex Differences in Earnings." *Social Forces* 66: 970–993.

Creed, Peter A., Juanita Jean Muller, and Wendy Patton. 2003. "Leaving High School: The Influence and Consequences for Psychological Well-Being and Career-Related Confidence." *Journal of Adolescence* 26:295–311.

Crittenden, Ann. 2001. *The Price of Motherhood: Why the Most Important Job in the World Is Still the Least Valued*. New York: Henry Holt.

Crow, Stephen M., Lillian Y. Fok, and Sandra J. Hartman. 1998. "Who Is at Greatest Risk of Work-Related Discrimination—Women, Blacks, or Homosexuals?" *Employee Responsibilities and Rights Journal* 11 (1): 15–26.

Csikszentmihalyi, Mihaly, and Barbara Schneider. 2000. *Becoming Adult: How Teenagers Prepare for the World of Work.* New York: Basic Books.

Cuddy, Amy J. C., Susan T. Fiske, and Peter Glick. 2004. "When Professionals Become Mothers, Warmth Doesn't Cut the Ice." *Journal of Social Issues* 60 (4):701–718.

D'Amico, Ronald. 1984. "Does Employment during High School Impair Academic Progress?" *Sociology of Education* 57:152–164.

D'Amico, Ronald, and Paula Baker. 1984. *Pathways to the Future.* Columbus: Ohio State University Center for Human Resource Research.

Davidson, Adam. 2012. "The Best Nanny Money Can Buy." *New York Times Magazine,* March 20. Available at http://www.nytimes.com/2012/03/25/magazine/the-best-nanny-money-can-buy.html.

Davis, Alyssa, and Elise Gould. 2015. "Closing the Pay Gap and Beyond: A Comprehensive Strategy for Improving Economic Security for Women and Families." Economic Policy Institute Briefing Paper 412. Available at http://www.epi.org/publication/closing-the-pay-gap-and-beyond/.

Dellinger, Kirsten, and Christine L. Williams. 2002. "The Locker Room and the Dorm Room: Workplace Norms and the Boundaries of Sexual Harassment in Magazine Editing." *Social Problems* 49 (2): 242–257.

DeSilver, Drew. 2015. "For Young Americans, Unemployment Returns to Pre-recession Levels." Pew Research Center, May 8. Available at http://www.pewresearch.org/fact-tank/2015/05/08/for-young-americans-unemployment-returns-to-pre-recession-levels/.

Desmond, Sharon M., James H. Price, Christopher Hallinan, and Daisy Smith. 1989. "Black and White Adolescents' Perceptions of their Weight." *Journal of School Health* 59:353–358.

DeVault, Marjorie L. 1991. *Feeding the Family: The Social Organization of Caring as a Gendered Work.* Chicago: University of Chicago Press.

———. 1999. "Comfort and Struggle: Emotion Work in Family Life." *Annals of the American Academy of Political and Social Science* 561:52–63.

Dill, Barry Thornton. 1994. "Fictive Kin, Paper Sons, and Compadrazgo: Women of Color and the Struggle for Family Survival." In *Women of Color in US Society,* edited by Maxine Baca Zinn and Bonnie Thornton Dill, 149–170. Philadelphia: Temple University Press.

Dodson, Lisa, and Rebekah M. Zincavage. 2015. "It's Like a Family: Caring Labor, Exploitation, and Race in Nursing Homes." *Gender and Society* 21 (6): 905–928.

Douglas, Mary. 1966. *Purity and Danger.* London: Routledge and Kegan Paul.

Duffy, Mignon. 2005. "Reproducing Labor Inequalities: Challenges for Feminists Conceptualizing Care at the Intersections of Gender, Race, and Class." *Gender and Society* 19 (1): 66–82.

———. 2011. *Making Care Count.* New Brunswick, NJ: Rutgers University Press.

Duffy, Mignon, Randy Albelda, and Clare Hammonds. 2013. "Counting Care Work: The Empirical and Policy Applications of Care Theory." *Social Problems* 60 (2): 145–167.

Duffy, Mignon, Amy Armenia, and Clare L. Stacey. 2015. *Caring on the Clock: The Complexities and Contradictions of Paid Care Work.* New Brunswick, NJ: Rutgers University Press.

Duncan, Kevin C. 1996. "Gender Differences in the Effect of Education on the Slope of Experience-Earnings Profiles: NLSY, 1979–1988." *American Journal of Economics and Sociology* 55 (4): 457–471.

Eagly, Alice H. 2007. "Female Leadership Advantage and Disadvantage: Resolving the Contradictions." *Psychology of Women Quarterly* 31:1–12.

Edwards, Kathryn Anne, and Alexander Hertel-Fernandez. 2010. "The Kids Aren't Alright: Labor Market Analysis of Young Workers." Economic Policy Institute Briefing Paper no. 258. Available at http://www.epi.org/publication/bp258.

Ehrenreich, Barbara. 2001. *Nickel and Dimed: On (Not) Getting By in America*. New York: Picador.

Ely, Robin J., and Debra Meyerson. 2000. "Theories of Gender in Organizations: A New Approach to Organizational Analysis and Change." *Research in Organizational Behavior* 22:103–151.

Engels, Fredrich. (1884) 1972. *The Origins of the Family, Private Property, and the State*. New York: International.

England, Paula. 1997. "The Sex Gap in Pay." In *Workplace/Women's Place*, edited by Dana Dunn, 74–87. Los Angeles: Roxbury.

———. 2005. "Gender Inequality in Labor Markets: The Role of Motherhood and Segregation." *Social Politics* 12:264–288.

———. 2010. "The Gender Revolution: Uneven and Stalled." *Gender and Society* 24 (2): 149–166.

England, Paula, Michelle Budig, and Nancy Folbre. 2002. "Wages of Virtue: The Relative Pay of Care Work." *Social Problems* 49 (4): 455–473.

England, Paula, and Nancy Folbre. 2005. "Gender and Economic Sociology." In *Handbook of Economic Sociology*, 2nd ed., edited by Neil J. Smelser and Richard Swedberg, 627–649. Princeton, NJ: Princeton University Press.

England, Paula, Joan M. Hermsen, and David A. Cotter. 2000. "The Devaluation of Women's Work: A Comment on Tam." *American Journal of Sociology* 105:1741–1751.

England, Paula, and Su Li. 2006. "Desegregation Stalled: The Changing Gender Composition of College Majors, 1971–2002." *Gender and Society* 20:657–777.

Entwisle, Doris R., Karl L. Alexander, and Linda Steffel Olson. 2000. "Early Work Histories of Urban Youth." *American Sociological Review* 65 (2): 279–297.

Epstein, Cynthia Fuchs. 2004. "Border Crossings: The Constraints of the Time Norms in Transgressions of Gender and Professional Roles." In *Fighting for Time: Shifting Boundaries of Work and Social Life*, edited by Cynthia Fuchs Epstein and Arne L. Kalleberg, 317–340. New York: Russell Sage Foundation.

Epstein, Cynthia Fuchs, Carroll Seron, Bonnie Oglensky, and Robert Saute. 1999. *The Part-Time Paradox: Time Norms, Professional Life, Family, and Gender*. New York: Routledge.

Erickson, Rebecca, and Clare L. Stacey. 2013. "Attending to Mind and Body: Engaging the Complexity of Emotion Practice among Caring Professionals." In *Emotional Labor in the 21st Century: Diverse Perspectives on Emotion Regulation at Work*, edited by A. A. Grandley, J. M. Diefendorff, and D. E. Rupp, 175–196. New York: Routledge.

Farrell, Warren. 2005. *Why Men Earn More: The Startling Truth behind the Pay Gap—and What Women Can Do about It*. New York: Amacom.

Feagin, Joe R. 2006. *Systemic Racism: A Theory of Oppression.* New York: Taylor and Francis.

Ferber, Marianne A., and Joe L. Spaeth. 1984. "Work Characteristics and the Male-Female Earnings Gap." *American Economic Review* 74:260–264.

Ferguson, Ann. 2013. "Making a Name for Yourself: Transgressive Acts and Gender Performance." In *Men's Lives*, edited by Michael S. Kimmel and Michael Messner, 80–93. Boston: Pearson.

Finch, Michael D., Michael J. Shanahan, Jeylan T. Mortimer, and Ryu Seongryeol. 1991. "Work Experience and Control Orientation in Adolescence." *American Sociological Review* 56:597–611.

Fisher, Cynthia D. 2000. "Mood and Emotions while Working: Missing Pieces of Job Satisfaction?" *Journal of Organizational Behavior* 21 (2): 185–202.

Fligstein, Neil, and Taekjin Shin. 2003. "Shareholder Value and the Transformation of the U.S. Economy, 1984–2000." *Sociological Forum* 22 (4): 399–424.

Folbre, Nancy. 2002. *The Invisible Heart: Economics and Family Values.* New York: New Press.

Folbre, Nancy, and Julie A. Nelson. 2000. "For Love or Money—or Both?" *Journal of Economic Perspectives* 14 (4): 123–140.

Fortin, Nicole M. 2008. "The Gender Wage Gap among Young Adults in the United States: The Importance of Money versus People." *Journal of Human Resources* 43 (4): 884–918.

Foucault, Michel. 1979. *Discipline and Punish: The Birth of the Prison.* New York: Vintage Books.

Fox, Suzy, and Paul E. Spector. 2000. "Relations of Emotional Intelligence, Practical Intelligence, General Intelligence, and Trait Affectivity with Interview Outcomes: It's Not All Just 'G.'" *Journal of Organizational Behavior* 21 (2): 203–220.

Freeman, Richard B. 1983. "Crime and Unemployment." In *Crime and Public Policy*, edited by James Q. Wilson, 89–106. San Francisco: Institute for Contemporary Studies Press.

Frenkel, Stephen J. 2003. "The Embedded Character of Workplace Relations." *Work and Occupations* 30 (2): 135–153.

Fuller, Rex, and Richard Schoenberger. 1991. "The Gender Salary Gap: Do Academic Achievement, Internship Experience, and College Major Make a Difference?" *Social Science Quarterly* 72:715–726.

Fuller, Sylvia. 2008. "Job Mobility and Wage Trajectories for Men and Women in the United States." *American Sociological Review* 73:158–183.

Furnham, Adrian, and Michael Argyle. 1998. *The Psychology of Money.* London: Routledge.

Gallagher, Dolores, Jonathon Rose, Patricia Rivera, Steven Lovett, and Larry W. Thompson. 1989. "Prevalence of Depression in Family Caregivers." *The Gerontologist* 29 (4): 449–456.

Garcia-Lopez, Gladys. 2008. "'Nunca Te Toman en Cuenta' [They never take you into account]: The Challenges of Inclusion and Strategies for Success of Chicana Attorneys." *Gender and Society* 22 (5): 590–612.

Gardecki, Rosella M. 2001. "Racial Differences in Youth Employment." *Monthly Labor Review* 124 (8): 51–67.

Garey, Anita Ilta, and Karen V. Hansen. 2011. "Introduction: An Eye on Emotion in the Study of Families and Work." In *At the Heart of Work and Family: Engaging the Ideas of Arlie Hochschild*, edited by Anita Ilta Garey and Karen V. Hansen, 1–14. New Brunswick, NJ: Rutgers University Press.

Gatta, Mary. 2009. "Restaurant Servers, Tipping, and Resistance." *Qualitative Research in Accounting and Management* 6 (1–2): 70–82.

———. 2011. "In the Blink of an Eye: American High-End Small Retail Businesses and the Public Workforce System." In *Retail Work*, edited by Irena Grugulis and Ödül Bozkurt, 49–67. London: Palgrave Macmillan.

———. 2014. *All I Want Is a Job*. Stanford, CA: Stanford University Press.

Gatta, Mary L., and Patricia A. Roos. 2005. "Rethinking Occupational Integration." *Sociological Forum* 20 (3): 369–402.

Gauchat, Gordon, Maura Kelly, and Michael Wallace. 2012. "Occupational Gender Segregation, Globalization, and Gender Earnings Inequality in US Metropolitan Areas." *Gender and Society* 26 (5): 718–747.

Gecas, Viktor. 1979. "The Influence of Social Class on Socialization." In *Contemporary Theories about the Family*, vol. 1, *Research-Based Theories*, edited by Wesley R. Burr, Reuben Hill, F. Ivan Nye, and Ira L. Reiss, 365–404. New York: Free Press.

George, Linda K., and Lisa P. Gwyther. 1986. "Caregiver Well-Being: A Multi-dimensional Examination of Family Caregivers of Demented Adults." *The Gerontologist* 26 (2): 253–260.

Girod, Roger, Yves Fricker, and Andras Korffy. 1973. "Counter-mobility." In *Social Stratification and Career Mobility*, edited by Walter Muller and Karl Ulrich, 17–27. Paris: Mouton.

Glaser, Barney G., and Anselm L. Strauss. 1965. *Awareness of Dying*. Chicago: Aldine.

———. 1967. *The Discovery of Grounded Theory: Strategies for Qualitative Research*. Chicago: Aldine.

Gneezy, Uri, Muriel Niederle, and Aldo Rustichini. 2003. "Performance in Competitive Environments: Gender Differences." *Quarterly Journal of Economics* 118 (3): 1049–1074.

Goldin, Claudia. 1990. *Understanding the Gender Gap: An Economic History of American Women*. New York: Oxford University Press.

Goldin, Claudia, and Lawrence F. Katz. 2007. "Long-Run Changes in the U.S. Wage Structure: Narrowing, Widening, and Polarizing." *Brookings Papers on Economic Activity* 2:135–165.

Goldin, Claudia, and Solomon Polachek. 1987. "Residual Differences by Sex: Perspectives on the Gender Gap in Earnings." *American Economic Review* 77 (2): 143–151.

Goldsmith, Arthur H., Jonathan R. Veum, and William Darity. 1997. "The Impact of Psychological and Human Capital on Wages." *Economic Inquiry* 35 (4): 815–829.

Goldstein, Bernard, and Jack Oldham. 1979. *Children and Work: A Study of Socialization*. New Brunswick, NJ: Transaction Books.

Gottfried, Heidi. 2003. "Temp(t)ing Bodies: Shaping Gender at Work in Japan." *Sociology: Journal of the British Sociological Association* 37:257–276.

———. 2013. *Gender, Work, and Economy: Unpacking the Global Economy*. Cambridge, MA: Polity.

Gould, Elise. 2015. "Child Care Workers Aren't Paid Enough to Make Ends Meet." Economic Policy Institute Issue Brief no. 405. Available at http://www.epi.org/publication/child-care-workers-arent-paid-enough-to-make-ends-meet.

Granovetter, Mark. 1973. "The Strength of Weak Ties." *American Journal of Sociology* 78 (6): 1360–1380.

Greenberger, Ellen, and Laurence D. Steinberg. 1983. "Sex Differences in Early Labor Force Experience: Harbinger of Things to Come." *Social Forces* 62 (2): 467–486.

———. 1986. *When Teenagers Work: The Psychological and Social Costs of Adolescent Employment.* New York: Basic Books.

Groshen, Erica L. 1991. "The Structure of the Female/Male Wage Differential. Is It Who You Are, What You Do, or Where You Work?" *Journal of Human Resources* 26 (3): 457–472.

Groves, Melissa Osborne. 2005. "How Important Is Your Personality? Labor Market Returns to Personality for Women in the US and UK." *Journal of Economic Psychology* 26 (6): 827–841.

Grugulis, Irena, and Ödül Bozkurt. 2011. *Retail Work.* London: Palgrave Macmillan.

Gruys, Kjerstin. 2012. "Does This Make Me Look Fat? Aesthetic Labor and Fat Talk as Emotional Labor in a Women's Plus-Size Clothing Store." *Social Problems* 49:481–500.

Guy, Mary E., and Meredith A. Newman. 2004. "Women's Jobs, Men's Jobs: Sex Segregation and Emotional Labor." *Public Administration Review* 64 (3): 289–298.

Hansen, David M., and Patricia Jarvis. 2000. "Adolescent Employment and Psychological Outcomes: A Comparison of Two Employment Contexts." *Youth and Society* 31 (4): 417–436.

Hansen, Karen, and Ilene Philipson. 1990. *Women, Class, and the Feminist Imagination: A Socialist Feminist Reader.* Philadelphia: Temple University Press.

Harlow, Roxana. 2003. "'Race Doesn't Matter, but . . .': The Effect of Race on Professors' Experiences and Emotion Management in the Undergraduate College Classroom." *Social Psychology Quarterly* 66 (4): 348–363.

Haveman, Heather A., and Lauren S. Beresford. 2012. "If You're So Smart, Why Aren't You the Boss? Explaining the Persistent Vertical Gender Gap in Management." *Annals of the American Academy of Political and Social Science* 639:114–130.

Hearn, Jeff, and Wendy Parkin. 2001. *Gender, Sexuality and Violence in Organizations.* Thousand Oaks, CA: Sage.

Heckman, James, Jora Stixrud, and Sergio Urzua. 2006. "The Effects of Cognitive and Noncognitive Abilities on Labor Market Outcomes and Social Behavior." *Journal of Labor Economics* 24 (3): 411–482.

Hegewisch, Ariane, and Angela Edwards. 2012. "The Gender Wage Gap: 2011." *Institute for Women's Policy Research Fact Sheet*, September. Available at https://iwpr.org/wp-content/uploads/wpallimport/files/iwpr-export/publications/C350%20September%202012%20update.pdf.

Hegewisch, Ariane, and Claudia Williams. 2013. "The Gender Wage Gap: 2012." *Institute for Women's Policy Research Fact Sheet*, September. Available at https://iwpr.org/wp-content/uploads/wpallimport/files/iwpr-export/publications/Gender%20Wage%20Gap%20FS%20Sep%202013_FINAL2.pdf.

Henson, Kevin, and Jackie Krasas Rogers. 2001. "'Why Marcia You've Changed!' Male Clerical Temporary Workers Doing Masculinity in a Feminized Occupation." *Gender and Society* 15 (2): 218–238.

Herman, Alexis M. 2000. "Report on the Youth Labor Force." Available at https://www.bls.gov/opub/rylf/pdf/rylf2000.pdf.

Hersch, Joni, and Leslie L. Stratton. 1997. "Housework, Fixed Effects, Wages of Married Workers." *Journal of Human Resources* 32 (2): 285–307.

Herzog, A. Regula. 1982. "High School Students' Occupational Plans and Values: Trends in Sex Differences 1976 through 1980." *Sociology of Education* 55 (1): 1–13.

Higgins, Monica C., and Kathy E. Kram. 2001. "Reconceptualizing Mentoring at Work: A Developmental Network Perspective." *Academy of Management Review* 26:264–288.

Himmelweit, Susan. 1999. "Caring Labor." *Annals of the American Academy of Political Science* 561:52–63.

Hirschman, Charles, and Irina Voloshin. 2007. "The Structure of Teenage Employment: Social Background and the Jobs Held by High School Seniors." *Research in Social Stratification and Mobility* 25:189–203.

Hochschild, Arlie Russell. 1979. "Emotion Work, Feeling Rules, and Social Structure." *American Journal of Sociology* 85 (3): 551–575.

———. 1983. *The Managed Heart: Commercialization of Human Feeling.* Berkeley: University of California Press.

———. 1989. *The Second Shift.* New York: Viking Penguin.

———. 2003. *The Commercialization of Intimate Life: Notes from Home and Work.* Berkeley: University of California Press.

Hodson, Randy, and Paula England. 1986. "Industrial Structure and Sex Differences in Earnings." *Industrial Relations* 25 (1): 16–32.

Hogue, Mary, Cathy L. Z. DuBois, and Lee Fox-Cardamone. 2010. "Gender Differences in Pay Expectations: The Roles of Job Intention and Self-View." *Psychology of Women Quarterly* 34 (2): 215–227.

Hondagneu-Sotelo, Pierrette. 2007. *Domestica: Immigrant Workers Cleaning and Caring in the Shadows of Affluence.* 2nd ed. Berkeley: University of California Press.

Horend, I., and L. Perdue. 1990. "Bingeing, Purging, and Developmental Changes in Parental Concern for Achievement." Paper presented at the annual meeting of the American Psychological Association, Boston, August 10–14.

Horton, John J., David G. Rand, and Richard J. Zeckhauser. 2011. "The Online Laboratory: Conducting Experiments in a Real Labor Market." *Experimental Economics* 14:399–425.

Horvath, Michael, and Ann Marie Ryan. 2003. "Antecedents and Potential Moderators of the Relationship between Attitudes and Hiring Discrimination on the Basis of Sexual Orientation." *Sex Roles* 48:115–130.

Huddleston, Prue. 2011. "'It's Alright for Saturdays, but Not Forever': The Employment of Part-Time Student Staff in the Retail Sector." In *Retail Work*, edited by Irena Grugulis and Ödül Bozkurt, 109–128. London: Palgrave Macmillan.

Huffman, Matt L., and Philip N. Cohen. 2004. "Occupational Segregation and the Gender Gap in Workplace Authority: National versus Local Labor Markets." *Sociological Forum* 19:121–147.

Hultin, Mia. 2003. "Mechanisms of Inequality: Unequal Access to Organizational Power and the Gender Wage Gap." *European Sociological Review* 19:143–159.

Ibarra, Herminia, Nancy M. Carter, and Christine Silva. 2010. "Why Men Still Get More Promotions than Women." *Harvard Business Review* 88:80–85.

Jacobs, Jerry. 1989. *Revolving Doors.* Stanford, CA: Stanford University Press.

Jacobs, Jerry A., and Kathleen Gerson. 2004. *The Time Divide*. Cambridge, MA: Harvard University Press.

Jacobs, Jerry A., David Karen, and Katherine McClelland. 1991. "The Dynamics of Young Men's Career Aspirations." *Sociological Forum* 6:609–639.

Jacobs, Jerry A., and Ronnie J. Steinberg 1990. "Compensating Differentials and the Male-Female Wage Gap: Evidence from the New York State Comparable Worth Study." *Social Forces* 69 (2): 439–468.

Johnson, Monica Kirkpatrick. 2001. "Change in Job Values during the Transition to Adulthood." *Work and Occupations* 28:315–345.

———. 2002. "Social Origins, Adolescent Experiences, and Work Value Trajectories during the Transition to Adulthood." *Social Forces* 80 (4): 1307–1340.

Kalleberg, Arne L. 1977. "Work Values and Job Rewards: A Theory of Job Satisfaction." *American Sociological Review* 42:124–143.

———. 2011. *Good Jobs, Bad Jobs: The Rise of Polarized and Precarious Employment Systems in the United States 1970s to 2000s*. New York: Russell Sage Foundation.

Kalleberg, Arne L., Barbara F. Reskin, and Ken Hudson. 2000. "Bad Jobs in America: Standard and Nonstandard Employment Relations and Job Quality." *American Sociological Review* 65 (2): 256–278.

Kaman, Vicki S., and Charmine E. J. Hartel. 1994. "Gender Differences in Anticipated Pay Negotiation Strategies and Outcomes." *Journal of Business and Psychology* 9:183–197.

Kane, Michael. 1991. "The Existence of Gender Biased Counseling of Female Students by High School Guidance Counselors." Available at http://files.eric.ed.gov/fulltext/ED350492.pdf.

Kang, Miliann. 2003. "The Managed Hand: The Commercialization of Bodies and Emotions in Korean Immigrant-Owned Nail Salons." *Gender and Society* 17 (6): 820–839.

———. 2010. *The Managed Hand: Race, Gender, and the Body in Beauty Service Work*. Oakland: University of California Press.

Kang, Sonia K., Katherine A. DeCelles, András Tilcsik, and Sora Jun. 2016. "Whitened Résumés: Race and Self-Presentation in the Labor Market." *Administrative Science Quarterly* 61 (3): 469–502.

Kanter, Rosabeth Moss. (1977) 1993. *Men and Women of the Corporation*. 2nd ed. New York: Basic Books.

Kerfoot, Deborah, and David Knights. 1996. "The Best Is yet to Come? The Quest for Embodiment in Managerial Work." In *Men as Managers, Managers as Men: Critical Perspectives on Men, Masculinities and Managements*, edited by D.L. Collinson and J. Hearn, 659–679. London: Sage.

Kilbourne, Jean. 1994. "Toward a New Model for the Prevention of Eating Disorders." In *Feminist Perspectives on Eating Disorders*, edited by P. Fallon, M. A. Katzman, and S. C. Wooley, 395–419. New York: Guilford.

Killing Us Softly 4: Advertising's Image of Women. 2010. Directed by Sut Jhally. Northampton, MA: Media Education Foundation.

Kimmel, Michael. 1994. "Masculinity as Homophobia: Fear, Shame, and Silence in the Construction of Gender Identity." In *Theorizing Masculinities*, edited by Harry Brod and Michael Kaufman, 119–142. Thousand Oaks, CA: Sage.

———. 2000. *The Gendered Society*. New York: Oxford University Press.

————. 2015. *The Gendered Society.* 5th ed. New York: Oxford University Press.

————. 2016. *The Gendered Society.* 6th ed. Boston: Pearson.

King, Gary, Michael Tomz, and Jason Wittenberg. 2000. "Making the Most of Statistical Analyses: Improving Interpretation and Presentation." *American Journal of Political Science* 44 (2): 341–355.

King, Laura A., and Robert A. Emmons. 1990. "Conflict over Emotional Expression: Psychological and Physical Correlates." *Journal of Personality and Social Psychology* 58 (5): 864–877.

Kittay, Eva. 1999. *Love's Labor: Essays on Women, Equality, and Dependency.* New York: Routledge.

Korczynski, Marek, and Cameron Macdonald. 2008. *Service Work: Critical Perspectives.* New York: Routledge.

Kuhn, Peter, and Catherine Weinberger. 2005. "Leadership Skills and Wages." *Journal of Labor Economics* 23 (3): 395–436.

Kumanyika, Shiriki, Judy F. Wilson, and Marsha Guilford-Davenport. 1993. "Weight-Related Attitudes and Behaviors of Black Women." *Journal of the American Dietetic Association* 93:416–422.

Lareau, Anette. 2003. *Unequal Childhoods.* Oakland: University of California Press.

Lareau, Anette, and Elliot B. Weininger. 2008. "Time, Work, and Family Life." *Sociological Forum* 23:419–454.

Laslett, Barbara, and Johanna Brenner. 1989. "Gender and Social Reproduction: Historical Perspectives." *Annual Review of Sociology* 15:381–404.

Latu, Ioana M., Tracie L. Stewart, Ashley C. Myers, Claire G. Lisco, Sarah Beth Estes, and Dana K. Donahue. 2011. "What We 'Say' and What We 'Think' about Female Managers: Explicit versus Implicit Associations of Women with Success." *Psychology of Women Quarterly* 35:252–266.

Lee, Jennifer C., and Jeremy Staff. 2007. "When Work Matters: The Varying Impact of Adolescent Work Intensity on High School Drop-Out." *Sociology of Education* 80:158–178.

Leidner, Robin. 1993. *Fast Food, Fast Talk: Service Work and the Routinization of Everyday Life.* Berkeley: University of California Press.

Leslie, Deborah. 2002. "Gender, Retail Employment and the Clothing Commodity Chain." *Gender, Place and Culture* 9 (1): 61–76.

Leventhal, Tama, Julia A. Graber, and Jeanne Brooks-Gunn. 2001. "Adolescent Transitions to Young Adulthood: Antecedents, Correlates, and Consequences of Adolescent Employment." *Journal of Research on Adolescence* 11:297–323.

Levitt, Steven D. 2001. "Alternative Strategies for Identifying the Link between Unemployment and Crime." *Journal of Quantitative Criminology* 17 (4): 377–390.

————. 2004. "Understanding Why Crime Fell in the 1990s: Four Factors That Explain the Decline and Six That Do Not." *Journal of Economic Perspectives* 18 (1): 163–190.

Lewin-Epstein, Noah. 1981. *Youth Employment during High School.* Chicago: National Center for Education Statistics.

Lewis, Kristi M. 2000. "When Leaders Display Emotion: How Followers Respond to Negative Emotional Expression of Male and Female Leaders." *Journal of Organizational Behavior* 21 (2): 221–234.

Liben, Lynn S., Rebecca S. Bigler, and Holleen R. Krogh. 2001. "Pink and Blue Collar Jobs: Children's Judgments of Job Status and Job Aspirations in Relation to Sex of Workers." *Journal of Experimental Child Psychology* 79 (4): 346–363.

Liebel, Manfred. 2004. *A Will of Their Own: Cross-cultural Perspectives on Working Children*. London: Routledge.

Lindsay, Paul, and William E. Knox. 1984. "Continuity and Change in Work Values among Young Adults." *American Journal of Sociology* 89:918–931.

Lippman, Laura, Renee Ryberg, Rachel Carney, and Kristin A. Moore. 2015. "Key 'Soft Skills' That Foster Youth Workforce Success: Toward a Consensus across Fields." Available at https://childtrends-ciw49tixgw5lbab.stackpathdns.com/wp-content/uploads/2015/06/2015-24AWFCSoftSkillsExecSum.pdf.

Lively, Kathryn. 2000. "Reciprocal Emotion Management: Working Together to Maintain Stratification in Private Law Firms." *Work and Occupations* 27 (1): 32–63.

Longest, Kyle C., and Michael J. Shanahan. 2007. "Adolescent Work Intensity and Substance Use: The Mediational and Moderational Roles of Parenting." *Journal of Marriage and Family* 69 (3): 703–720.

Lorber, Judith. 1994. *Paradoxes of Gender*. New Haven, CT: Yale University Press.

Lovejoy, Meg. 2001. "Disturbances in the Social Body: Differences in Body Image and Eating Problems among African American and White Women." *Gender and Society* 15 (2): 239–261.

Lueptow, Lloyd B. 1980. "Social Change and Sex-Role Change in Adolescent Orientations toward Life, Work and Achievement: 1965–1975." *Social Psychology Quarterly* 43:48–59.

Lynch, Kathleen. 2010. "Affective Equality: Who Cares?" Paper presented at the Seventeenth ISA World Congress of Sociology, Gothenburg, Sweden, July 11–17. Available at http://wide-switzerland.ch/wp-content/uploads/2016/09/Lynch.pdf.

Lyness, Karen S., and Michael K. Judiesch. 1999. "Are Women More Likely to Be Hired or Promoted into Management Positions?" *Journal of Vocational Behavior* 54:158–173.

Macdonald, Cameron Lynn. 2015. "Ethnic Logics: Race and Ethnicity in Nanny Employment." In *Caring on the Clock: The Complexities and Contradictions of Paid Care Work*, edited by Mignon Duffy, Amy Armenia, and Clare L. Stacey, 153–164. New Brunswick, NJ: Rutgers University Press.

Macdonald, Cameron Lynne, and Carmen Sirianni. 1996. *Working in the Service Society*. Philadelphia: Temple University Press.

MacKinnon, C. 1979. *Sexual Harassment of Working Women: A Case of Sex Discrimination*. New Haven, CT: Yale University Press.

Malhotra, Deepak, and Max Bazerman. 2007. *Negotiation Genius: How to Overcome Obstacles and Achieve Brilliant Results at the Bargaining Table and Beyond*. New York: Bantam Dell.

Manning, Alan; and Joana Swaffield. 2008. "The Gender Gap in Early-Career Wage Growth." *Economic Journal* 118 (530): 983–1024.

Manning, Wendy D. 1990. "Parenting Employed Teenagers." *Youth and Society* 22:184–200.

Marini, Margaret M. 1989. "Sex Differences in Earnings in the United States." *Annual Review of Sociology* 15:343–380.

Marini, Margaret Money, Pi-Ling Fan, Erica Finley, and Ann M. Beutel. 1996. "Gender and Job Values." *Sociology of Education* 69 (1): 49–65.

Marsh, Herbert W. 1991. "Employment during High School: Character Building and Subversion of Academic Goals." *Sociology of Education* 64:172–189.

Marsh, Herbert W., and Sabina Kleitman. 2005. "Consequences of Employment during High School: Character Building, Subversion of Academic Goals, or a Threshold?" *American Educational Research Journal* 42:331–369.

Martin, Jack K., and Steven A. Tuch. 1993. "Black-White Differences in the Value of Job Rewards Revisited." *Social Science Quarterly* 74:884–901.

Martin, Joanne. 1990. "Deconstructing Organizational Taboos: The Suppression of Gender Conflict in Organizations." *Organization Science* 1 (4): 1–21.

———. 1994. "The Organization of Exclusion: Institutionalization of Sex Inequality, Gendered Faculty Jobs and Gendered Knowledge in Organization Theory and Research." *Organization* 1 (2): 401–432.

Martin, Patricia Yancey. 2001. "Mobilizing Masculinities: Women's Experiences of Men at Work." *Organizations* 8:587–618.

———. 2003. "'Said and Done' versus 'Saying and Doing': Gendering Practices, Practicing Gender at Work." *Gender and Society* 17 (3): 342–366.

Maume, David J., Jr., 1999. "Glass Ceiling and Glass Escalators: Occupational Segregation and Race and Sex Differences in Managerial Promotions." *Work and Occupations* 26:483–509.

Maxfield, Sylvia. 2005. "Modifying Best Practices in Women's Advancement for the Latin American Context." *Women in Management Review* 20:249–261.

McGuire, Gail M. 2002. "Gender, Race, and the Shadow Structure: A Study of Informal Networks and Inequality in a Work Organization." *Gender and Society* 16:303–322.

McMorris, Barbara, and Christopher Uggen. 2000. "Alcohol and Employment in Transition to Adulthood." *Journal of Health and Social Behavior* 41:276–294.

McNeal, Ralph B., Jr. 1997. "Are Students Being Pulled Out of High School? The Effect of Adolescent Employment on Dropping Out." *Sociology of Education* 70:206–220.

Mears, Ashley. 2014. "Aesthetic Labor for Sociologies of Work, Gender, and Beauty." *Sociological Compass* 8:1330–1343.

Medrich, Elliott A., Judith A. Roizen, Victor Rubin, and Stuart Buckley. 1982. *The Serious Business of Growing Up: A Study of Children's Lives Outside of School*. Berkeley: University of California Press.

Mendez, Jennifer Bickham, and Diane Wolf. 2001. "Where Feminist Theory Meets Feminist Practice: Border-Crossing in a Transnational Academic Feminist Organization." *Organization* 8 (4): 723–750.

Merluzzi, Jennifer, and Stanislav D. Dobrev. 2015. "Unequal on Top: Gender Profiling and the Income Gap among High Earner Male and Female Professionals." *Social Science Research* 53:45–58.

Merton, Robert K. 1996. *On Social Structure and Science*. Chicago: University of Chicago Press.

Meyer, Madonna Harrington. 2000. *Care Work: Gender, Labor, and the Welfare State*. New York: Routledge.

Meyer, Robert, and David Wise. 1983. "The Effects of the Minimum Wage on the Employment and Earnings of Youth." *Journal of Labor Economics* 1 (1): 66–100.

Mihalic, Sharon W., and Delbert Elliot. 1997. "Short- and Long-Term Consequences of Adolescent Work." *Youth and Society* 28:464–498.

Mincer, Jacob. 1962. "On-the-Job Training: Costs, Returns and Some Implications." *Journal of Political Economy* 70 (5): 50–79.

Mincer, Jacob, and Haim Ofek. 1982. "Interrupted Work Careers: Depreciation and Restoration of Human Capital." *Journal of Human Resources* 17:3–24.

Mirchandani, Kiran. 2000. "'The Best of Both Worlds' and 'Cutting My Own Throat': Contradictory Images of Home-Based Work." *Qualitative Sociology* 23:159–181.

———. 2003. "Challenging Racial Silences in Studies of Emotion Work: Contributions from Anti-racist Feminist Theory." *Organizational Studies* 24 (5): 721–742.

Misra, Joya, and Kyla Walters. 2016. "All Fun and Cool Clothes? Youth Workers' Consumer Identity in Clothing Retail." *Work and Occupations* 43 (3): 294–325.

Morris, J. Andrew, and Daniel C. Feldman. 1996. "The Dimensions, Antecedents, and Consequences of Emotional Labor." *Academy of Management Review* 21: 986–1010.

Morrison, Todd G., Elayne M. Bell, Melanie A. Morrison, Charles A. Murray, and Wendy O'Connor. 1994. "An Examination of Adolescents' Salary Expectations and Gender-Based Occupational Stereotyping." *Youth and Society* 26 (2): 178–193.

Mortimer, Jeylan T. 2005. *Working and Growing Up in America.* Cambridge, MA: Harvard University Press.

Mortimer, Jeylan T., and Michael D. Finch. 1986. "The Effects of Part-Time Work on Adolescent Self-Concept and Achievement." In *Becoming a Worker,* edited by Kathryn M. Borman and Jane Reisman, 66–89. Norwood, NJ: Ablex.

Mortimer, Jeylan T., and Donald S. Kumka. 1982. "A Further Examination of the 'Occupational Linkage Hypothesis.'" *Sociological Quarterly* 23:3–16.

Mortimer, Jeylan T., and Jon Lorence. 1979. "Work Experience and Occupational Value Socialization: A Longitudinal Study." *American Journal of Sociology* 84:1361–1385.

Mortimer, Jeylan T., Jon Lorence, and Donald S. Kumka. 1986. *Work, Family, and Personality: Transition to Adulthood.* Norwood, NJ: Ablex.

Mortimer, Jeylan T., Ellen Efron Pimentel, Seongryeol Ryu, Katherine Nash, and Chaimun Lee. 1996. "Part-Time Work and Occupational Value Formation in Adolescence." *Social Forces* 74:1405–1418.

Mortimer, Jeylan T., Michael Shanahan, and Seongryeol Ryu. 1993. "The Effects of Adolescent Employment on School-Related Orientation and Behavior." In *Adolescence in Context: The Interplay of Family, School, Peers and Work in Adjustment,* edited by Rainer K. Silbereisen and Eberhard Todt, 304–326. New York: Springer.

Mortimer, Jeylan T., Jeremy Staff, and Sabine Oesterle. 2003. "Adolescent Work and the Early Socioeconomic Career." In *Handbook of the Life Course,* edited by J. T. Mortimer and M. J. Shanahan, 437–459. New York: Kluwer Academic/Plenum.

Moss-Racusin, Corinne A., Julie E. Phelan, and Laurie A. Rudman. 2010. "When Men Break the Gender Rules: Status Incongruity and Backlash toward Modest Men." *Psychology of Men and Masculinity* 11:140–151.

Mouw, Ted, and Arne L. Kalleberg. 2010. "Occupations and the Structure of Wage Inequality in the United States, 1980s to 2002." *American Sociological Review* 75 (3): 402–431.

Mroz, Thomas A., and Timothy H. Savage. 2006. "The Long-Term Effects of Youth Unemployment." *Journal of Human Resources* 41 (2): 259–293.

Muñoz, Carolina Bank. 2008. *Transnational Tortillas: Race, Gender, and Shopfloor Politics in Mexico and the United States.* Ithaca, NY: Cornell University Press.

National Science Foundation. 2007. "Science and Engineering Degrees: 1966–2004." Available at https://wayback.archive-it.org/5902/20160210223704/http://www.nsf.gov/statistics/nsf07307/pdf/nsf07307.pdf.

Nickson, Dennis, Scott A. Hurrell, Chris Warhurst, and Johanna Commander. 2011. "Labour Supply and Skills Demand in Fashion Retailing." In *Retail Work*, edited by Irena Grugulis and Ödül Bozkurt, 66–87. London: Palgrave Macmillan.

Nickson, Dennis, Chris Warhurst, and Eli Dutton. 2004. "Aesthetic Labour and the Policy-Making Agenda: Time for a Reappraisal of Skills?" SKOPE Research Paper no. 48. Available at http://www.skope.ox.ac.uk/wp-content/uploads/2014/04/SKOPEWP48.pdf.

Nickson, Dennis P., and Chris Warhurst. 2001. *Looking Good and Sounding Right: Style Counselling and the Aesthetics of the New Economy.* London: Industrial Society.

Oaxaca, Ronald. 1973. "Male-Female Wage Differentials in Urban Labor Markets." *International Economic Review* 14 (3): 693–709.

O'Neill, June. 2003. "The Gender Gap in Wages, circa 2000." *American Economic Review* 93 (2): 309–314.

Orbach, Susie. 1986. *The Hunger Strike.* New York: Norton.

O'Regan, Katherine, and John Quigley. 1996a. "Spatial Effects on Employment Outcomes: The Case of New Jersey Teenagers." *New England Economic Review*, May–June, pp. 41–57.

———. 1996b. "Teenage Employment and the Spatial Isolation of Minority and Poverty Households." *Journal of Human Resources* 31 (4): 692–702.

Osgood, D. Wayne. 1999. "Having the Time of Their Lives: All Work and No Play?" In *Transitions to Adulthood in a Changing Economy: No Work, No Family, No Future?* edited by Alan Booth, Ann C. Crouter, and Michael J. Shanahan, 176–186. Westport, CT: Praeger.

Otis, Eileen M. 2011. *Markets and Bodies: Women, Service Work, and the Making of Inequality in China.* Stanford, CA: Stanford University Press.

———. 2016. "Bridgework: Globalization, Gender, and Service Labor at a Luxury Hotel." *Gender and Society* 30 (6): 912–934.

Owens, Sherry Lynn, Bobbie C. Smothers, and Fannye E. Love. 2003. "Are Girls Victims of Gender Bias in Our Nation's Schools?" *Journal of Instructional Psychology* 30 (2): 131–136.

Pabilonia, Sabrina Wulff. 2001. "Evidence on Youth Employment, Earnings, and Parental Transfers in the NLSY 1997." *Journal of Human Resources* 36 (4): 795–822.

Padavic, Irene, and Barbara Reskin. 2002. *Women and Men at Work.* 2nd ed. Thousand Oaks, CA: Pine Forge Press.

Pager, Devah, and Lincoln Quillian. 2005. "Walking the Talk? What Employers Say versus What They Do." *American Sociological Review* 70 (3): 355–380.

Paglin, Morton, and Anthony M. Rufolo. 1990. "Heterogeneous Human Capital, Occupational Choice, and Male-Female Earnings Differences." *Journal of Labor Economics* 8 (1): 123–144.

Paolacci, Gabriele, and Jesse Chandler. 2014. "Inside the Turk: Understanding Mechanical Turk as a Participant Pool." *Current Directions in Psychological Science* 23 (3): 184–188.

Parker, Sheila, Mimi Nichter, Mark Nichter, Nancy Vuckovic, Colette Sims, and Cheryl Ritenbaugh. 1995. "Body Image and Weight Concerns among African-American and White Adolescent Females: Differences That Make a Difference." *Human Organization* 54:103–114.

Parkinson, Brian. 1991. "Emotional Stylists: Strategies of Expressive Management among Trainee Hairdressers." *Cognition and Emotion* 5 (5–6): 419–434.

Parks, Jennifer A. 2003. *No Place Like Home? Feminist Ethics and Home Health Care.* Bloomington: Indiana University Press.

Parrenas, Rhacel Salazar. 2008. *The Force of Domesticity: Filipina Migrants and Globalization.* New York: New York University Press.

Pascoe, C. J. 2007. *Dude, You're a Fag: Masculinity and Sexuality in High School.* Berkeley: University of California Press.

Paternoster, Raymond, Shawn Bushway, Robert Brame, and Robert Apel. 2003. "The Effect of Teenage Employment on Delinquency and Problem Behaviors." *Social Forces* 82 (1): 297–335.

Perlick, Deborah, and Brett Silverstein. 1994. "Faces of Female Discontent: Depression, Disordered Eating, and Changing Gender Roles." In *Feminist Perspectives on Eating Disorders,* edited by P. Fallon and M. Katzman, 77–94. New York: Guilford.

Pettinger, Lynne. 2004. "Brand Culture and Branded Workers: Service Work and Aesthetic Labour in Fashion Retail." *Consumption, Markets and Culture* 7 (2): 165–184.

———. 2006. "On the Materiality of Service Work." *Sociological Review* 54 (1): 48–65.

Pew Research Center. 2015. "The American Middle Class Is Losing Ground: No Longer the Majority and Falling Behind Financially." December 9. Available at http://www.pewsocialtrends.org/2015/12/09/the-american-middle-class-is-losing -ground/.

Pierce, Jennifer. 1995. *Gender Trials: Emotional Lives in Contemporary Law Firms.* Berkeley: University of California Press.

Pinkley, Robin L., and Gregory B. Northcraft. 2000. *Get Paid What You're Worth: The Expert Negotiator's Guide to Salary and Compensation.* New York: St. Martin's.

Plankey-Videla, Nancy. 2012. *We Are in This Dance Together: Gender, Power, and Globalization at a Mexican Garment Factory.* New Brunswick, NJ: Rutgers University Press.

Polachek, Solomon W. 1981. "Occupational Self-Selection: A Human Capital Approach to Sex Differences in Occupational Structure." *Review of Economics and Statistics* 63 (1): 60–69.

Pozas, María de los Ángeles. 2002. *Estrategia internacional de la gran empresa mexicana en la década de los noventa* [International strategy of the great empress of Mexico in the nineties]. Mexico City: El Colegio de México.

Price-Glynn, Kimberly, and Carter Rakovski. 2012. "Who Rides the Glass Escalator? Gender, Race and Nationality in the National Nursing Assistant Study." *Work, Employment and Society* 26 (5): 699–715.

Prokos, Anastasia, and Irene Padavic. 2005. "An Examination of Competing Explanations for the Pay Gap among Scientists and Engineers." *Gender and Society* 19 (4): 523–543.

Pyke, Karen D., and Denise L. Johnson. 2003. "Asian American Women and Racialized Femininities: 'Doing' Gender across Cultural Worlds." *Gender and Society* 17 (1): 33–53.

Quinn, Beth A. 2002. "Sexual Harassment and Masculinity: The Power and Meaning of 'Girl Watching.'" *Gender and Society* 16 (3): 386–402.

Radhakrishnan, Smitha. 2011. *Appropriately Indian.* Durham, NC: Duke University Press.

Rafaeli, Anat, and Robert I. Sutton. 1987. "Expression of Emotion as Part of the Work Role." *Academy of Management Review* 12 (1): 23–37.

———. 1989. "The Expression of Emotion in Organizational Life." In *Research in Organizational Behavior,* vol. 11, edited by L. L. Cummings and B. M. Staw, 1–42. Greenwich, CT: JAI Press.

Rand, Colleen S. W., and John M. Kuldau. 1990. "The Epidemiology of Obesity and Self-Defined Weight Problem in the General Population: Gender, Race, Age, and Social Class." *International Journal of the Eating Disorders* 9 (3): 329–343.

Rantalaiho, Liisa, Tuula Heiskanen, Paivi Korvajarvi, and Marja Vehvilainen. 1997. "Introduction." In *Gendered Practices in Working Life,* edited by L. Rantalaiho and T. Heiskanen, 3–15. New York: St. Martin's.

Rees, Albert, and Wayne Gray. 1982. "Family Effects in Youth Unemployment." In *The Labor Market Problem: Its Nature, Causes and Consequences,* edited by Richard B. Freeman and David A. Wise, 453–474. Chicago: University of Chicago Press.

Reskin, Barbara F. 1993. "Sex Segregation in the Workplace." *Annual Review of Sociology* 19:241–270.

———. 2002. "Motives and Mechanisms in Explaining Ascriptive Inequality." Presidential address presented at the annual meeting of the American Sociological Association, Chicago, August 16–19.

Reskin, Barbara F., and Denise D. Bielby. 2005. "A Sociological Perspective on Gender and Career Outcomes." *Journal of Economic Perspectives* 19:71–86.

Reskin, Barbara, and Heidi I. Hartmann. 1986. *Women's Work, Men's Work, Sex Segregation on the Job.* Washington, DC: National Academy Press.

Reskin, Barbara F., and Debra Branch McBrier. 2000. "Why Not Ascription? Organizations' Employment of Male and Female Managers." *American Sociological Review* 65:210–233.

Reskin, Barbara, and Irene Padavic. 1994. *Women and Men at Work.* Thousand Oaks, CA: Pine Forge Press.

Reskin, Barbara, and Patricia Roos. 2002. *Job Queues, Gender Queues: Explaining Women's Inroads into Male Occupations.* Philadelphia: Temple University Press.

Ribas, Vanesa, Janette Dill, and Philip Cohen. 2012. "Mobility for Care Workers: Job Changes and Wages for Nurse Aides." *Social Science and Medicine* 75 (12): 2183–2190.

Ridgeway, Cecilia. 2001. "Gender, Status, and Leadership." *Journal of Social Issues* 57 (4): 637–655.

———. 2009. "Framed Before We Know It: How Gender Shapes Social Relations." *Gender and Society* 23 (2): 145–160.

Ridgeway, Cecilia L., and Chris Bourg. 2004. "Gender as Status: An Expectation States Theory Approach." In *The Psychology of Gender,* edited by A. H. Eagly, A. E. Beall, and R. J. Sternberg, 217–241. New York: Guliford Press.

Ridgeway, Cecilia L., and Shelley J. Correll. 2004. "Unpacking the Gender System: A Theoretical Perspective on Cultural Beliefs in Social Relations." *Gender and Society* 18:510–531.

Rindfuss, Ronald R. 1991. "The Young Adult Years: Diversity, Structural Change, and Fertility." *Demography* 28:493–512.

Rindfuss, Ronald R., Elizabeth Cooksey, and Rebecca A. Sutterlin. 1999. "Young Adult Occupational Achievement." *Work and Occupations* 26:220–263.

Ritzer, George. 2000. *The McDonaldization of Society: An Investigation into the Changing Character of Social Life.* Newbury Park, CA: Pine Forge.

Rivera, Lauren A., and Andras Tilcsik. 2016. "Class Advantage, Commitment Penalty: The Gendered Effect of Social Class Signals in an Elite Labor Market." *American Sociological Review* 81 (6): 1097–1131.

Roberts, Christine. 2012. "Most 10 Year-Olds Have Been on a Diet: Study." *New York Daily News* July 3. Available at http://www.nydailynews.com/news/national/diets -obsess-tweens-study-article-1.1106653.

Rollins, Judith. 1985. *Between Women: Domestics and their Employers.* Philadelphia: Temple University Press.

Romero, Mary. 1992. *Maid in the USA.* New York: Routledge.

———. 2011. *The Maid's Daughter: Living Inside and Outside the American Dream.* New York: New York University Press.

Roos, Patricia A., and Mary Lizabeth Gatta. 1999. "The Gender Gap in Earnings: Trends, Explanations, and Prospects." In *Handbook of Gender and Work*, edited by Gary Powell, 95–123. Thousand Oaks, CA: Sage.

Root, Maria P. P., Patricia Fallon, and William N. Friedrich. 1986. *Bulimia: A Systems Approach to Treatment.* New York: Norton.

Rose, Stephen, and Heidi Hartmann. 2004. *Still a Man's Labor Market: The Long-Term Earnings Gap.* Washington, DC: Institute for Women's Policy Research.

Ross, Catherine E. 1987. "The Division of Labor at Home." *Social Forces* 65:816–833.

Rossi, Peter H., and Andy B. Anderson. 1982. "The Factorial Survey Approach: An Introduction." In *Measuring Social Judgments: The Factorial Survey Approach*, edited by P. H. Rossi and S. L. Nock, 15–68. Beverly Hills, CA: Sage.

Rothblum, Esther D. 1994. "'I'll Die for the Revolution but Don't Ask Me Not to Diet': Feminism and the Continuing Stigmatization of Obesity." In *Feminist Perspectives on Eating Disorders*, edited by P. Fallon, M. A. Katzman, and S. C. Wooley, 53–76. New York: Guilford.

Rowe, Reba, and William E. Snizek. 1995. "Gender Differences in Work Values—Perpetuating the Myth." *Work and Occupations* 22 (2): 215–229.

Rucker, Clifford E., and Thomas F. Cash. 1992. "Body Images, Body Size Perceptions, and Eating Behaviors among African-American and White College Women." *International Journal of Eating Disorders* 12 (3): 291–299.

Rudman, Laurie A., and Peter Glick. 1999. "Feminized Management and Backlash toward Agentic Women: The Hidden Costs to Women of a Kinder, Gentler Image of Middle Managers." *Journal of Personality and Social Psychology* 77 (5): 1004–1010.

Ruhm, Christopher. 1997. "Is High School Employment Consumption or Investment?" *Journal of Labor Economics* 15:735–776.

Ruijter, Judith M. P. de, Anneke van Doorne-Huiskes, and Joop J. Schippers. 2003. "Size and Causes of the Occupational Gender Wage-Gap in the Netherlands." *European Sociological Review* 19 (4): 345–360.

Safron, Deborah J., John E. Schulenberg, and Jerald G. Bachman. 2001. "Part-Time Work and Hurried Adolescence: The Links among Work Intensity, Social Activities, Health Behaviors and Substance Abuse." *Journal of Health and Social Behavior* 42 (2): 425–449.

Salzinger, Leslie. 2003. *Genders in Production: Making Workers in Mexico's Global Factories.* Berkeley: University of California Press.

Sayer, Liana C. 2005. "Gender, Time, and Inequality: Trends in Women's and Men's Paid Work, Unpaid Work, and Free Time." *Social Forces* 84:285–303.

Schaefer, Kayleen. 2010. "New Policies Exterminating Teen Mall Rats." *ABC News,* September 23. Available at http://abcnews.go.com/Business/shopping-malls-increasingly-putting-restrictions-teens/story?id=11701470.

Schaubroeck, John, and James R. Jones. 2000. "Antecedents of Workplace Emotional Labor Dimensions and Moderators of Their Effects on Physical Symptoms." *Journal of Organizational Behavior* 21 (2): 163–183.

Scheper-Hughes, Nancy, and Margaret M. Lock. 1987. "The Mindful Body: A Prolegomenon to Future Work in Medical Anthropology." *Medical Anthropology* 1:6–41.

Schilt, Kristen, and Matthew Wiswall. 2008. "Before and After: Gender Transitions, Human Capital, and Workplace Experiences." *B.E. Journal of Economic Analysis and Policy* 8 (1): 1–28.

Schippers, Mimi. 2007. "Recovering the Feminine Other: Masculinity, Femininity, and Gender Hegemony." *Theory and Society* 36 (1): 85–102.

Schneider, Barbara, and David Stevenson. 1999. *The Ambitious Generations: America's Teenagers, Motivated but Directionless.* New Haven, CT: Yale University Press.

Schoenhals, Mark, Marta Tienda, and Barbara Schneider. 1998. "The Educational and Personal Consequences of Adolescent Employment." *Social Forces* 77 (2): 723–761.

Scott, Alison MacEwan. 1994. "Gender Segregation in the Retail Industry." In *Gender Segregation and Social Change: Men and Women in Changing Labour Markets,* edited by Alison MacEwan Scott, 235–270. Oxford: Oxford University Press.

Shanahan, Michael J., and Brian P. Flaherty. 2001. "Dynamic Patterns of Time Use in Adolescence." *Child Development* 72:385–401.

Shanahan, Michael J., Jeylan T. Mortimer, and Helga Krüger. 2002. "Adolescence and Adult Work in the Twenty-First Century." *Journal of Research on Adolescence* 12 (1): 99–120.

Sherman, Rachel. 2007. *Class Acts: Service and Inequality in Luxury Hotels.* Oakland: University of California Press.

———. 2010. "Time Is Our Commodity: Gender and Struggle for Occupational Legitimacy among Personal Concierges." *Work and Occupations* 37 (1): 81–114.

Shotter, John. 1984. *Social Accountability and Selfhood.* Oxford: Oxford University Press.

Silverstein, Brett, Lauren Perdue, Cordulla Wolf, and Cecelia Pizzolo. 1988. "Bingeing, Purging, and Estimates of Parental Attitudes Regarding Female Achievement." *Sex Roles* 19:723–733.

Silverstein, Brett, Deborah Perlick, Joanne Clauson, and Elizabeth McKoy. 1993. "Depression Combined with Somatic Symptomology among Adolescent Females Who Report Concerns regarding Maternal Achievement." *Sex Roles* 28:637–653.

Skillsmart. 2007. *Sector Skills Agreement Stage One: Assessment of Current and Future Skills Needs.* London: Skillsmart.

Small, Deborah, Michele Gelfand, Linda Babcock, and Hilary Gettman. 2007. "Who Goes to the Bargaining Table? The Influence of Gender and Framing on the Initiation of Negotiation." *Journal of Personality and Social Psychology* 93 (4): 600–613.

Smith, Ryan. A. 2002. "Race, Gender, and Authority in the Workplace: Theory and Research." *Annual Review of Sociology* 28:509–542.

Smith, Vicki. 2012. "'You Get the Economy You Choose': The Political and Social Construction of the New Economy." *Work and Occupations* 39 (2): 148–156.

Snyder, Karrie A., and Adam I. Green. 2008. "Revisiting the Glass Escalator: The Case of Gender Segregation in a Female Dominated Occupation." *Social Problems* 55 (2): 271–299.

Snyder, Kieran. 2014. "The Abrasiveness Trap: High-Achieving Men and Women Are Described Differently in Reviews." *Fortune*, August 26. Available at http://fortune.com/2014/08/26/performance-review-gender-bias.

Solberg, Eric, and Teresa Laughlin. 1995. "The Gender Pay Gap, Fringe Benefits, and Occupational Crowding." *Industrial and Labor Relations Review* 48 (4): 692–708.

Solnick, Sara J. 2001. "Gender Differences in the Ultimatum Game." *Economic Inquiry* 39:189–200.

Stacey, Clare L. 2011a. "The Caring Self: The Work Experiences of Paid Family Caregivers." *Qualitative Sociology* 35 (1): 47–64.

———. 2011b. *The Caring Self: Work Experiences of Home Care Aides.* Ithaca, NY: Cornell University Press.

Stacey, Clare L., and Lindsey L. Ayers. 2015. "Caught between Love and Money: The Experiences of Paid Family Caregivers." In *Caring on the Clock: The Complexities and Contradictions of Paid Care Work*, edited by Mignon Duffy, Amy Armenia, and Clare L. Stacey, 201–212. New Brunswick, NJ: Rutgers University Press.

Staff, Jeremy, Emily E. Messersmith, and John E. Schulenberg. 2009. "Adolescents and the World of Work." In *Handbook of Adolescent Psychology*, 3rd. ed., edited by Richard Lerner and Laurence Steinberg, 270–314. Hoboken, NJ: John Wiley and Sons.

Staff, Jeremy, and Jeylan T. Mortimer. 2007. "Educational and Work Strategies from Adolescence to Early Adulthood: Consequences for Educational Attainment." *Social Forces* 85 (3): 1169–1194.

Staff, Jeremy, John E. Schulenberg, and Jerald G. Bachman. 2010. "Adolescent Work Intensity, School Performance, and Academic Engagement." *Sociology of Education* 83:183–200.

Staff, Jeremy, and Christopher Uggen. 2003. "The Fruits of Good Work: Early Work Experiences and Adolescent Deviance." *Journal of Research on Crime and Delinquency* 40 (3): 263–290.

Steinberg, Laurence, and Sanford M. Dornbusch. 1991. "Negative Correlates of Part-Time Employment during Adolescence: Replication and Elaboration." *Developmental Psychology* 27:304–313.

Steinberg, Laurence, Suzanne Fegley, and Sanford Dornbusch. 1993. "Negative Impact of Part-Time Work on Adolescent Adjustment: Evidence from a Longitudinal Study." *Developmental Psychology* 29 (2): 171–180.

Steinberg, Ronnie J. 1990. "Social Construction of Skill: Gender, Power, and Comparable Worth." *Work and Occupations* 17 (4): 449–482.

Stephenson, Stanley P., Jr. 1976. "The Economics of Youth Job Search Behavior." *Review of Economics and Statistics* 58:104–111.

————. 1980. "In-School Work and Early Postschool Labor Market Dynamics." Working paper, Pennsylvania State University, State College.

————. 1981. "In School Labour Force Status and Post-school Wage Rates of Young Men." *Applied Economics* 13:279–302.

Stern, David, and Yoshi-Fumi Nakata. 1989. "Characteristics of High School Students' Paid Jobs, and Employment Experience After Graduation." In *Adolescence and Work: Influences of Social Structure, Labor Markets, and Culture*, edited by David Stern and Dorothy Eichorn, 189–234. Hillsdale, NJ: Lawrence Erlbaum Associates.

Sternheimer, Karen. 2016. "The Privilege of a Summer Job." *Everyday Sociology* (blog), July 21. Available at http://www.everydaysociologyblog.com/2016/07/the-privilege-of-a-summer-job.html.

Stevens, Constance J., Laura A. Puchtell, Ryu Seongryeol, and Jeylan T. Mortimer. 1992. "Adolescent Work and Boys' and Girls' Orientations to the Future." *Sociological Quarterly* 33 (2): 153–169.

Stevens, Cynthia K., Anna G. Bavetta, and Marilyn E. Gist. 1993. "Gender Differences in the Acquisition of Salary Negotiation Skills: The Role of Goals, Self-Efficacy, and Perceived Control." *Journal of Applied Psychology* 78:723–735.

Stone, Deborah. 2000. "Caring by the Book." In *Carework: Gender, Labor, and the Welfare State*, edited by Madonna Harrington Meyer, 89–111. New York: Routledge.

Stone, Pamela. 2008. *Opting Out? Why Women Really Quit Careers and Head Home.* Oakland: University of California Press.

Story, Louise. 2005. "Many Women at Elite Colleges Set Career Path to Motherhood." *New York Times*, September 20. Available at http://www.nytimes.com/2005/09/20/us/many-women-at-elite-colleges-set-career-path-to-motherhood.html.

Story, Mary, Simone A. French, Michael D. Resnick, and Robert W. Blum. 1995. "Ethnic/Racial and Socioeconomic Differences in Dieting Behaviors and Body Image Perceptions in Adolescents." *International Journal of Eating Disorders* 18:173–179.

Storz, Nancy, and Walter H. Greene. 1983. "Body Weight, Body Image, and Perceptions of Fad Diets in Adolescent Girls." *Journal of Nutrition Education* 15 (1): 15–19.

Subich, Linda M., Gerald V. Barrett, Dennis Doverspike, and Ralph A. Alexander. 1989. "The Effects of Sex-Role-Related Factors on Occupational Choice and Salary." In *Pay Equity: Empirical Inquiries*, edited by R. Michael, H. Hartmann, and B. O'Farrell, 91–104. Washington, DC: National Academy Press.

Sullivan, Paul. 2015. "Finding a Nanny Who Fits with Your Family." *New York Times*, January 23. Available at https://mobile.nytimes.com/2015/01/24/your-money/finding-a-nanny-who-fits-with-your-family.html.

Tang, Thomas Li-Ping, Jwa K. Kim, and David Shin-Hsiung Tang. 2000. "Does Attitude toward Money Moderate the Relationship between Intrinsic Job Satisfaction and Voluntary Turnover?" *Human Relations* 53 (2): 213–246.

Taylor, Phil, and Peter Bain. 2002. "Call Centre Organizing in Adversity: From Excell to Vertex." In *Union Organising*, edited by G. Gall, 163–182. London: Routledge.

Theriot, Nancy M. 1988. "Psychosomatic Illness in History: The 'Green Sickness' among Nineteenth-Century Adolescent Girls." *Journal of Psychohistory* 15:461–480.

Thomas, Veronica G., and Leslie C. Shields. 1987. "Gender Influences on Work Values of Black Adolescents." *Adolescence* 22:37–43.

Thompson, Becky W. 1992. "'A Way Outa No Way': Eating Problems among African-American, Latina, and White Women." *Gender and Society* 6:546–561.

Thompson, Derek. 2009. "It's Not Just a Recession; It's a Mancession!" *The Atlantic*, July 9. Available at https://www.theatlantic.com/business/archive/2009/07/its-not-just-a-recession-its-a-mancession/20991.

Thurow, Lester. C. 1969. *Poverty and Discrimination*. Washington, DC: Brookings Institute.

Tilcsik, András. 2011. "Pride and Prejudice: Employment Discrimination against Openly Gay Men in the United States." *American Journal of Sociology* 117 (2): 586–626.

Tilly, Chris, and Françoise Carré. 2011. "Endnote: Perceptions and Reality." In *Retail Work*, edited by Irene Grugulis and Ödül Bozkurt, 297–306. London: Palgrave Macmillan.

Tomaskovic-Devey, Donald, and Sheryl Skaggs. 2002. "Sex Segregation, Labor Process Organization, and Gender Earnings Inequality." *American Journal of Sociology* 108 (1): 102–128.

Treas, Judith, and Eric D. Widmer. 2000. "Married Women's Employment over the Life Course: Attitudes in Cross-national Perspective." *Social Forces* 78: 1409–1436.

Tronto, Joan. 1993. *Moral Boundaries: A Political Argument for an Ethic of Care*. New York: Routledge.

Tuominen, Mary. 2003. *We Are Not Babysitters: Family Child Care Providers Redefine Work and Care*. New Brunswick, NJ: Rutgers University Press.

Uggen, Christopher, and Sara Wakefield. 2007. "What Have We Learned from Longitudinal Studies of Work and Crime?" In *The Long View of Crime: A Synthesis of Longitudinal Research*, edited by Liberman Akiva, 191–216. New York: Springer.

Uttal, Lynet, and Mary Tuominen. 1999. "Tenuous Relationships: Exploration, Emotion, and Racial Ethnic Significance in Paid Child Care Work." *Gender and Society* 13:758–780.

Valian, Virginia. 1999. *Why So Slow? The Advancement of Women*. Cambridge, MA: MIT Press.

Vallas, Steven P., William Finlay, and Amy S. Wharton. 2009. *The Sociology of Work: Structures and Inequalities*. Oxford: Oxford University Press.

Van Maanen, John, and Gideon Kunda. 1989. "'Real Feelings': Emotional Expression and Organizational Culture." In *Research in Organizational Behavior*, vol. 11, edited by L. L. Cummings and B. M. Staw, 43–103. Greenwich, CT: JAI Press.

Waddell, Glen R. 2006. "Labor Market Consequences of Poor Attitude and Low Self-Esteem in Youth." *Economic Inquiry* 44 (1): 69–97.

Wade, Lisa, and Myra Max Ferree. 2015. *Gender: Ideas, Interactions, Institutions*. New York: W. W. Norton.

Wade, Mary E. 2001. "Women and Salary Negotiation: The Costs of Self-Advocacy." *Psychology of Women Quarterly* 25:65–76.

Waldfogel, Jane. 1998. "The Family Gap for Young Women in the United States and Britain: Can Maternity Leave Make a Difference?" *Journal of Labor Economics* 16 (3): 505–545.

Warhurst, Chris, and Dennis Nickson. 2007. "Employee Experience of Aesthetic Labour in Retail and Hospitality." *Work, Employment, and Society* 21:103–120.

Warren, John Robert, and Jennifer C. Lee. 2003. "The Impact of Adolescent Employment on High School Dropout: Differences by Individual and Labor-Market Characteristics." *Social Science Research* 32:98–128.

Warren, John Robert, Paul C. LePore, and Robert D. Mare. 2000. "Employment during High School: Consequences for Students' Grades in Academic Courses." *American Educational Research Journal* 37:943–969.

Weinberg, Bruce A., Patricia B. Reagan, and Jeffrey J. Yankow. 2000. "Do Neighborhoods Matter? Evidence from the NLSY79." Available at http://citeseerx.ist.psu .edu/viewdoc/download?doi=10.1.1.361.3846&rep=rep1&type=pdf.

West, Candace, and Don Zimmerman. 1987. "Doing Gender." *Gender and Society* 1:13–37.

Wharton, Amy S., and Rebecca J. Erickson. 1993. "Managing Emotions on the Job and at Home: Understanding the Consequences of Multiple Emotional Roles." *Academy of Management Review* 18:457–486.

———. 1995. "The Consequences of Caring: Exploring the Links between Women's Job and Family Emotion Work." *Sociological Quarterly* 36 (2): 273–296.

Wharton, Amy S., Thomas Rotolo, and Sharon R. Bird. 2000. "Social Context at Work: A Multilevel Analysis of Job Satisfaction." *Sociological Forum* 15:65–90.

White, Evelyn. 1991. "Unhealthy Appetites: Large Is Lovely, unless You're Unhappy Overeating and Unable to Lose Weight." *Essence*, September 28, pp. 28–30.

White, Lynn K., and David B. Brinkerhoff. 1981. "The Sexual Division of Labor: Evidence from Childhood." *Social Forces* 60 (1): 170–181.

Whitehead, Stephen. 1998. "Disrupted Selves: Resistance and Identity Work in the Managerial Arena." *Gender and Education* 10:199–215.

Williams, Christine. 1992. "The Glass Escalator: Hidden Advantages for Men in the 'Female' Professions." *Social Problems* 39 (3): 253–267.

———. 1995. *Still a Man's World: Men Who Do "Women's Work."* Berkeley: University of California Press.

———. 2006. *Inside Toyland: Working, Shopping, and Social Inequality.* Berkeley: University of California Press.

Williams, Christine, and Catherine Connell. 2010. "Looking Good and Sounding Right: Aesthetic Labor and Social Inequality in the Retail Industry." *Work and Occupations* 37:349–377.

Williams, Christine L., Chandra Muller, and Kristine Kilanski. 2012. "Gendered Organizations in the New Economy." *Gender and Society* 26:549–573.

Williams, Joan C. 2000. *Unbending Gender.* Oxford: Oxford University Press.

Williams, Melissa J., Elizabeth L. Paluck, and Julie Spencer-Rodgers. 2010. "The Masculinity of Money: Automatic Stereotypes Predict Gender Differences in Estimated Salaries." *Psychology of Women Quarterly* 34:7–20.

Willis, Paul. 1977. *Learning to Labor: How Working Class Kids Get Working Class Jobs.* New York: Columbia University Press.

Wingfield, Adia Harvey. 2009. "Racializing the Glass Escalator: Reconsidering Men's Experiences with Women's Work." *Gender and Society* 23 (1): 5–26.

———. 2012. *No More Invisible Man: Race and Gender in Men's Work.* Philadelphia: Temple University Press.

———. 2015. "Are Some Emotions White-Only? Feeling Rules in Professional Work-places." In *Working in America*, edited by Amy Wharton, 201–213. New York: Taylor and Francis.

Winslow, Sarah. 2010. "Gender Inequality and Time Allocations among Academic Faculty." *Gender and Society* 24:769–793.

Witz, Anne, Chris Warhurst, and Dennis Nickson. 2003. "The Labour of Aesthetics and Aesthetics of Organization." *Organization* 10:33–54.

Wolf, Naomi. 2002. *The Beauty Myth: How Images of Beauty Are Used against Women.* New York: Harper Perennial.

Wood, Robert G., Mary E. Corcoran, and Paul N. Courant. 1993. "Pay Differentials among the Highly Paid: The Male-Female Earnings Gap in Lawyers' Salaries." *Journal of Labor Economics* 11 (3): 417–441.

Wright, David. 2005. "Commodifying Respectability: Distinctions, at Work in the Bookshop." *Journal of Consumer Culture* 5 (3): 295–314.

Wright, Erik O., and Janeen Baxter. 2000. "The Glass Ceiling Hypothesis: A Com-parative Study of the United States, Sweden, and Australia." *Gender and Society* 14:275–294.

Yoder, Janice, and Patricia Aniakudo. 1997. "Outsider within the Firehouse: Subor-dination and Difference in the Social Interactions of African American Women Firefighters." *Gender and Society* 11 (3): 324–341.

Zabludovsky, Gina. 2004. "Women in Management in Mexico." In *Women in Manage-ment Worldwide*, edited by Marilyn J. Davidson and Ronald J. Burke, 183–205. Burlington, VT: Ashgate.

Zelizer, Viviana. 2005. *The Purchase of Intimacy.* Princeton, NJ: Princeton University Press.

Zerbe, W., and L. Falkenberg. 1989. "The Expression of Emotion in Organizational Life: Differences across Occupations." *Proceedings of the Annual Conference of the Administrative Sciences Association of Canada* 10 (5): 87–96.

Zimmer-Gembeck, Melanie J., Heather M. Chipuer, Michelle Hanisch, Peter A. Creed, and Leanne Mcgregor. 2006. "Relationships at School and Stage Environ-ment Fit as Resources for Adolescent Engagement and Achievement." *Journal of Adolescence* 29:911–933.

Index

Yasemin Besen-Cassino is Professor of Sociology at Montclair State University. She is the author of *Consuming Work: Youth Labor in America* (Temple); coauthor (with Dan Cassino) of *Consuming Politics: Jon Stewart, Branding, and the Youth Vote in America*; and coeditor (with Michael Kimmel) of *The Jessie Bernard Reader.*